MARCEL MAUSS   24·9·99

Methodology and History in Anthropology

General Editor: David Parkin, Director of the Institute of Social and Cultural Anthropology, University of Oxford

Volume 1
Marcel Mauss: A Centenary Tribute. Edited by Wendy James and N.J. Allen

Volume 2
Franz Baerman Steiner. Selected Papers
Taboo. Franz B. Steiner. Edited and with an Introduction by Jeremy Adler and Richard Fardon

Volume 3
Franz Baerman Steiner. Selected Papers
Orientalism, Value, and Civilization. Franz B. Steiner. Edited and with an Introduction by Jeremy Adler and Richard Fardon

Volume 4
The Problem of Context: Perspectives from Social Anthropology and Elsewhere. Edited by R.M. Dilley

MARCEL MAUSS

A CENTENARY TRIBUTE

Edited by
Wendy James and N. J. Allen

Berghahn Books
New York • Oxford

First published in 1998 by

Berghahn Books

Library of Congress Cataloging-in-Publication Data
Marcel Mauss : a centenary tribute / edited by Wendy James and N.J.
Allen.
      p.   cm. -- (Methodology and history in anthropology ; v. 1)
    Includes bibliographical references and index.
    ISBN 1-57181-703-4 (alk. paper). -- ISBN 1-57181-705-0
(alk. paper)
    1. Mauss, Marcel, 1872-1950.   2. Anthropology--Philisophy.
3. Gifts. 4. Ceremonial exchange. I. James, Wendy. II. Allen,
N. J. III. Series.
GN21.M33M37   1998
301'.01--dc21   98-28121
                                           CIP

British Library Cataloguing in Publication Data

Marcel Mauss : a centenary tribute. – (Methodology & history in
    anthropology ; v. 1)
    1. Mauss, Marcel   2. Ethnologists – History and criticism
    I. James, Wendy, 1940-   II. Allen, N. J.
    306'.092

ISBN 1571817050

Hommage à Claudette Kennedy

Mrs Claudette Kennedy, née Raphaël, born at Bourg-la-Reine (Paris) in 1910, great-niece of Emile Durkheim, cousin of Marcel Mauss, survivor of Auschwitz. Resident in Oxford since 1986, and friend of the British Centre for Durkheimian Studies.

Frontispiece: Marcel Mauss.
Photograph taken during the Great War
*(Courtesy of Etienne Halphen and the
British Centre for Durkheimian Studies)*

CONTENTS

PREFACE

This volume offers a set of essays which re-evaluate the importance of the writings and inspiration of Marcel Mauss, the nephew and younger colleague of Emile Durkheim. One of the few scholars in Durkheim's circle to survive the Great War, Mauss continued teaching and publishing until the late 1930s, and he played a key part in the survival of the Durkheimian tradition in the social sciences. This is already well recognised, but it is only in recent years that a fresh generation of scholars and students has begun to recognise his distinctive contribution to, and reshaping of, that tradition. The essays presented here explore not only the context of Mauss's work and his influence on other writers, but also the resonance of some of his key themes for the concerns of today's anthropology and sociology.

Recent publications testify to the awakening realisation of the power of Mauss's writings in France and the French-speaking world. We should make special mention here of the substantial biographical work by Marcel Fournier from the University of Montreal, *Marcel Mauss* and his edited volume *Marcel Mauss: écrits politiques*, as well as the theoretical commentaries by Bruno Karsenti *Marcel Mauss: le fait social total* and *L'homme total* (for details see the select bibliography at the end of this volume). The correspondence between Durkheim and Mauss is being edited by Philippe Besnard, Marcel Fournier, and Christine Delangle, and is expected to appear in the near future. The *Revue européenne des sciences sociales* devoted a special issue (1996) to the proceedings of a 1995 conference 'Mauss: hier et aujourd'hui' held in Lausanne, Switzerland. Maurice Godelier published *L'énigme du don* in 1996, a major reassessment of Mauss's essay on the forms of exchange, and it is expected that this will shortly appear in English translation.

Interest in Mauss has also grown in Britain, and more generally in the world of Anglophone anthropology. The present volume is among the results of a conference on 'Marcel Mauss Today' held at Oxford University in September, 1996. It was organised by the British Centre for Durkheimian Studies, the Institute of Social and Cultural Anthropology, and the Maison Française. The meetings drew a wide attendance from students as well as professional scholars in anthropology and related fields. Some twenty-eight papers were presented, about half in French and half in English. Participants came from several European countries as well as further afield.

From the wide range of papers discussed at the conference, it was decided to select those which would form a coherent set of studies and would appeal most to an English-language readership interested in the current relevance of Mauss's work. Most of the present chapters were originally written in English, but those by the French scholars Alain Testart, Claudine Haroche, and Bruno Karsenti are included here in translation, along with that of the Russian scholar Alexander Gofman (also originally presented in French). Together they re-evaluate Mauss's work from a number of complementary angles, and illustrate how fruitfully his ideas can be brought into current fields of theoretical discussion and research practice in the social sciences. We believe the publication of this book is very timely for British and American anthropology in particular, and we hope it will be found a worthy complement to the new publications which are appearing in French. We believe also that it will carry forward a long-standing acknowledgement of theoretical indebtedness on the part of English-speaking anthropologists towards the French tradition, and trust that it will be found serviceable as a teaching guide.

The editors, Wendy James and Nicholas Allen, are both based at Oxford University's Institute of Social and Cultural Anthropology, and are committee members of the British Centre for Durkheimian Studies (founding organiser W.S.F. Pickering) which is located there. The Centre has already overseen the publication of several volumes arising from former conferences, mostly relating to Durkheim. This is the first with a dominantly anthropological tone, and the first concerned specifically with Mauss. It is particularly appropriate that it has been possible to include it in Berghahn Books' new series 'Methodology and History in Anthropology', under the general editorship of David Parkin, Director of the Institute of Social and Cultural Anthropology.

ACKNOWLEDGEMENTS

As editors of this volume, and on behalf of W.S.F. Pickering and the British Centre for Durkheimian Studies, we would like to express our gratitude to all those who presented papers to the conference 'Marcel Mauss Today' in 1996. We are sorry that we were not able to include a wider range of papers in the present volume, though all texts submitted have been deposited in the archive collection of the Centre. We are grateful to those who chaired sessions at the conference and guided the discussions, in particular R.H. Barnes, Gérald Berthoud, Philippe Besnard, John Davis, Maurice Godelier, Raymond Jamous, Josep Llobera, David Parkin, Peter Rivière, and Willie Watts-Miller. For full collaboration in the planning of the conference and generous assistance in every aspect of its becoming a reality, as well as for welcoming us to the Maison Française, we are greatly indebted to its Director, Jean-Claude Vatin and his staff. We greatly appreciated John Davis's kindness in inviting participants to an opening reception at All Souls College. We benefited from the support of St Cross College in providing facilities for the conference dinner, as well as that of St Anne's College in providing accommodation for some guests. General assistance with the running of the conference was provided by a team of graduate students. We were very pleased that two members of the family, Mme. Claudette Kennedy and M. Pierre Mauss, were able to join us on the occasion of this conference marking the centenary of the journal to which Marcel Mauss contributed so much.

David Parkin gave us helpful guidance at various stages in the evolution of this volume. In the editorial task of translating four of the papers here from their original French, we were very glad to have the assistance of Jacqueline Redding and the contributors themselves. The

Institute of Social and Cultural Anthropology provided the basic
facilities for producing the manuscript, and we occasionally needed
help from the administrative staff there. We would like to make special
mention of the support given us by the librarian Mike Morris, as well
as Isabella Birkin, Sue Shayler, and Gina Burrows. Loïc Wacquant
kindly provided bibliographic advice. Finally we would like to
acknowledge financial support from an ESRC research seminar grant
to the Durkheim Centre, a grant from the CNRS in Paris via the Maison
Française, and (in connection with the expenses of producing the
book) some assistance from the Faculty Board of Anthropology and
Geography in the University of Oxford.

We gladly acknowledge the permission granted by Cambridge
University Press and Philippe Besnard for including a revised version
of Marcel Mauss's 'Intellectual self-portrait', first published in Philippe
Besnard's edited volume *The sociological domain*, Cambridge, 1983.
Finally, we would like to offer special thanks to Sir Raymond Firth, who
was glad to hear that this book was under way and spoke very warmly
of meeting Mauss in the 1920s and 1930s. He very kindly made a
written note of his memories for us, and this may be found towards the
end of the Introductory Essay, chapter 1 below.

WJ, NJA
5 May 1998

Introductory essay

'ONE OF US':

MARCEL MAUSS AND 'ENGLISH' ANTHROPOLOGY

Wendy James

The links between social anthropology as it developed in Britain (together with its cousins in the wider Anglophone world) and the work of several generations of French scholars are many and subtle. One of the key connections, which this volume carries forward, was forged by E.E. (later Sir Edward) Evans-Pritchard, Professor of Social Anthropology at Oxford from 1946 to 1970. Throughout his career he promoted a greater awareness of Durkheim's sociology and the ideas and writings of his colleagues as represented in the journal they founded in 1898, *L'Année sociologique*. The present volume marks not only the centenary of the first appearance of this journal, but of Marcel Mauss's first visit to Oxford, when he presented the first volume to Professor (later Sir) Edward Tylor over dinner; this same copy remains in the library of the Institute of Social and Cultural Anthropology, inscribed in Mauss's hand: 'A Monsieur le Prof. Tylor. Avec la permission de Mr Durkheim. Hommages & profond respect de Marcel Mauss. Oxford. 6 juin 1898.'

The work of the Durkheimian school became a standard reference point in the teaching of social anthropology at Oxford and elsewhere, and in many ways has shaped much research and theoretical debate in the discipline over the last half-century. Evans-Pritchard's effort itself continued a history of close contacts between the French school of Durkheim, especially as represented in the figure of Marcel Mauss, and the world of Anglophone anthropology. These contacts were very

significant in Britain, but also in other English-speaking countries
where anthropology was expanding, including the United States of
America. In this essay, I do not attempt to indicate the influence of
English anthropology upon Mauss; rather the other way around, in
order to highlight some of the ways in which his work has been
appreciated by the English-reading community of anthropologists,
and continues to be so.

French sociology was by no means the only source of 'modern'
social anthropology in Britain. There were, for example, the
established museums which had inspired much of the initial
professional activities of anthropologists in the late nineteenth
century (Sir Edward Tylor, for example, holding the position of Reader
in Anthropology at the Pitt Rivers Museum from 1883, and Professor
from 1896, while in Cambridge Haddon fostered systematic study at
the Museum of Anthropology and Archaeology). There were
important contributions from the 'science' side, including the work of
Rivers in the field of psychology. There were important connections
with archaeology, ancient history, and the classics (Sir James Frazer
was actively based at Trinity College, Cambridge, and at Oxford the
archaeologist and historian R.R. Marett was appointed Reader in
Social Anthropology in 1910, fostering these links for a further three
decades). In London, Seligman and Malinowski at the LSE had created
a standard in the 1920s for the 'fieldworking' side of social
anthropology's methods, and Malinowski in particular flew the flag
for 'participant observation' and for the need to establish
anthropology as something quite distinct from history and from the
museums. A.R. Radcliffe-Brown, as the first holder of the Oxford Chair
from 1937, represented a strong pull towards the 'natural science'
ideal for the discipline.

Evans-Pritchard drew upon all these sources, and the work of
many of these men (themselves in many cases indebted to the French
school for inspiration and practical support), in formulating his own
approach and in establishing what became the largest and most
influential of the British anthropology departments in the years
following the Second World War. One of the features that marked his
vision of the discipline, however, was an explicit rejection of the claims
for a 'natural science' status pressed by some of his contemporaries;
while not endorsing the older, evolutionary conceptions which had
shaped much anthropology, he was clear in his appeals for social
anthropology to admit, and foster, its character as one of the
humanities. He pointed to its affinity with history, its means of
working being through language, through the translation of
meanings, and through the constructive activity of the ethnologist as
personal interpreter of the particular society being studied. He dealt

critically with one generalising system of theory after another, rejecting the pretentions of scholars who remained entangled in the language of their own preconceptions rather than engaging seriously with the language of those being studied. I believe that Evans-Pritchard has too often been bracketed with the 'systematising' efforts of what we are now pleased to call 'structural-functionalism', while his primary concern with the integrity of the ethnographic data, its historical specificity, and the human agency of those it describes and represents, has not always been sufficiently recognised.

As a part of the reestablishment of anthropology after the war, Evans-Pritchard endeavoured to construct a historical lineage for modern anthropology (something that very few of his colleagues attempted at the time). He lectured regularly on figures such as Montesquieu, Saint-Simon, Comte, Adam Ferguson, etc.[1] It was in this context that he gave Durkheim a central place. But in relation to Durkheim's actual writings, especially *The elementary forms of religious life*, Evans-Pritchard's lectures and papers were never uncritical: rather to the contrary. He was scathing of the notion that religion could be reduced to sociological explanation; and in other ways distanced himself (in his own words) from received Durkheimian theory, as from other generalising social theories.[2] He called upon his colleagues and students, most famously in lectures of the 1950s and 1960s, to abandon the false promise of the natural sciences and to embrace the methods and philosophy rather of history. One of the key figures he invoked to his support in this campaign was R.G. Collingwood, historian of Roman Britain, academic sceptic, and philosopher.[3]

I believe it was in the same spirit of rebuilding anthropology in the mould of the humanities that Evans-Pritchard responded to the writings of Marcel Mauss. Here too he found a writer who sought out the materiality of social forms in time and place, the interconnection of language, action, and experience, and the rootedness of what we might now call psychological dispositions. Collingwood certainly resisted the systematising positivism of his colleagues in academic philosophy, turning rather to a vision of history, conceived as the past forms of human life and thought, as the proper subject-matter for a reflexive and critical philosopher.[4] Mauss, while not actually rejecting Durkheim's positivism and formalism, did seek out other ways of investigating and comparing what he often referred to as the 'concrete' phenomena of social life. He not only collaborated with Emile Durkheim in the establishment of a distinctive French tradition of comparative sociology in the first years of the twentieth century, but carried this tradition forward in the inter-war period. He was a key figure in the shaping, even reshaping, of Durkheimian ideas about the phenomena of social life in the French academy itself — the main theme of Bruno Karsenti's recent work, including his chapter in this volume. As it was, Mauss continued to rework aspects of the Durkheimian heritage in such an engaging and persuasive manner that they retained a fresh appeal even after the Second World War, and profoundly influenced the modern discipline of social and cultural anthropology as it was expanding rapidly at that time both in French and English language scholarship, research, and teaching. There are parallels between the ways in which Collingwood, Evans-Pritchard, and Mauss seemed to seek out complexity, rather than easy generalisation in the study of human life. Further, and especially with reference to the ethnographers, I believe that we can roughly equate Evans-Pritchard's call for anthropologists to see their ethnographic material in the kind of way that a historian would with Mauss's advocacy of the need to study the forms of social life in all the specificity of their 'concrete' existence.

The appeal of the Durkheimian group to British anthropology stemmed mainly from the fact of their commitment to the integrity of evidence about the remoter peoples of the world. No other major writer or school of writing in the nineteenth century which claimed to encompass the broad principles of history, government, morality, or the nature of human beings paid such sustained and professionally expert attention to the ethnographic record (compare, for example, Marx and Weber). There was already a strong empirical tradition in British anthropology, as I have indicated. What the *Année* group offered to those seeking to develop a philosophical framework for social anthropology as one of the humanities was their combination of respect for empirical detail, linguistic sensitivity, and the promise of sophisticated, deep-level comparison. These were the qualities apparent in the work of Marcel Mauss and other colleagues which became much better known to Anglophone anthropologists through the series of translations of essays from the *Année* promoted by Evans-Pritchard after the war (discussed in detail below). Their reception also provided part of the context in which the work of Claude Lévi-Strauss began later to be read, taught, and translated.[5] The affinity was evident; and for many British anthropologists in the 1960s, it seemed that the earlier generation of French works were likely to be put in the shade for ever by the dazzling abstractions of Lévi-Straussian structuralism. But while the way in which anthropological questions are framed has been profoundly and permanently affected by Lévi-Strauss's vision, the older French texts, and particularly the ethnographically-grounded essays, have remained fresh, suggestive, and often pointedly relevant to post-structuralist concerns. Anglophone anthropology has expanded enormously, in several directions, and it has moved closer in some of its guises to the disciplines of psychology, history, and Marxism — the very disciplines against which Durkheim tried to define sociology, and from which structuralism seems insulated. But at the same time, the work of Marcel Mauss has seemed to reassert its claim on our attention, the work of a man who was first nephew, pupil, and collaborator to Durkheim, and later a major influence on Lévi-Strauss.

On Mauss's visit to England in 1898, he decided to proceed to Oxford, where his work put him in contact with Indologist Moriz Winternitz. He also met Tylor, to whom he presented some of his own work along with the first volume of *L'Année sociologique*. Marcel Fournier's recent biography gives a wealth of detail about Mauss's contacts and exchanges with British, as well as American anthropologists over the next four decades. He established very warm relations with Sir James and Lady Frazer, who visited him on several occasions in Paris. He made visits to England, for example in 1905, and again in 1912 when he spent a couple of months working at the British Museum, learning of the work of A.R. Radcliffe-Brown and meeting Rivers and Haddon at Cambridge, Marett at Oxford, and Seligman in London. He addressed the Aristotelian Society in 1920 on 'The problem of nationality', spent another short period in London in 1921, and then in 1924 came back to reestablish his relationships with British institutions and colleagues as a part of the postwar effort to revive the *Année sociologique*. On this occasion he was again able to meet several anthropologists, including Balfour and Malinowski. In 1926 he made a tour of the United States, his heavy programme including seminar series at Harvard and Chicago. A couple of years later he was invited back to London to give a series of three lectures at the LSE, on prayer in Australia.[6]

In a testimonial letter, written much later in 1936 in connection with Radcliffe-Brown's application for the Chair at Oxford, Mauss referred to his first visit to Oxford and claimed to count himself, if not actually a pupil, at least a disciple of the late Sir Edward Tylor. He also claimed connections and friendship with a range of British anthropologists, including Haddon and Rivers through whom he was introduced to Radcliffe-Brown, as well as Balfour and Marett, who had carried forward the tradition established by Tylor.[7] Mauss's personal relationship with Radcliffe-Brown seems to have been quite informal and relaxed; in an earlier letter to him written in 1935, he commented, obviously in response to something Radcliffe-Brown put to him: 'Je sais le despotisme de Malinowski. La faiblesse de la Rockefeller vis-à-vis de lui est probablement la cause de son succès. La faiblesse, dûe à l'âge et à l'élégance des autres Anglais, ceux de Londres aussi bien que ceux de Cambridge et d'Oxford lui laissent le champ libre en Angleterre; mais soyez-en bien sûr, même les jeunes qu'il protège savent le juger. Ce sont des royautés qui ne durent pas.'[8] Mauss goes on to suggest that while his major works on magic and agriculture are a very good exposition of facts, and while the Rockefeller grants have enabled him to ensure that his army of followers will carry out a large body of work, his theoretical weakness and total lack of erudition will eventually become evident. In a later paragraph, Mauss interestingly and cryptically says 'Je crois qu'Evans-Pritchard a quelque chance du côté d'Oxford.' Mauss had also been asked to write on behalf of A.M. Hocart, then Professor at the University of Cairo, for whose book on *Les Castes* he was at about this time preparing a very warm introduction; and on behalf of the much younger Evans-Pritchard, whose writings he evidently admired.[9] Radcliffe-Brown, as the senior man, was in the event appointed (though an appointment was also found as a result of Marett's efforts for Evans-Pritchard, as a Research Lecturer in African Sociology). Through all these and other contacts and exchanges, Marcel Mauss was made an Honorary Fellow of the Royal Anthropological Institute about the same time, and invited to deliver the Huxley Memorial Lecture in London in 1938.[10]

R.R. Marett has recorded an interestingly different angle on the development of these English/French connections. In his autobiography of 1941, he tells us that his relations with anthropology in France had been more obscure than those he had cultivated with Germany. He admitted that in the early years of the century, while Durkheim had founded the *Année sociologique* some years back, he had not come across it. However, when he eventually read Hubert and Mauss's essay on magic, he noted that

> [T]hey posited *mana* as basic for magic; very much as I had done for religion, or rather for all transactions with the supernatural conceived or perceived as a wonder-working power. Now I doubt if they had ever heard of me, even as I had never heard of them, when we severally arrived at what was roughly the same conclusion. But I had the almost unfair advantage of priority. Both of us had evidently hit the same bird, and theirs was the heavier shot; but I fired first.[11]

He then observed that he had written a paper in 1904 about how both magic and religion had evolved out of the same '"theoplasm or god-stuff"', as Hartland was for calling it' and 'Even then I had not heard of the similar views of my French colleagues, as the references prove; though a third paper contributed to the Tylor volume in 1907 shows that I had studied them in the meantime.'[12] Marett then reminisced about his search for the *Année sociologique* — when he first heard of it there was no copy to be found in the Oxford libraries, and he had to buy the set of volumes for himself. 'And very glad I was that I had done so.' So far he had done his best to cope with the vast literature, 'a great deal of it in English', that embodied what travellers and other first-hand observers had to say about primitive life. 'But of the theorists, more especially those hailing from the Continent, I knew little, perhaps even congratulating myself on the virgin state of my mind in this respect. But here was a key to all the latest thought about man in society.... True, they were sociologists, not to say socialistic in tendency.' Up to a point, however, he accepted that their insistence on the social element — language being a very good example — was needed to counteract the opposite tendency running through so much of British work, 'Tylor's included'. One was apt, he said, to picture an imaginary being known as 'the savage' who, exactly as if here were an Oxford professor, sat and mused on the nature of things. The French sociologists, even if they tended to go too far the other way, were very enlightening. Marrett claimed to have derived from them his view that religion stood for all the socially approved, and magic for all the antisocial, ways of dealing with the supernormal powers as conceived by a given community. 'In the Sociological Review for January, 1908, I defined my attitude towards this school of thought as carefully as I could, but perhaps failed to indicate the full extent of my debt to their remarkable labours.'[13]

T.K. Penniman, later Curator of the Pitt Rivers Museum, published a book in 1935 entitled *A hundred years of anthropology*. It referred, though only very briefly, to the work of Durkheim and the *Année sociologique*. By the time of the second edition in 1952, however, when an extra substantial chapter was added on 'Anthropology since 1935', the new attention being paid to the French school was commented on at length. 'During the time that has elapsed since the first edition of this book, the influence of Emile Durkheim and of his pupils has greatly increased in England and in the Dominions, mainly through the earlier work of Malinowski, and the later work of Radcliffe-Brown.'[14] Some of the wording comes in fact from the typescript of Evans-Pritchard's BBC lectures — the loan of which Penniman gratefully acknowledges, and the publication of which he considered a most 'important contribution to the history, theory, and aims of the subject'.[15] In developing his account Penniman also refers to Evans-Pritchard's Marett Lecture for 1950, his calls for anthropology to recognise its historical rather than 'natural science' character, and his own historical work.[16] Indeed Evans-Pritchard's efforts at reshaping the discipline also included an explicit focus upon religion, values, symbols and moral ideas, a decisive shift towards the study of language as a vehicle of meaning, and the philosophical implications of translation and interpretation. In these respects, the work of the Durkheimians, and of Lucien Lévy-Bruhl, provided inspiration of a quality well beyond what could be found in Anglophone anthropology.[17]

It was very soon after his taking up the Oxford Chair that Evans-Pritchard sought to strengthen existing academic, institutional, and personal links with the French school. Louis Dumont, a former pupil of Mauss, was appointed to a lecturership at Oxford in 1951. From the early 1950s Evans-Pritchard launched the series of translations which above all else secured the continuing attention of Anglophone scholars, especially in the now rapidly growing discipline of social anthropology, to the *Année* school. The first to appear, in 1953, was a set of three texts by Durkheim himself, translated by David Pocock as *Sociology and philosophy* and introduced by John Peristiany, also teaching at the Oxford Institute.[18] The work of Marcel Mauss, however, came to occupy a central place in this series, which nearly half a century on is still being taken forward through the efforts of the British Centre for Durkheimian Studies (an English version of the essay by Hubert and Mauss on 'Time' is in preparation as we go to press with this volume[19]). The various introductions to these translated texts together constitute an overview of the lasting inspiration which English readers have found in the ideas and methods of the *Année* school.

Evans-Pritchard invited Ian Cunnison to undertake the translation of Mauss's *Essai sur le don*, possibly around 1950 or even before (he noted that it was some years since he first suggested the project); Cunnison was not only a French scholar but an experienced fieldworking anthropologist, who had a particular interest in history and had already worked both in what is now Zambia and in the northern Sudan.[20] In introducing Cunnison's translation of *The gift* in 1954, Evans-Pritchard emphasised its place in the wider context of the French school. He referred, for example, to the essays on sacrifice, classification, magic, and the seasonal variations of the Eskimo as related works, in which Mauss had collaborated with other members of the school.[21] Evans-Pritchard noted how much of the work which the *Année* group pursued had been of this collaborative kind, and the consequent setback resulting from the terrible loss of so many in the 1914-18 war.

> Had it not been for these disasters Mauss might have given us in ampler measure the fruits of his erudition, untiring industry, and mastery of method. But he not only wrote about social solidarity and collective sentiments. He expressed them in his own life. For him the group of Durkheim and his pupils and colleagues had a kind of collective mind.... On the few occasions I met Mauss I received the impression that this was how he thought and felt, and his actions confirmed it. He took over the labours of his dead colleagues.... He undertook also, in 1923-24, the even heavier task of reviving his beloved *Année*, which had ceased publication after 1913.[22]

Evans-Pritchard reminds us that although Mauss had become a Sanskrit scholar and a historian of religions at the same time as he became a sociologist, the obligations he felt towards the journal, especially its re-launching after the war, and to editing the work of his former colleagues meant that he produced few major works after 1906. 'His projected works on Prayer, on Money and on the State were never completed.'[23]

Evans-Pritchard declared that Mauss was in the line of philosophical tradition running from Montesquieu through the philosophers of the Enlightenment — Turgot, Condorcet, St. Simon — to Comte and then Durkheim, 'a tradition in which conclusions were reached by analysis of concepts rather than of facts'. He added 'While that is true, it is also true that Mauss was far less a philosopher than Durkheim. In all his essays he turns first to the concrete facts and examines them in their entirety and to the last detail.' This was the main theme of an 'excellent' lecture on Mauss which had recently been delivered at Oxford (1952) by one of his former pupils, Louis Dumont. Dumont had pointed out that though Mauss, out of loyalty and affection, studiously avoided open criticism of Durkheim, such criticism is nevertheless implicit in his writings, which are so much more empirical than Durkheim's. 'Mauss sought only to know a limited range of facts and then to understand them, and what Mauss meant by understanding comes out very clearly in the Essay. It is to see social phenomena — as, indeed, Durkheim taught that they should be seen — in their totality. "Total" is the key word of the Essay.' Evans-Pritchard went on to ask what were the means to be used in reaching such an understanding of institutions, and rhetorically to answer: 'They are those employed by the anthropological fieldworker who studies social life from both outside and inside.... Mauss demonstrated that, given enough well documented material, he could do this without leaving his flat in Paris. He soaked his mind in ethnographical material... Mauss did in his study what an anthropologist does in the field.... We social anthropologists regard him as one of us.'[24]

Evans-Pritchard emphasised Mauss's devotion to original sources; 'one must be a scholar'; not only was Mauss able to offer insights to professional Sanskritists and Roman lawyers, but could also advance the interpretation of Malinowski's ethnography of the Trobriand Islands. 'He could do this because of his vast knowledge, which Malinowski lacked, of Oceanic languages and of the native societies of Melanesia, Polynesia, America and elsewhere, which enabled him to deduce by a comparative study of primitive institutions what the fieldworker had not himself observed.'[25]

Not all the texts which became part of the series involved Mauss directly, though in spirit they were all very close to his work. For example, in 1960, two essays by his younger colleague Robert Hertz were published in English, those on 'Death' and 'The right hand' (translated by Rodney and Claudia Needham).[26] In his introduction Evans-Pritchard noted: 'In the last few years there have been published translations by past and present members of the Institute of Social Anthropology at Oxford of two minor classics of the French sociological school.... A third volume is now presented.... These essays I have greatly admired, and I have lectured on them at Oxford for a number of years.... We hope [these translations] may be the beginning of a series of such translations — of essays which have a close theoretical relationship'. The British interest in Hertz has indeed continued, and is still doing so with further translation work and evaluative studies by Robert Parkin.[27] As Evans-Pritchard proclaimed: 'If the essays are still worth reading they are worth translating, for there are many people in the world, among them students of sociology and social anthropology, who have English as a mother or second tongue and have no, or a very inadequate, knowledge of the French language; and I believe that they are still worth reading, although written many years ago, for their historical, methodological, and theoretical interest.'[28] There follows quite a substantial discussion of the 'comparative method', in which Evans-Pritchard develops with some ambition his vision of the place of anthropology in the wider field of scholarship and social theory.[29] Anthropology was more than a fieldworking subject, a search for empirical data; it required a body of theoretical ideas, and this is where the French school was so important. 'It is a fact, which none can deny, that the theoretical capital on which anthropologists today live is mainly the writings of people whose research was entirely literary, who brought to bear great ability, much learning, and rigorous methods of scholarship on what others had observed and recorded.' He recorded his own sense of commitment: 'When that capital is exhausted we are in danger of falling into mere empiricism, one field study after another adding to the number of known facts, but uninspired and uninspiring. If a personal note be allowed, I would, though with serious reservations, identify myself with the Année school if a choice had to be made and an intellectual allegiance to be declared.'[30]

The essay on 'Primitive classification' appeared in 1963, Needham's translation of a text by Durkheim and Mauss, whose connection with Hertz's work was evident. It appeared not long after Franz Steiner's study *Taboo*, which also had close links with the Maussian tradition; and it was soon followed by Mary Douglas's well known *Purity and danger*.[31] I would venture to say that *Primitive classification*, after *The gift*, has been the most heavily used of the whole series of *Année* translations in the teaching of anthropology in Britain. Nick Allen has recently provided a re-evaluation of the lasting importance of this essay, despite some of the critical observations offered in the translator's introduction. Allen offers a defence of its broadly historical character, its role as a source for Granet's work on Chinese thought, and indirectly at least for the work of Dumézil. He clarifies the essay's implications for a study of those cosmological forms of classification in which entities that are classified 'horizontally' or syntagmatically (for instance, males classified into clans) are at the same time classified 'vertically' or paradigmatically as being linked with a particular totemic species or cardinal point or colour. The 'vertical' linkages, based on 'affective' qualities, are more or less absent in the 'flatter' world of modern 'developed' systems of science and philosophy, where the effort is made to base classifications on purely intellectual judgements of sameness or difference. He argues that the original intention of the essay was to explore the prehistory of scientific classification, via the specific cases of the Australians, the Zuñi, the Chinese and so forth.[32]

A translation of the essay by Hubert and Mauss on 'Sacrifice' appeared soon after, in 1964.[33] Evans-Pritchard had explicitly drawn on this essay in his work on Nuer religion, and in introducing it he wrote that it was 'one of the gems of the Année.... [A]s a study of the structure, or one might almost say the grammar, of the sacrificial rite the Essay is superb.' He suggested that while little reference to the Essay had been made, this was perhaps due to a lack of interest among sociologists and social anthropologists in religion; but 'Interest in the subject appears to be reviving, and it would seem an appropriate time therefore for publication in an English translation of this remarkable piece of scholarly analysis.'[34]

The year 1972 saw the publication of Hubert and Mauss's essay on 'Magic' in English.[35] This text has had perhaps the least obvious connections with, and influence on, Anglophone anthropology. It is very different in tone, and in approach, to the extremely influential work of Evans-Pritchard himself on Azande witchcraft. I think it very unlikely that Evans-Pritchard had Hubert and Mauss's work in mind in the 1930s when he was working on this topic. David Pocock, in his introduction, did not really deal directly with the text itself, relying rather on some of the comments which Lévi-Strauss had already published. He suggested that the essay contributes to the 'dissolution' of magic, though admits that this was not really Mauss's intention.[36] He emphasises that Mauss treats magic as an action (and here signals perhaps the different furrow that had been ploughed by British anthropology in treating it as part of an intellectual or belief system).[37] Pocock brought some of his own material from India into line with Mauss's analysis, but confessed, 'One can on occasion become irritated with Mauss as with a contemporary'.[38] In English anthropology, the field of 'magic and witchcraft' was still in the 1970s dominated by

African ethnographic contributions, themselves coloured markedly by the 'intellectualist' concerns established by Evans-Pritchard's own earlier work. For myself as a British-trained anthropologist, it was puzzling to find virtually no reference to African data in this book when it appeared, and it was equally difficult to relate the ideas in it to the 'received' standard understanding of Durkheim's dualistic theory about religion as a society-wide phenomenon and 'magic' as an individualistic and antisocial activity.[39] It may be possible at some later date, however, for anthropologists to re-engage with the ideas of this essay: ideas of a undeniably 'phenomenological' kind about personal force, felt power, and its ritual enactment in social relations.[40]

The series continued in 1979 with the appearance of two volumes. One was James Fox's translation of the essay on the seasonal variations of the Eskimo, prepared by Mauss in collaboration with Beuchat.[41] Fox, who had taken his doctorate at Oxford, provided a substantial foreword, in itself a fine essay on Mauss and the *Année* school as a source of influence on British anthropology. In particular, Fox shows how 'clear and unmistakable' was the influence of Mauss and Beuchat's essay about the Eskimo upon the formation of Evans-Pritchard's classic study *The Nuer* of 1940. It is worth noting also that several introductory anthropology books of the 1970s make special reference to the interest of the Eskimo essay, for example those by David Pocock, Ioan Lewis and Edmund Leach.[42] Fox acutely observes that the 'modernity' of Mauss's thought, already noted by Lévi-Strauss, poses its own problems. 'So many of Mauss's ideas have borne fruit that there is a temptation to render them in a language and terminology of a later date. This would be a disservice to Mauss, whose ideas at the time were still in a crucial formative phase.' Therefore, Fox explains, he has endeavoured to keep as close to Mauss's own terminology and mode of phrasing as 'the demands of fluent English would allow'.[43] We have recognised the problem, and tried in the presentation of the essays here to follow this lead.

The second volume was the translation by Ben Brewster of a set of short but very suggestive pieces by Mauss, consisting of his lectures on relations between sociology and psychology, on the collective suggestion of the idea of death, on the notion of the person and on body techniques (the text on body techniques had appeared first in *Economy and society*). The major essay on 'the person' had originally been presented in London and published in the *Journal of the Royal Anthropological Institute*. There had as yet been no translation, although both Meyer Fortes and John Middleton had made contributions to this topic, in a French edited volume on concepts of 'the person' in Africa.[44] Real interest in Mauss's essay among English and American scholars was created only in the late 1970s, when Nick

Allen's conversations about it with Michael Carrithers and others led
to an interdisciplinary seminar series at Wolfson College, Oxford, in
1980. This bore fruit in 1985, in a book devoted to the implications of
the essay. Here was included a fresh translation by W.D. Halls, an
appreciation of the piece by Nick Allen, and a set of case studies by
anthropologists, historians and philosophers drawing on evidence
from many civilisations and historical periods. These were designed to
bear on Mauss's chief proposition: that the *category* of the self-
directed, privately conscious, individual human person, congruent
with the public endorsement of individual identity and agency, is not
a human universal but itself a product of Western history. The debates
surrounding this question, cast rather differently from contemporary
burgeoning concerns about 'the self' in popular scholarship have also
formed a significant part of exchanges between anthropology and
psychology. They have set in a wider historical and cultural context the
kinds of attention now commonly given to 'the individual', the
cultural construction of 'personhood' and consciousness, and to
subjective experience in the processes of doing ethnographic research
and writing it up.[45] Mauss's essay on the person can now be seen quite
clearly as one influential source for Dumont's developing arguments
about the particular circumstances of the rise of individualism in the
West, and the contrast with those modes of social hierarchy so well
exemplified in India. Implicitly, too, one can place Marilyn Strathern's
critique of Western individualism contained in her masterly study of
the social, and gendered, formation of 'persons' in Melanesia
alongside Dumont's work as an endorsement and elaboration of
Mauss's position.[46]

Of the four pieces in Brewster's collection, the first two and the last,
dealing with psychological, bodily, and experiential aspects of the
human being, have been relatively neglected in Anglophone
anthropology up to now, but are given particular attention by several
contributors to the present volume. Touching on themes of human
consciousness and engaging with issues in medicine, psychology, and
philosophy, they also present particular problems for the translator. Here
we find, for example, Mauss's clearest, though still tentative, portrayal of
the image of *l'homme total* as the proper focus of anthropological study,
and his explicit divergence from the body/soul, individual/society
dualism of Durkheim. The conception of *l'homme total,* discussed for
example in the chapters here by Gofman, Karsenti, Schlanger, and
Haroche, is not that of 'the individual' as a complete totality; it is more
a conception of the 'totality of the human condition', encompassing as
it does, within each individual and across the collectivity, the
intersecting planes, or dimensions, of organic, psychological, and social
existence. In French, of course, while *l'homme* takes the masculine

grammatical form, it cannot be translated today simply as 'man', partly because it never has been in itself a gendered conception in the same way as its English equivalent, but mainly because of the strong modern currents against 'sexism' in language which have changed the way we use English. In handling the sensitivities of translating this term, we have decided not to adopt any fixed English formula. According to context, we sometimes leave the expression in French; sometimes use 'total', 'complete', or 'whole human being', or sometimes a phrase such as 'totality of the human condition' in order to avoid the suggestion of closure or completeness within the individual as such. We have also avoided using the term 'person' in translating *l'homme total*, because of the potential confusion with Mauss's own arguments in his essay treating the modern, Western conception of the autonomous person and the private self in its historical context.

The momentum of interest in Mauss's work continued, with a fresh translation in 1990 of *The gift* (also by W.D. Halls). A new introduction by Mary Douglas indicated in its range of reference the wide influence of the essay, which by this time had become a central and influential teaching requirement in British departments and beyond. Douglas remarked on anthropology since *The gift*: 'Nothing has been the same since. The big developments stem from this work. Before we had *The gift*'s message unfolded for us, we anthropologists, if we thought of the economy at all, treated it almost as a separate aspect of society, and kinship as separate again, and religion as a final chapter at the end.' She suggested that Evans-Pritchard had Mauss's teaching very much at heart when he described the marriage dues of the Nuer as a strand in the total circulation of cattle, and wives, and children, and men: 'every single relationship had its substantiation in a gift.'[47] Douglas went on to discuss her own efforts to apply Mauss's ideas to modern society, echoing the Durkheim scholar Steven Lukes on the return of the old 'enemy' of utilitarianism, and the renewed quest for trust and solidarity.

Not all the British responses to Mauss's anthropology have wholeheartedly endorsed his virtues. Some leading figures have expressed reservations. For example, Raymond Firth has repeated his as recently as 1993 (but compare the warmth of his personal memories, below). After indicating that Malinowski and Radcliffe-Brown, leaders of the field in the 1920s, 'shared a respect for the French sociological tradition' and that he and fellow students were well acquainted with the work of Durkheim and Mauss, Firth goes on to say, 'You know, there are enormous fashions in social anthropology, particularly in the teaching of social anthropology. *The gift* by Marcel Mauss is a very interesting and important work, but I don't think it is either as interesting or as important as the reading lists of all the universities would seem to show.

To us at that time, it was really a kind of development of Malinowski's thesis.'[48] Nevertheless it gained a central place in the textbooks as exemplifying the apparently general or even universal way in which the circulation of goods helps to create a framework of moral and social relations. See, for example, the references in John Beattie's *Other cultures* of 1964.[49]

In the world of English-language anthropology, and even beyond, Mauss's essay *The gift* is by far the best known of his texts. While we have emphasised in this book how much larger is the scope of his contribution, we include a set of papers specifically taking their starting point from this essay. They too have a historical thrust: they all eschew the easy and 'naturalistic' generalisations which have sometimes been drawn from readings of *The gift*. Alain Testart questions the facile assumptions of universality behind the apparent general logic of exchange and reciprocity; what can these mean in any one concrete instance; what can it mean to speak, literally, of an 'obligation to return'? As a general principle, it does not exist. Ilana Silber looks sceptically at the usefulness of recent 'exchange' theory in analysing the very 'personal' and competitive forms of wealth donation in the U.S.A. Is there not something of Maussian 'totality' in modern American philanthropy?

Against these questionings it is significant that in his essay for Evans-Pritchard's memorial volume, Godfrey Lienhardt chose to emphasise Mauss's insights into the less benign aspects of social life — indeed into reciprocal enmity and aggression, on which Evans-Pritchard had also written.[50] This theme of the negative, hurtful, and hostile aspects of 'the gift' and its refusal was present in Mauss's main study, and also developed in a separate paper playing on the ambiguities of the word *gift*, which in various Germanic languages can mean either gift or poison. The ambivalences of gift giving, or its denial, are currently being reconsidered by several scholars. See, for example, Alan Schrift's introduction to a recent collection of old and new papers by both French and Anglophone anthropologists, which itself includes a translation of Mauss's essay 'Gift, gift'; and also Maurice Godelier's recent work, about to appear in English.[51] The idea of reciprocity denied has also played a key role in work on the general sociology of exchange by Marshall Sahlins in America, Frederik Barth in Norway, and John Davis in Britain (as well as by Jonathan Parry in the very particular case of India); and it receives further commentary here in several chapters.[52] Mauss on gift giving has perhaps been over-discussed in Anglophone anthropology, especially as part of a quest for principle — how far are gifts voluntary, how far do they create positive moral bonds, etc.; to the point where some of the dimensions of Mauss's insights have been overlooked, especially where they do not sit very comfortably with a bourgeois outlook on the niceness of making social relationships. Things are not easily given away, nor do people always make ties by marrying out. Paul Dresch's hard look at the Middle East and its high evaluations of auonomy and endogamy in his chapter here reveals something of the discomfort which that ethnographic region presents to any easy reading of Durkheim, Mauss, or indeed Lévi-Strauss on the general social rationality of 'reciprocity', in the division of labour, in commerce, or in marriage. Mauss's argument even in *The gift* is actually more difficult than this, Tim Jenkins' chapter probes a deeper Maussian concern with pre-categorical forces of compulsion in human life, forces which ethnography can help reveal to sociology and to philosophy.

It is interesting that of all the contributions to Evans-Pritchard's memorial volume, the only one which referred to any of Mauss's writings other than *The gift* was the piece by Louis Dumont, itself in fact an English translation of his introduction to the French translation of *The Nuer*. Here Dumont refers to Evans-Pritchard's thought as having been 'nourished by French sociology', and to the translation series he fostered. In elucidating the significance of Evans-Pritchard's analysis of Nuer society, Dumont refers to Mauss's concept of the 'double morphology' of seasonal rhythm (as worked out initially for the Eskimo).[53] He follows David Pocock's formulation of the difference between the functionalist concern for 'social integration' and Evans-Pritchard's search for 'relations defined in terms of social situations, and relations between these relations', the contexts in which he sets the relativities of Nuer terminology.[54] Dumont considers that the shift achieved by Evans-Pritchard, in part the result of his drawing on the ideas of Durkheim and Mauss, was 'important for the history of the subject in England'.[55] He notes that it was not in *The Nuer* that Evans-Pritchard made explicit his difference from Radcliffe-Brown and functionalism: it was in the Marett Lecture of 1950. This raised a storm, while *The Nuer* continued to be accepted and praised; Dumont asks whether we can identify in it, therefore, an element corresponding to 'the predominant trends of English anthropology' alongside another 'which, in contrast, is the author's own, even opposed to current thought?' His answer is naturally in the affirmative; and he comments that 'strictly the structural aspect of *The Nuer* has never really taken root in England'.[56] He goes on to compare Evans-Pritchard's work with what Mauss had been teaching in Paris in the 1930s, suggesting that in *The Nuer* Evans-Pritchard presented a whole series of differentiations where Mauss had simply spoken of 'politico-domestic organization'. Evans-Pritchard had also specifically introduced a widening of the category of the 'political', very much in the spirit of Mauss's emphasis as far back as 1897 when he criticised Steinmetz for not defining, but simply classing according to the common notions. Dumont emphasises that these must be transcended. 'It is not enough to 'adopt modern or western categories, even with modifications; rather the modes of thought of the two universes must be subsumed under categories that fit them both.'[57] A concern for the political, over which there is some ambiguity in *The Nuer*, has sometimes led in later English anthropology to the naive reintroduction of 'the modern individual' into a subject 'where this very book, like other master-books, has shown us the opposite path, that of relationships.'[58] What is especially noteworthy here is the insistence of Dumont, student of Mauss and younger colleague of Evans-Pritchard, on the intellectual sympathy between these two, and the radical difference between their thought and that of Radcliffe-Brown.

Given that there has been so much sustained interest in Mauss and the *Année* school, the 'influence' of *The gift* in particular being so widely acknowledged, we might ask whether it is necessary to return again to the original writings. Of course it will always be possible to suggest that this or that further piece deserves reading, or translating. But beyond this, it is possible to ask whether the full complexity and suggestiveness of the original writings have always been recognised by those who have taken them up. It is in relation to the concept of 'exchange', however, that we see particularly clearly how a very wide range of authors, and teachers, pay lip service to Mauss's essay without necessarily accepting all its implications. A good deal of work on 'exchange' in the social sciences operates at what Edwin Ardener would once have called the level of 's-structures', that is (following de Saussure and the linguistic structuralists) the syntagmatic, or synchronic, chain of events or signs; to restrict one's image of exchange to this literal level of buying, bartering, and conversing is to see society as no more than the sum of these actions and events. The contrast is drawn by structuralists, broadly conceived, with less visible but enduring principles and categories which shape surface actions and events as the grammatical forms of a language govern possible sentences, or as Marxian axioms of the unequal relation between capital and labour govern the apparently free transactions of the market place. Ardener called this paradigmatic level that of 'p-structures', and sought to specify the articulation between the two levels.[59] In the kinds of 'exchange' theory that flowered in economic anthropology particularly in the 1950s and 1960s, it was the surface level of behavioural interaction which engaged the attention of analysts; for example, this perspective marks the work of the whole 'school' of 'transactionalism'.[60] Ardener once called this the 'higher functionalism'; it flows from the utilitarian tradition in the social sciences which remains very strong and is reflected today in such fields as 'rational choice theory'. It was, however, one of Mauss's aims to find an alternative to the world of utilitarianism, and hence his effort to identify the historical contexts from which it had become differentiated. The historicality of *The gift* and its treatment of the notion of *totality* in social phenomena reach beneath the level of specific events and personal actions to those more enduring compulsions, as Jenkins or Dresch would call them, that structure the forms of social life of a given period or region.

Marcel Mauss, of all the *Année* group, seems to have sought out the local connectedness of form and content, the historically specific pattern, the tangible aspect of human life in the movements of social encounter, not only in relation to 'exchange' but also in relation to the body and its material experience, the techniques of work, and the rhythmic enactment of ritual and symbolic performance. He was the first to call this level of the material or corporeal life and its public face by the Latin term *habitus*, originally a medical usage referrring to the external appearance of the body and face in relation to the internal state of health or sickness. The term was later much developed by Pierre Bourdieu to cover the tangible, environmentally and socially situated practical forms of human activity, and in this sense it has now become almost a standard part of anthropological language.[61] It is possible to regard the 'totality' of social phenomena, a theme which runs through much of Mauss's work, as firmly based on this 'grounded' level of social 'reality'. Mauss, like Marx, often appealed to the 'concrete' phenomena of history and human life, rather than seeking abstractions of a formal or transcendent kind. The 'totality' of social phenomena lay not in some bland integrative principle, but in the paradigmatic engagement of the material, the organic and bodily, the psychological and political in a wider choreography of social form which itself had a lasting historical character.

In his treatment of both social and individual life, Mauss avoided endorsing the dualism so characteristic of Durkheim: the categorical opposition of the sacred and the profane, the individual and society, the body and the soul. He also avoided developing the notions of system and the congruence of systemic social facts, notions for which Durkheim is particularly remembered. W.S.F. Pickering's chapter here explores the possibility that Mauss's Jewish background and upbringing played a role in the distinctive development of his thought about society and religion in general, by comparison with that of Durkheim, though so much was common to them. Pickering suggests that some of the divergences of emphasis between the two men's work stem from a fundamentally contrasting conception of the field of religion.

The positive alternatives to 'Durkheimian' theory offered in Mauss's own work often remain implicit, tentative, and partial, but they are present, they are sometimes clearly signalled, and their appeal can be recognised today. The distinctiveness of Mauss's anthropology, and its lasting interest, have been discussed in particular by Nick Allen in a number of contexts; already mentioned above are his papers on 'The person' and on 'Primitive classification'. He has also offered a 'Maussian approach' to Durkheim's *Division of labour,* arguing among other things that Mauss had a more persuasive view of the internal complexity of the most elementary conceivable form of human society than had Durkheim. Cleavages, cross-cutting criteria of differentiation, and reciprocities were built in, as it were, to the most kinship-based and seemingly amorphous forms of 'mechanical' solidarity. Having demonstrated the presence of these principles in Mauss's commentaries on social cohesion and segmentation,[62] Allen is able to show how close he came to formulating a model of early human society that can also be derived from other principles (in particular through the comparative study of kinship terminology): a model of differentiation by sex, by descent moiety, and by alternating generation categories, such that the alternating generation moieties constitute each other's membership by the exchange of children.[63] Allen has continued to extend his re-evaluation of vital themes in Mauss's work, another recent paper, for example, considering the way in which Mauss took seriously and carried forward the *Année's* primary aim of exploring the social history of the Aristotelian categories of thought. In this general endeavour, he argues, lies the coherence of Mauss's *oeuvre* as a whole.[64]

Nick Allen's chapter here is also concerned with Mauss's sense of the 'historical'. One of the books that Mauss planned to write but never did would have explored the category of 'substance' and shown its connection with vernacular theories and representations of food in India, Greece, and elsewhere, ideas which underlie the modern scientific concept of matter. For Mauss, as Allen notes, categories are abstractions from the mode of thinking and feeling current in a historically given society (i.e., not, *pace* some philosophers, entities transcending social history). The argument was present to some degree in the essay on primitive classification; and can be developed with respect, Allen argues, to the evidence for the prevalence of five-fold structures of classification in Indo-European history. Mauss aspired to 'a *sociologie* combining ethnography with philology and history', and Allen comments that while there is still a vast amount to do, Mauss's vision remains inspirational.

The essays of several contributors to the present volume pick up and elaborate themes in Mauss's writings that have hitherto had little attention, at least in British and American anthropology. For example, Schlanger develops the importance of Mauss's perception of the field of 'technology' as the study of the effective use of the human body itself, a topic that leads directly into the effectiveness of the way the body uses tools. The material level of cultural transmission and the learning of such techniques is a profoundly important element in Mauss's argument that the 'nation' cannot be identified with a pure ideal origin; peoples have borrowed, lent, and adapted techniques over all historical time and modern nations are all cultural hybrids. Haroche develops the theme of the communicative significance of human gesture and other organised bodily actions, and the way in which participation in systems of gestural communication defines in some ways what constitutes a society, or a civilisation. James develops the distinctively 'historical' dimensions of Mauss's work, especially in his response to African ethnography. Not only does he perceive the time depth of older, internal patterns whereby African societies have interacted and affected one another culturally and politically over long periods, but (unlike Durkheim) he draws this longer history into a manageable relation to the changes resulting from the recent historical disruption of quite another order, produced by the colonial appropriation of most of Africa. Jonathan Parry's appraisal of Mauss as the fundamental theoretical influence lying behind Dumont's work on India, and on hierarchy and its historically specific western counterpart of individualism, demonstrates the continuing vitality of the Maussian vision, itself rooted partly in his studies of ancient India. The long-term historical dimension is present here too; and we could perhaps see a significant contrast with Australia, the type case of religion which Durkheim selected as the basis for *The elementary forms*, and for which the evidence quite lacked any sense of internal, ancient history; at the same time it rarely incorporated the dimension of modern historical time as it was affecting Australian society. Tim Jenkins emphasises in his critique of Derrida (which reflects sceptically also on the formalism and the universal, ahistorical abstractions of Durkheim and Lévi-Strauss) the irreducibly empirical 'inertia' of ethnographic texts and the practices they report, arguing that to take the ethnography seriously entails a moral confrontation that cannot be dissipated by the abstract manipulations of language.

As we were completing the preparation of this volume, I found myself by chance in conversation with Sir Raymond Firth at the annual conference of the Association of Social Anthropologists of the Commonwealth, of which he is Life President. I told him of this project, and he was glad to reminisce about his and Rosemary Firth's memories of meeting Marcel Mauss on several occasions. He graciously agreed to write a few words for us to include here to add a personal note to our collective tribute.

> I first met Mauss in (I think) 1926. With Malinowski I went to his apartment in Paris, to be greeted by a burly man with a black beard, hospitable, intellectually exuberant, and talking fairly good English with a slight American accent. He welcomed me as a New Zealander, having as I

gathered, served as an interpreter for American and British troops, including some New Zealanders, in the course of the First World War. His apartment held many exotic objects, including as I remember a West African sculpture of a leopard. His conversation, mainly with Malinowski, was scholarly and stimulating, and they argued amicably, but strongly, about some anthropological matters which I cannot now recall. Mauss was obviously an enthusiast for ideas.

I met him on several other occasions in Paris and London. Perhaps he had a special interest in me because I had worked with Maori people, and he seemed to fancy himself somewhat as an interpreter of Maori thought. In his *Essai sur le don* he had taken a Maori text as the pivot of his argument about reciprocity in the gift. But I felt he did not really understand the Maori, and in fact he glossed one word of the text quite wrongly. The Maori elder spoke of a gift having an immaterial essence which demanded a proper return. Mauss misread this as implying that part of the personality of the giver was involved. But while this distorted the Maori view, Mauss's concept proved extremely stimulating. My critique was published first in 1929, soon after his own essay.[65] But he did not take it amiss, and our relations remained very friendly. In 1937 he wrote a letter in support of my (unsuccessful) application for the chair of anthropology at Cambridge.

In the autumn of 1937, as we remember with great pleasure, he dined my wife and me in his Paris apartment, cooking the meal himself — 'a beautiful steak' says Rosemary — in the intervals of attending to his wife, who was ill in an adjoining room and could not appear. Lively in talk, he was gentle and most courteous to Rosemary. This was the last time I saw him and I retain warm memories of his wide range of knowledge, his sparkling intellect and his generous nature.

(signed) *Raymond Firth, 7-IV-98.*

Sir Raymond's particular recollections serve as a reminder that there are numerous angles to the 'English' reception of Marcel Mauss's anthropology. This introductory essay has sketched only a few. I hope at least that it has indicated that our indebtedness to Mauss goes much further than his acknowledged masterpiece, *The gift;* and the chapters which follow take up several fresh and important themes that have a direct bearing on some of the live questions of today's anthropology. We have allowed space first, however, for Mauss himself to outline his intellectual concerns, in a revised translation of a little-known and out-of-print piece. We are confident that the resonance between this piece, and our collection as a whole, will be heard.

NOTES

1. See, for example, E.E. Evans-Pritchard's BBC lectures of 1950, published as *Social anthropology*, London, 1951; and *A history of anthropological thought*, ed. A. Singer, London, 1981.

2. E. Durkheim, *The elementary forms of religious life* [1912], trans. K.E. Fields, New York, 1995. E.E. Evans-Pritchard, *Theories of primitive religion*, London, 1965, chap. 3; *A history of anthropological thought*, chap. 14.

3. See E.E. Evans-Pritchard, 'Social anthropology: past and present', the Marett Lecture, 1950, and 'Anthropology and history', the Simon Lecture, 1961, both reprinted in *Essays in social anthropology*, London, 1962. See also the select bibliography of *Social anthropology*, which includes Collingwood's posthumously published *The idea of history*, Oxford, 1946.

4. R.G. Collingwood, *An essay on philosophical method*, Oxford, 1933; *An essay on metaphysics*, Oxford, 1940; *The idea of history* [1946], revised edn, Oxford, 1993.

5. See, for example, C. Lévi-Strauss, *Tristes tropiques* [1955], trans. J. Russell, London, 1961; *Totemism* [1962], trans. R. Needham, London, 1964; *The savage mind* [1962], London, 1966; *The elementary structures of kinship* [1947], trans. J.H. Bell, J.R. von Sturmer, and R. Needham (editor), London, 1969.

6. I have drawn on the wealth of information in M. Fournier, *Marcel Mauss*, Paris, 1994, pp. 125-34, 153-5, 289-90, 306-7, 351-2, 472-6, 496, 524, 530, 548. Further information on Mauss's contacts in Britain and America can be found, for example, at pp. 563, 635-7, 649-50.

7. M. Mauss, testimonial letter of 23 September 1936, sent to Oxford University and copied to Radcliffe-Brown. Institute of Social and Cultural Anthropology archives, RB 1/1/10, Oxford.

8. Letter from Marcel Mauss to A.R. Radcliffe-Brown, 2 January 1935, Institute of Social and Cultural Anthropology archives, RB 1/1/10, Oxford. Quoted in part in Fournier, *Marcel Mauss*, p. 637 n. 1.

9. Ibid., p. 650, n. 1. M. Mauss, Introduction to A.M. Hocart, *Les castes*, trans. from the English manuscript by E.J. Lévy and J. Auboyer, and first published in Paris, 1938.

10. 'Une catégorie de l'esprit humaine: la notion de personne, celle de "moi"', The Huxley Memorial Lecture for 1938, *JRAI* vol. 68, 1938, pp. 263-81.

11. H. Hubert and M. Mauss, 'Esquisse d'une théorie générale de la magie', *L'Année sociologique*, vol.7, 1902-3, pp. 1-146. R.R. Marett, *A Jerseyman at Oxford*, London, 1941, p. 161.

12. Marett, *Jerseyman at Oxford*, p. 161.

13. Ibid, pp. 162-3.

14. T.K. Penniman, *A hundred years of anthropology* [1935], 2nd edn, London, 1952, pp. 444-5.

15. Published as E.E. Evans-Pritchard, *Social anthropology*.

16. E.E. Evans-Pritchard, 'Social anthropology: past and present'; *The Sanusi of Cyrenaica*, Oxford, 1949.

17. See, for example, E.E. Evans-Pritchard, 'The Intellectualist (English) Interpretation of Magic', *Bull. of the Faculty of Arts*, University of Cairo, I, Pt. 2, 1933, pp. 1-21. 'Lévy-Bruhl's theory of primitive mentality', *Bull. of the Faculty of Arts*, University of Cairo, II, Pt. 2, 1934, pp. 1-26, repr. in *Journal of the Anthropological Society of Oxford*, I, 1970, pp. 39-60. 'Science and Sentiment: an Exposition and Criticism of the Writings of Pareto', *Bull. of the Faculty of Arts*, University of Cairo, III, Pt. 2, 1936, pp. 163-92.

18. E. Durkheim, *Sociology and philosophy* [1924], trans. D. F. Pocock, London, 1953.

19. H. Hubert, 'Etude sommaire de la représentation du temps dans la religion et dans la magie', Ecole pratique des Hautes Etudes, Section des sciences religieuses, Paris, 1905, pp. 1-39; reprinted under the names of H. Hubert and M. Mauss, in their *Mélanges d'histoire des religions*, Paris, 1909, pp. 189-229. An English translation is in preparation, to be published under the auspices of the British Centre for Durkheimian Studies.

20. M. Mauss, *The gift: forms and function of exchange in archaic societies* [1925], trans. I. Cunnison, London, 1954.

21. E.E. Evans-Pritchard, introduction to *The gift*, 1954, p. v.
22. Ibid., p. vi.
23. Ibid., pp. v-vi.
24. Ibid., pp. vii-viii.
25. Ibid., pp. viii-ix.
26. R. Hertz, *Death and the right hand* [1907, 1909], trans. R. and C. Needham, London, 1960. cf. A. van Geenep, *The Semi-scholars* [1911], trans. R. Needham, London, 1967, and L. Lévy-Bruhl, *The notebooks on primitive mentality* [1949], trans. P. Rivière, Oxford, 1975.
27. E.E. Evans-Pritchard, introduction to *Death and the right hand*, p. 9. See Robert Hertz, *Sin and expiation in primitive societies* [1922], trans. R. Parkin, with a preface by W. S. F. Pickering, Occasional papers 2, British Centre for Durkheimian Studies, Oxford, 1994; and R. Parkin, *The dark side of humanity: the work of Robert Hertz and its legacy*, Amsterdam, 1996.
28. Evans-Pritchard, introduction to *Death and the right hand*, p. 10.
29. Ibid., pp. 12-24.
30. Ibid., p. 24.
31. E. Durkheim and M. Mauss, *Primitive classification* [1903], trans. R. Needham, London, 1963. F. Steiner, *Taboo*, London, 1956. M. Douglas, *Purity and danger: an analysis of concepts of pollution and taboo*, London, 1966.
32. N.J. Allen, '*Primitive classification*: the argument and its validity', in W.S.F. Pickering and H. Martins, eds, *Debating Durkheim*, London, 1994, pp. 40-65.
33. H. Hubert and M. Mauss, *Sacrifice: its nature and function* [1898], trans. W.D. Halls, London, 1964.
34. E.E. Evans-Pritchard, foreword to *Sacrifice*, pp. vii-viii. Cf. E.E. Evans-Pritchard, *Nuer Religion*, Oxford, 1956, chap. 8.
35. M. Mauss and H. Hubert, *A general theory of magic* [1902-3], trans. R. Brain, London, 1972.
36. D.F. Pocock, Foreword to *Magic*, p. 2.
37. Ibid., p. 4.
38. Ibid., p. 6.
39. W. James, review of Marcel Mauss [Hubert & Mauss], *A general theory of magic*, trans. R. Brain, in *African affairs* 73, 1974, pp. 234-5.
40. See, for example, S. Martelli, 'Mana ou sacré? La contribution de Marcel Mauss à la fondation de la sociologie religieuse', in G. Berthoud and G. Busino, eds, *Mauss: hier et aujourd'hui*, special issue of *Revue européenne des sciences sociales*, 34, 1996, pp. 51-66.
41. M. Mauss and H. Beuchat, *Seasonal variations of the Eskimo: a study in social morphology*, trans. J.J. Fox, London, 1979.
42. J.J. Fox, foreword to *Seasonal variations of the Eskimo*, pp. 13-14. Cf. D.F. Pocock, *Understanding social anthropology*, London, 1975, pp. 146-7; I.M. Lewis, *Social anthropology in perspective: the relevance of social anthropology*, Harmondsworth, 1976, pp. 156-8; E. R. Leach, *Culture and communication: the logic by which symbols are connected. An introduction to the use of structuralist analysis in social anthropology*, Cambridge, 1976, p. 3.
43. Fox, foreword to *Seasonal variations*, pp. 15-16.
44. M. Mauss, *Sociology and psychology: essays by Marcel Mauss*, trans. B. Brewster, London, 1979. Cf. M. Fortes, 'On the concept of the person among the Tallensi', and J. Middleton, 'The notion of the person among the Lugbara', both in G. Dieterlen, ed., *La notion de personne en Afrique noire*, Paris, 1973.
45. M. Carrithers, S. Collins, and S. Lukes, eds, *The category of the person: anthropology, philosophy, history*, Cambridge, 1985. For a specific appreciation of Mauss's arguments, see chap. 2 by N.J. Allen, 'The category of the person: a reading of Mauss's last essay', pp. 26-45. Compare, for example, P. Heelas and A. Lock, eds, *Indigenous*

psychologies: the anthropology of the self, London, 1981; W. James, *The listening ebony: moral knowledge, religion, and power among the Uduk of Sudan*, Oxford, 1988, chap. 2 on 'Persons', pp. 68-142, and Postscript to Part I, 'On moral knowledge', pp. 143-56; A.P. Cohen, *Self consciousness: an alternative anthropology of identity*, London, 1994.

46. L. Dumont, *Homo hierarchicus: the caste system and its implications* [1979], Chicago, 1980. M. Strathern, *The gender of the gift*, Chicago, 1988.

47. M. Douglas, introduction to *The gift: the form and reason for exchange in archaic societies*, trans. W.D. Halls, 1979, pp. xiv-xv.

48. D. Quigley, 'Raymond Firth on social anthropology', interview, *Social anthropology*, 1, 1993, pp. 207-22, at p. 213.

49. J.H.M. Beattie, *Other cultures: aims, achievements and methods in social anthropology*, London and New York, 1964, esp. at pp. 200-1.

50. R.G. Lienhardt, 'Getting your own back: themes in Nilotic myth', in J.H.M. Beattie and R.G. Lienhardt, eds, *Studies in social anthropology: essays in memory of E.E. Evans-Pritchard by his former colleagues*, pp. 213-37, at p. 213.

51. M. Mauss, 'Gift, gift' [1924], in *Oeuvres* vol. 3, pp. 46-51. A.D. Schrift, ed., *The logic of the gift: toward an ethic of generosity*, London and New York, 1997 (including an edited translation of excerpts from 'Gift, gift' at pp. 28-32). M. Godelier, *L'énigme du don*, Paris, 1996.

52. M.D. Sahlins, *Stone age economics*, Chicago, 1972; F. Barth, *Models of social organisation*, Occasional papers of the RAI, 23, London, 1966; J. Davis, *Exchange*, Buckingham, 1992; J. Parry, ' *The gift*, the Indian gift and "The Indian gift"', *Man* 21, 1986, pp. 453-73.

53. L. Dumont, 'Preface to the French edition of the Nuer', trans. M. and J. Douglas, in *Studies in social anthropology*, pp. 328-42; at pp. 329, 331.

54. Ibid., p. 331-3; cf. D.F. Pocock, *Social anthropology*, London, 1961.

55. L. Dumont, 'Preface', pp. 332-3

56. Ibid., p. 334.

57. Ibid., pp. 336-7.

58. Ibid., p. 342.

59. E.W. Ardener, *The voice of prophecy*, London, 1989.

60. B. Kapferer, ed., *Transactional anthropology*, London, 1976.

61. Mauss, *Sociology and psychology*, p. 101. Cf. P. Bourdieu, *Outline of a theory of practice*, Cambridge, 1977.

62. See especially M. Mauss, 'La cohésion sociale dans les sociétés polysegmentaires' [1931], in *Oeuvres*, vol. 3, pp. 11-26.

63. N.J. Allen, 'The division of labour and the notion of primitive society: a Maussian approach', *Social anthropology*, 3, 1995, pp. 49-59.

64. N.J. Allen, 'Mauss and the categories', *Durkheimian studies*, forthcoming.

65. R. Firth, *Economics of the New Zealand Maori* [1929], 2nd edn, Wellington, 1959, pp. 420-21.

The scholar and his time

Chapter 2

AN INTELLECTUAL SELF-PORTRAIT

Marcel Mauss

This unpublished manuscript by Mauss is apparently a confidential memorandum intended for Charles Andler and Sylvain Lévi. It was almost certainly written in 1930 when he was a candidate for election to the Collège de France. It has been published in French, as 'L'oeuvre de Mauss par lui-même', in the *Revue française de sociologie*, vol. 20, 1979, pp. 209-20, and in the *Revue européenne des sciences sociales*, vol. 34, 1996, pp. 225-36. What follows derives from the translation by A. Bailey and J. Llobera published in P. Besnard, ed., *The sociological domain*, Cambridge, 1983. It has been substantially revised here by N.J. Allen, who has added the material in square brackets.

It is impossible to detach me from the work of a school. If there is any individuality here, it is immersed within a voluntary anonymity. Perhaps what characterises my scientific career, perhaps even more today than formerly, is the sense of working as a member of a team, and the conviction that collaboration with others is a force that stands opposed both to isolation and to the pretentious quest for originality.

There are two reasons for my behaviour.

First, a theoretical one. As a positivist, believing only in facts, I go so far as to maintain that descriptive sciences attain greater certainty than theoretical sciences (in the case of phenomena that are too complex). Thus if I practise theoretical science — and reasonably well perhaps — I believe that it is only of interest in so far as, extracted from certain facts, it can help us observe and record other facts, and classify them in different ways; in so far as it deepens understanding rather than generalising, in so far as it gives itself firm contours and weighs itself down with content rather than soaring upwards to build elaborate constructions from historical hypotheses or metaphysical ideas. But a vast knowledge of the facts is only possible through the collaboration of numerous specialists. Deprived though it is of laboratory facilities, sociology does not lack the means to verify its facts, provided that one can bring into one's comparisons all the social phenomena of history, as understood by the specialists in each branch of that discipline. But this task is impossible for a single individual. The only way to achieve solid results is for scholars mutually to verify each others' work, criticising each other relentlessly, each party to an argument equally making use of facts.

Secondly, a factual reason. The progress made by sociology in France in the twenty years from 1893 to 1914 would have been impossible if we had not been a group working together. We were not a mere school of disciples blindly gathered around a teacher and a philosopher. Of course, Durkheim was full of ideas, and far-reaching ones. But what drew us together around him was our knowledge that here was a real scholar, that his methods were totally sound, and that his range of knowledge was vast and scrupulously verified. The aspects of his mind that most seduced me and the rest of us were his Cartesianism, his ever realistic and rationalist search for facts, and his ability to know and grasp those facts. These are the qualities that I believe I have consciously and conscientiously developed in myself, in my friends, and in my students. Every science is the product of collective work. Made by individuals who partake together in the real world, the science emerges from the facts and ideas brought by these individuals to a single market place. This is just what happened in our effort to create sociology. We required an enormous amount of data and a precise language in which to record them. All this presupposes a group and consensus within it. But from another point of view, in exploring this domain of the social, only just opened up to science, we were like lost souls who can only find their way by calling out to one another in the forest. Simply to describe a phenomenon[1] or pinpoint questions raised endless difficulties that could only be resolved by an ongoing group. All by himself in Bordeaux, Durkheim was painfully aware of the enormity of his task and of his relative impotence. However great his genius, he could only master from a distance the data of history, of the past and of research into contemporary societies. I set an example and became Durkheim's recruiting agent in Paris between 1895 and 1902. That is how we came to form a group of competent and specialised scholars, and overcame in an atmosphere of confidence the first problems in our science.

This sort of workshop requires a considerable degree of self-sacrifice. A laboratory is no good without a leader, but it also requires high-quality members, that is, friends young and old, with hypotheses to work on, lots of ideas, and wide knowledge, but above all, it requires people who are ready to contribute all of these to a common fund, to join in the work of the longer-standing members and to help launch the work of the newcomers, just as everyone joins in their work. We formed such a team. It is alive and even reviving. Neither Durkheim nor myself were sparing with our efforts or our ideas. His work would have been impossible had we not devoted ourselves to it without any feeling of self-sacrifice, and if I were not continuing to do so.

From all this have come two features of my life. First of all, I have perhaps worked too much in collaboration with others. This indeed takes up the greater part of my time. I contributed to Durkheim's *Suicide* (quantitative method, classification of 26,000 suicides individually filed on cards and distributed in seventy-five compartments).[2] I collaborated in everything he did, just as he collaborated with me; often he even rewrote entire pages of my work. I published two articles in collaboration with him, including our essay on *Primitive classification* [1903], for which I supplied all the data. With Hubert, I published one essay on *Sacrifice* [1899] and another on *Magic* [1904], and the preface to our *Mélanges d'histoire des religions* [1908-9]. Generally, I took part in everything he did that was not strictly criticism or archaeology. He always checked what I wrote. Although I had planned to do no more than collaborate with Beuchat, I had to rework from start to finish our *Seasonal variations of the Eskimo* [1906]. The number of times I have collaborated in the work of my students and friends is not to be counted. If I am somewhat overwhelmed by the burden at present, it is because I have accepted the enormous task of publishing the mass of unpublished work left behind by Durkheim, Henri Hubert, and Hertz. Thanks to me, their works are reaching the public at a rate of one or two volumes per year. My teaching and supervision of research at the Ecole des Hautes Etudes and at the Institut d'Ethnologie have perhaps been excessive, and have also contributed to the delay of my own publications. But am I to blame if my professional conscience is excessively demanding? The quality and number of my students all over the world are proof that this teaching has not been without value. The research for which I assigned the topics, ensured the successful completion, corrected drafts and proofs, inspired the orientation, demonstrate that my work here has not been negligible. Had it not been for the war, it would perhaps have been glorious.

[Secondly,] the great tragedy of my scientific life was not the interruption of my work by the four-and-a-half years of war, nor the year lost due to illness (1921-2), nor even my sense of complete despair at the premature deaths of Durkheim and Hubert [1917 and 1927]; it was the loss during those painful years of my best students and my best friends. One could say that it was a loss for this branch of French science;

but for me, it was catastrophe. Perhaps the best that I had been able to give of myself disappeared with them. The renewed success of my teaching since the war, and the foundation and success of the Institut d'Ethnologie (which is surely more than half owing to me), prove again what I can still do in this direction; but they do not replace what I lost.

But before leaving this topic, I should like to dispel a prejudicial misconception about me that I know to be current. It has been suggested that I have slanted my teaching in favour of sociology. Nothing could be further from the truth. However fruitful they may or may not have been, however free they may or may not have left me for my own research, my lectures have never entirely coincided with my research. In my chair of 'The History of Religions of Non-Civilised Peoples', I have been faithful to its baroque title and to the spirit of the Ecole des Hautes Etudes. In that context I have strictly limited my teaching to a historical, critical, and noncomparative point of view, even when the facts that I was studying only interested me from a comparative point of view. I have never in that place been a propagandist for sociology. Being responsible for teaching descriptive ethnology at the Institut d'Ethnologie, where I myself drew up the statutes, and where, along with Rivet and Lévy-Bruhl, I oversee the teaching, publications and overall activities — in this context I have always confined my teaching to the purely descriptive. Perhaps this conscientiousness and impartiality can be accounted a scientific merit.

In any event, these factors explain why, towards the end of my career, I wish to teach exactly what I have always worked on: the comparative history of societies and especially of religions. At my age, it is quite legitimate to make my teaching coincide with the oral presentation of my preliminary and definitive researches, either unpublished, or published but not taught. I am even thinking of adding to my teaching programme the unpublished work left by my best friends; in this way, its publication would be facilitated, their memory would be better preserved, and my more general teaching could have a wider effect; it would be not only mine, but theirs as well. I would be teaching not only my own work, but also the ideas and the evidence for those ideas elaborated by my friends, from Durkheim and Hubert to Doutté and Maurice Cahen.

Published work

My published work is somewhat piecemeal. I do not greatly believe in scientific systems and have never needed to express more than partial truths. However, in addition to a continuity in orientation, my work has not been without continuity of a material kind; there exists a link between these scattered fragments. It lies in the publication of the *Année sociologique* and of the *Travaux de l'Année sociologique*. The continuity of my efforts is shown by the fact that after a hiatus of ten years it has been possible to revive these publications, and that I have done so, and that I have published in the Collection of the *Travaux* two to four volumes each year.

It is good to judge my efforts under this head. That is where their unity appears.

The Année sociologique

If one measures things by quantity, the greater part of my work — of our collective work — has been devoted to the writing, editing, and publishing of the *Année sociologique*. I have published there about 2,500 octavo pages out of the 10,000-11,000 pages of the fourteen volumes published or in press (400 pages in vol. 1 of the new series and 300 pages in vol. 2 of that series, if I include my bibliographic contributions to all the different sections). I shall not discuss the value of this bibliography, the work of selection it presupposes, the labour of keeping up with current developments, maintaining personal contacts and correspondence, and so on.

However, I would like to justify my personal efforts as part of this collective effort, and stress the value of our joint work at the same time as my own contribution. Some have thought that its scale was exaggerated, that the results were disproportionate to the effort, that the aims were not achieved and were impossible. Nothing could be more wrong.

Durkheim founded the *Année* [1898] to enable us and himself systematically to put forward our point of view on all sorts of sociological topics. However, in all our minds, it soon became something quite different from a vehicle for propagating a method or a platform for opposing the various schools of economists, historians of religion, theoreticians of jurisprudence, and so on. Under Durkheim's direction, and I might add, to some extent under my own impulsion, we all agreed to try to organise in the journal not merely ideas but above all facts. From vol. 2 onwards, it became a kind of reasonably up-to-date storehouse for the different sociological specialities. Naturally, the vagaries of the publications that appeared and of our own research and inclinations, and above all, the magnitude of our ignorance have sometimes led us astray. The correct balance of the facts and the exact importance of the ideas have not always been perfectly appreciated.

The development of theories, however, has always been carefully recorded. For anyone who wishes to keep up with advances in learning, we have certainly been useful and, in the French-speaking world, perhaps even indispensable. This applies even to advances in disciplines that are merely neighbours to our own (for example, philosophy and psychology of religion), and all the more so to advances in our own discipline and in neighbouring specialities (law, economics, human geography, etc.). But, above all, we attempted, and myself particularly, to incorporate the facts within sociological theory, and simultaneously to organise them, and present analyses of the raw data provided by the descriptive branches of our sciences. My own personal effort over ten years, then the shared effort of my students and myself, and finally my (again) almost solitary effort over the last four years have precisely been to promulgate and often to establish the facts deriving from unclassified civilisations.

Most of my reviews and some of my bibliographical notes have been theoretical. Some of them record facts that are not easily accessible. Thus, one can still read with profit my reviews of de Groot's *Religious system of China* (in seven volumes) [1899, 1903, 1910, 1913], and of Spencer and Gillen, of which, as a young man, I was the first to recognise the importance and even to elucidate the content [1900, 1905]. Other reviews contain theoretical discoveries, for instance, those of the books by Dieterich [1906], van Ossenbruggen [1906] and Elsdon Best, where I pointed out the significance of systems of first names within the clan. The sum total of the reviews concerning North American Indians contain in germ all that we have done since on the potlatch and on the legal institutions of those tribes. In some other reviews, Durkheim and I resolved the problem of Polynesian and Micronesian kinship terminologies [cf. *A.S.* vol. 8, pp. 386-8]. Others again present syntheses on general problems such as the relation between anthropology and history of religions, and between the sociology and the psychology of religion, and so on. Finally, some show how geographical groupings of phenomena are constituted — for example, the religious systems of Africa.

The basic point is that, while constantly remaining on the level of facts adequate to the ideas explored, we have been able to distribute notions logically and pragmatically within sound frameworks, which are now used everywhere and by almost everyone, even our critics. Our system of classification has been generally adopted in phenomenological accounts within the history of religions. The system used consistently by the *Année sociologique* is followed so slavishly by everyone that I have had to express Durkheim's and my own reservations on their value (see my paper [1927] on 'The divisions and proportions of divisions of sociology' and the series of general reviews that follows it). Finally, although we had never intended this, the *Année* provides a considerable service to the French public. It is a sort of handbook, continually updated, of one of the most recent and important sciences; it is the ongoing expression of the work of what the whole world calls the French Sociological School (see

Malinowski's article on 'Social anthropology' in the latest edition of the *Encyclopaedia Britannica*).

I shall not consider here the considerable number of my reviews that have appeared in other journals.

Theoretical work

There remains my theoretical work per se, which may appear rather piecemeal. It is somewhat scattered, especially in recent years when I have had to represent sociology in a variety of different milieux. But these appearances are superficial, for my work has its own logical unity. The overall scheme that Hubert and I have followed is stated in our preface to the *Mélanges d'histoire des religions* [1909], and I have only added a few points since then.

But the order in which the questions were posed followed the course of my life and my discipline. Thus some biographical details concerning Durkheim as well as myself will find their way into the account.

During my student years, I wavered between three things: studies that would now be termed quantitative (the collaboration with Durkheim), suicide, urban history, human spatial distribution — the last of which is echoed in my work on *Seasonal variations* [1906]; secondly, the study of law (three years); and finally the sociology of religion. It was through a taste for philosophy and also by a conscious decision that I followed the suggestion of Durkheim and specialised in the study of religious phenomena, to which I have dedicated myself almost entirely for my whole life. Durkheim delivered his course at Bordeaux on the origins of religion (1894-5) for my benefit and for himself. Together we were trying to locate my endeavours in the place where they would give best service to the nascent science and plug its most serious gaps. We both felt that the study of institutions, the family, and law, were sufficiently developed, and that studies of ritual were sufficiently advanced except on one point. At that time, we were content with the work of Frazer and, above all, Robertson Smith. Only oral ritual and religious ideation appeared to us more or less untouched. Even before my *agrégation*, I had sufficiently prepared myself for the topic by solid historical and philological studies in addition to my *agrégation* in philosophy, and by my familiarity with the works of foreign writers. The subjects for my theses were already decided. One was to be on Leo the Hebrew and Spinoza, whose close relations I had *discovered* in 1893, but it was a subject I became fed up with in 1897 following an indiscretion that enabled M. Couchoud to take the gloss off it and ruin it. The other thesis was to be on prayer in all its aspects. This choice of subject shows the naivety and boldness with which we proceeded at the time. In order to treat it, I embarked on philological studies [1895] that I thought would have to be brief: Vedic and Classical Sanskrit, Pali, Ancient Hebrew (talmudic and liturgic), Christian liturgy, Avestan, 1902, 1907.[3] They quickly showed me the way that, in its depth and refinement, leads to more general perspectives, and does so by surer means, than purely ideological procedures can. A year of study in Holland and in England, with my ethnographic and museographic apprenticeship [1898-9], made my standards even more demanding. The contact that I established with Henri Hubert, who was to be my professional 'twin' (*jumeau de travail*), also taught me to widen my perspective and to deepen my analysis, despite the scantiness of the ethnographic data available at the time. Social phenomena thus appeared to us on the one hand more complex and more material, and on the other more spiritual and moral. The observation of the social domain, and the social domain of the world of religion appeared to us vast and more varied than we had expected. At the time when we met and came to be on close terms with each other, H. H. and I lived in a condition of intellectual exhilaration. Together we discovered the human worlds of the prehistoric, the primitive, the exotic, and the Semitic and Indian universes, in addition to the Ancient and Christian worlds that we knew already. When we established a division of labour in our studies and specialised in order to know these worlds better, we were perhaps almost delirious. Yet by sheer good sense and hard work, I believe, we accomplished what we set out to do. Only with the death of Hubert has the project lapsed. But for that, with the help of all our students and the support of the Musée de Saint-Germain, the Institut d'Ethnologie and the *Année sociologique*, by confronting the latest results of our own researches with those of other scholars in our sciences who work in ever-increasing numbers, especially abroad, we were on the point of reaping the belated benefits of our efforts.

During this period we were filling the compartments of sociology with facts. We encouraged the search for new phenomena, we reclassified those that had been poorly classified, and we re-analysed those that had been badly described. Discoveries and novelties were a constant delight. Apart from our labours as reviewers and the proper tributes we paid to our predecessors, we never published anything that was a repetition of what was already known, or even a straightforward verification of it. When we drafted such material, we did not inflict it on the public. So I count for nothing all the work I have done spreading knowledge of other people's ideas, and in my bibliography I have not even mentioned the apprentice writings of my youth on Andrew Lang, the Inca Empire, etc.[4]

Institutions

My work as a whole falls fairly easily under four rubrics to which I have contributed quite a number of new ideas and new facts. While pursuing my studies in the sociology of religion, I have never lost sight of the studies of institutions with which I had begun my professional life. In any case, one part of our method consists precisely in relating institutional and structural phenomena to mental phenomena and vice versa.

Before leaving this field of my early training, in the conclusion to a lengthy review article [1896] on Steinmetz's *Ethnologische Studien zur ersten Entwicklung der Strafe*, (entitled 'Religion and the Origins of Penal Law'), I demonstrated what has now become a classical hypothesis. I proved that the feud, a phenomenon belonging to the politico-domestic sphere of law, is not the origin of our public criminal law, but the origin of our private civil law of responsibility. Our public criminal law derives from the system of ritual prohibitions and from the ritual sanctions on the crimes relating to the prohibitions. The character of the public indignation and response against these crimes is the same as the reaction to crimes against religion.

Similarly, helped by Beuchat, I showed that the Eskimo, and likewise many other societies (one can now say very many others), for instance, the early Slavs, have two social structures, one in summer and one in winter, and that in parallel they have two systems of law and religion [1906]. This particularly striking case demonstrates the close dependence of law and religion on phenomena of social mass and demographic patterns of settlement. Comparably, I have also indicated on several occasions, including in my forthcoming contribution to the Anesaki Festschrift, that the notion of the soul and of reincarnation is linked to that of the inheritance of first names within the clan and the family, and to the social position of the individual as manifested in his titles, masques, dances, etc. [see 1938].

On other occasions, I have tried to explain the reciprocities and antagonisms that develop in a society by pointing to the way in which it distributes men, women, and generations among its internal divisions [esp. 1932]. I have thus identified systems of moral phenomena of considerable importance: the widely distributed institution of joking relationships, which itself raises numerous problems [1926]; and, above all, the phenomena labelled by the term potlatch, within which I prefer to distinguish systems of total prestations and systems of agonistic prestations or potlatch proper [esp. 1925].

In connection with the latter, guided by Boas's admirable descriptions of the American Northwest [and?] by a suggestion from Durkheim, I was able to identify a whole system of phenomena that are extremely widespread in most archaic civilisations. I found signs of it throughout the whole of North America, the whole of Melanesia and Polynesia, and in practically the whole Indo-European, Semitic, and Berber worlds. From the whole system I drew out the idea of the gift as simultaneously religious, mythic, and contractual. I also drew out the idea of the total prestation from clan to clan and from generation to generation (usually with males and females out of alignment), from one sex to the other, and from one descent group to another (cf. Malinowski). I also analysed the collective nature of archaic forms (cf. Davy) and, above all, the notion of 'total facts' which set in motion the whole collectivity, as an entity simultaneously economic, moral and religious, aesthetic and mythic (cf. Granet). Superimposed on these reciprocities and antagonisms, there developed the system of pure rivalries, sumptuary, military, athletic etc., within the societies. Moreover, as was evident on the basis of the North American and Melanesian phenomena, we connected with this system the important phenomena of the development of religious brotherhoods and politico-religious aristocracies (cf. Davy, Granet and M. M.). The extension of these studies to the Indo-European world, and more particularly the Germanic and Roman worlds, is a personal contribution (for Greece, see Gernet).

In sum, my contribution has been to supplement older views of the simple structure of clan society — which were correct but insufficient — by building onto them an account of the allocation of rights and duties between groups defined by criteria that are simultaneously natural and social, criteria of age, sex, and generation [1932].

The idea of dual descent that Durkheim and I had elucidated in connection with Polynesia, and that I have identified in the Nigritian [West African] world — this too can look forward to rapid developments, which will pose in quite different terms the problem of the female and male lines.

All these matters go beyond and replace the previous ways of posing the questions. Not to mention that they allow us to glimpse certain solutions to general and even moral questions (Conclusion to *The gift*).

Religion and ideation

The bulk of my work, however, deals with ritual and religious representations. My major undertaking was a monograph on prayer. It soon became limited to the elementary forms of oral ritual (Australia). The initial project, on which I did some preparatory work, envisaged two additional volumes. One was to deal with the development of oral ritual (Melanesia, Polynesia, Vedic India); the other would have dealt with the mystic sublimation of prayer (Brahmanic and Buddhist India), its individualisation (Semites and Christians), and finally its regression and relapse into mechanistic repetition (India, Tibet, Christianity).

I have several times given courses on the substance of the first volume. Two fascicules of it were printed privately and provisionally in 1909, representing scarcely one quarter of the book. Publication was interrupted because meanwhile documents arrived from Strehlow (Aranda and Loritja tribes). They were shown to me; I made a copy; I corresponded with the author; I participated in their publication; but just as I was definitively settling down to the work, which the new material enabled me to tackle afresh and in greater depth, I was stopped short by the war.

But before all this, as a matter of sound method, I had to resolve two questions. Moreover, on both of them, Hubert too, having set off from different points of view, was developing concerns that linked up with my own. He wanted to work out an explanation for the sacrifice of the god — the object of his researches on the Semitic origins of Christian belief — while what I wanted was to see whether the ritual formulae of sacrifice depended so closely on the sacrifice that the oral ritual actually derived from it. In addition, we had to firm up our ideas on magic, which was then considered to be the primitive form of pseudo-science that had preceded religion.

In dealing with these two questions we became aware of others.

Our work on sacrifice [1899] enabled us to conclude that sacrificial ritual belonged to the very evolved forms of religious life, not to the primitive base. It was connected with the far more general system of consecrations. I do not analyse it. I do not describe the way in which we were able to envisage both the evolution that gave rise to sacrifice and the evolution that steered it towards the sacrifice of the god. The essential point is that, following Robertson Smith and Durkheim, we showed there a clear example of the functioning of the idea of the sacred. Thus the problem of the latter idea becomes fundamental. We encountered the problem again in the context of magic.

Among the phenomena classed as religious, magic at that time occupied a curious position. Like Max Müller, Frazer, and Farnell, we had originally believed that the primitive situation only involved magical formulae. We needed to see whether magic was an exception, whether it belonged to a different sphere of mentality, and whether it was the source of religion or itself too derived from the idea of the sacred or from something similar. In our essay on magic [1904], we identified a great number of elements common to magic and religion, and we proved that they set in motion the same mental mechanisms. In particular, however, at the base of magic as of religion, we detected a vast shared notion that we called *mana*, borrowing the term from Malayo-Polynesian. This idea of *mana* is perhaps more general than that of the sacred. Later, Durkheim tried to deduce it sociologically from the notion of the sacred. We were never sure that he was right, and I still continue to talk of the magico-religious base. In any case, like the notion of the sacred, *mana* presents itself in the manner of a category. This opened up a new problem. But at the same time everything took on a new aspect and formed a single system.

Of the notes to the essay on magic only a certain proportion were published in the text. The second part on magic and religion, where we explain the relations between these two systems of phenomena, is fully drafted and will be published. It consists of a demonstration that the mutual relations into which magic and religion have entered are of a juridical rather than a logical or cognitive nature, and that they have varied with different religions and societies.

Thus looming over all our work there arose two new questions of the utmost importance. One was the idea of the sacred, on which we have worked for a long time and on which I plan one day to make known the results of our studies. The second was the question of the categories of thought. We had already shared out these questions at a time when we still conflated them. Hubert was to study the sacred in time, which he did [1905]. I was to study the sacred in space, which I did in part, and which my student Czarnowski is in the process of doing definitively. However, in agreement with Durkheim, we soon isolated the problem of reason.

We have attacked the subject from many angles. The study of religious representations of a general order and of natural beings in every volume of the *Année sociologique* from vol. 2 onwards; number and cause (the essay on *The origin of magical powers* [1904]); space and time (in the monograph on the origin of the notion of time); the soul (and not simply the notion of animism); the world (the notion of orientation). Durkheim and I dealt with the subject in itself in our monograph on the notion of class, entitled *Primitive classification* [1903]. The question of space is there explicitly addressed, as is that of 'participations' and 'contrasts'. This effort was one of the most philosophical attempted by any school of sociologists. Durkheim pursued the subject in depth from a theoretical point of view in *The elementary forms of religious life* [1912].

Together, Hubert and I were preparing a series of converging studies on the notion of substance and on its history starting from ancient times. I hope to publish it in two or three volumes. (Henri Hubert — Gundestrup vessels; Marcel Mauss — Archaic form of the notion of food, Greece and Vedic India compared). Perhaps a third volume will pursue the research into the domain of patristics. Hubert published several fragments of his contribution. I published a difficult fragment of mine in the *Mélanges Sylvain Lévi* [1911].

Psychology and sociology

After the death of Durkheim, I was to some extent obliged to take his place. I have defended sociology almost all over the place, and from time to time engaged in diplomacy on its behalf. In any case, this problem of thought in common, action in common, and feeling in common was eventually taken up by the psychologists themselves (McDougall, Dumas, etc.). I even agreed to write on the subject in vol. 3 of the *Traité de psychologie* (2nd edn.). The contact between Dumas and myself [1923] on the topic of laughter, weeping, and the expression of feelings treated as signs, obliged me to take up a position. I did so on a number of occasions. I shall complete these discussions of fact and method this very year [in fact 1935] by a psycho-sociological consideration of what I call the 'techniques of the body' (walking, running, jumping, gymnastics, swimming, resting, breathing, sleeping, making love, etc.). The everlasting and rather empty debate between psychologists and sociologists can thus be taken up afresh on the basis of mutual understanding. For, to take an example, the classical theory of Mead, on the symbolic activity of the mind, accords perfectly with the theory that Durkheim and I attempted on the importance of the symbol — ritual, mythic, linguistic, or whatever.

I have added to these considerations others on the nature of what I call total phenomena, and the total human being, the only unit of study that the sociologist encounters. These reflections have met with fairly widespread acceptance. I was much touched by that of Kœhler in particular. I recall also my paper on 'Art and myth according to Mr Wundt' [1908].

Methodology

The public is still too fond of sociological methodology, while our students and collaborators are still too fixated on philosophical considerations about the legitimacy of our branch of study. It would be better to master the subject and move it forward than to engage in transcendental critiques of it. I have often had to resign myself to taking part in the latter. While Durkheim was still alive, Fauconnet and I drafted with him a whole slim volume on sociology. Only two parts of it have appeared: the article 'Sociology' in the *Grande Encyclopédie* [1901], which is still treated, after *The rules of sociological method*, as a manifesto of the whole school, and the article by Durkheim and Fauconnet, in reality written by all three of us, entitled 'History of sociology and the social sciences'. The third part has never been published. On several occasions I have again taken up this general theme, and I am still continuing to do so today, in vol. 2 of the *Année sociologique*, new series, in 'Divisions and proportions of the divisions of sociology' [1927]. It was desirable to explain how far we should go in accepting the new research (Foy and Graebner) and new hypotheses (Koppers and Schmitt) on the history of civilisations. I have done this many times (*Année sociologique*, vols. 8 to 12 inclusive and vols. 1 and 2 of the new series). I shall continue in vol. 3 of the new series with a global study of the notion of civilisation. A fragment of this has just been published in *Semaine de synthèse* (1929). My articles on 'Ethnology in France and abroad', published in the *Revue de Paris* [1913], show that this direction of my interests is of long standing.

Towards the end of the year I also plan to publish my Oslo lectures dealing with the use of the notion of 'primitive' in sociology and in the history of civilisation [cf. 1932/3]. They will show that, in agreement with Hubert, I relate the condition of one part of the so-called lower societies to the great Neolithic and Early Bronze Age civilisation.

Throughout my work, I have never lost sight of the only objective of the discipline to which I have devoted myself, namely to show and to make precise, by direct and maximally sensitive contact with the facts, the place of social life as such in the life of humanity.

I believe that I have contributed to advancing sociological awareness among historians, philologists, and the like, and to advancing historical and statistical awareness among sociologists.

Throughout this present account of my works, I have not said a word about my written interventions in the sphere of the normative. I do not believe, however, that such work as I have done in this domain is without scientific and philosophical interest. This includes my publications and even my scientific and didactic activities within the Cooperative Movement (statistics, Russian cooperatives, etc.), the excerpts I have published from a manuscript on Bolshevism (*Monde slave* [1925], *Revue de metaphysique et de morale* [1924]), and my communications on the concept of nation and internationalism [1920].

Nearly all of these belong to a major work on *The nation* (first principle of modern politics), which is nearly complete in manuscript form. This work will not even be published in the collection of the *Travaux de l'Année sociologique* — such is the strength of my desire to separate sociology as a pure science from even a totally disinterested [political] theory.

NOTES

1. [The word *fait* means both fact and phenomenon.]
2. Mauss understates the number of compartments, which ought to be 176 [French editor].
3. [The significance of these two dates is not clear.]
4. Mauss is referring to the booklet prepared on the occasion of his candidacy for the Collège de France: 'Notice sur les titres et travaux de M. Marcel Mauss', Presses Universitaires de France, 1930 [French editor].

Chapter 3

MAUSS'S JEWISH BACKGROUND:

A BIOGRAPHICAL ESSAY

W.S.F. Pickering

Although I began to write about the life of Marcel Mauss before the appearance of Fournier's extremely well documented book on him, much of what I intend to say may sound as if it were copied from Fournier. Of course I have used details drawn from what he has written, but some of the facts are well known anyway.[1]

Marcel Mauss was fourteen years younger than Emile Durkheim. Born in 1872 in Epinal, the family town of the Durkheims, he was the son of Rosine Durkheim, Emile Durkheim's elder sister, and Gerson Mauss. After considerable success in a *lycée* in Epinal, Marcel went to Bordeaux, where he was under the care of his uncle. His father died in 1896 when Marcel was about twenty-three years of age and had just arrived in Paris. After his father died, Durkheim became very much a father to him.

In character Mauss appears to have been very different from his uncle. He lacked the well-disciplined, serious-minded, ascetically inclined personality that is associated with Emile Durkheim. Mauss was a large man with a big beard and big hands and had, in fact, been an amateur boxer. People used to greet him by saying 'Here comes Tartarin [de Tarascon]'.[2] He was an ardent walker and had a great sense of humour, perhaps accentuated by his black beard and the carefully carelessly-tied cravat (*lavallière*) which he so often wore. Certainly in the 1920s and 1930s he was a very popular figure in the extended family. With his jokes and stories he was a man full of fun. He had a rough appearance but a warm heart. Compared with his uncle he was never considered to be a serious academic; indeed he was seen by the family as a bit of a joker. An incessant talker, he liked to show off, and might have been an actor. He was also something of a gourmet and knew all the best restaurants. He used to shop in the market on a Sunday and then entertain his students with his fine cooking. Something might be made out of the assertion that he did not take himself very seriously. Apart from how the family viewed him, he scarcely seemed to think of himself as a magisterial professor. This may account for the fact that he never completed his doctorate and was already fifty-nine years of age when he was awarded a professorship at the Collège de France in 1931.[3] And he was there for only eight years or so. Why did he then retire in 1939? After all, he was about sixty-eight and did not have to retire. He gave as his reason his desire to make way for a younger person.[4] After continuing for a short while as director of the Ecole Pratique des Hautes Etudes, Fifth section, he thought in 1940 that it was diplomatic to leave this post as well. Was it because he was Jewish and deemed it diplomatic to withdraw? Was he forced to do so under Nazi threats? That seems unlikely (see below). According to his own words he did not want the Ecole to be disadvantaged (perhaps worse) with a Jew as its director.[5] But some might suggest that perhaps he realised that his mind was losing its natural ability. This might also have accounted for his retirement from the chair at the Collège de France. We do know that in his last years his mental capacities waned and he was in many ways looked after by his brother, Henri Mauss, living very near the Cité Universitaire in Paris. Henri Mauss originally ran the family millinery business in Epinal. In any event, one might note that after he retired he published nothing. It is said that he just ceased to work.

Some might wonder whether he really did doubt that he was cut out to be a magisterial professor. After all, he had tried unsuccessfully for a professorship at the Collège de France in 1909, when he was thirty-seven years of age — an age when he was entering a high plateau of academic acumen. It was more than likely that he was ambivalent about being made a professor. On the one hand he knew he was academically well qualified, if not more so, but he did not want to be compared with his uncle, who had gone to the Sorbonne in 1902 and had entered fully into university politics and who presented the image of a totally dedicated professional. Yet rightly he desired recognition in the academic world.

As has just been hinted, the shadow of Emile Durkheim stood over him throughout his entire life. It had the advantage of giving him an automatic *entrée* into academic circles, but it also meant that he was seen as being not quite up to the intellectual stature of his uncle. To his face, Mauss's fellow students mischievously called Durkheim 'The Uncle'.[6] Clearly some feeling of inferiority was present in Mauss's psyche.

Becoming a professor only late in life did not mean he was without academic appointments of considerable responsibility and influence. In 1901 he was a director of studies in the prestigious Ecole Pratique des Hautes Etudes, in the Fifth section on the history of religions of noncivilised peoples. In 1925 he helped to found and was joint director of the Institut d'Ethnologie in Paris.

But to turn to another side of his life. For many years, it seems, he saw himself fitted to be a jovial bachelor. He married late in life, at the age of fifty-two, much to the surprise of his friends. It is said he was encouraged to marry for social reasons, for as a professor at the Collège de France he needed to have a wife! Marthe Dupret, whom he had known for some time, was born in 1886, and became his wife in 1934. She very soon became ill through gas poisoning, possibly an attempted suicide, and was never seen in public. Instead of looking after him — and we have in mind that he was not fit himself — poor Marcel was obliged to nurse her until her death in 1947, three years before he himself died. Why Marthe did not find herself fully part of the extended family was, it is said, because not only was she an invalid but also she did not match the family socially. From 1937 onwards Marcel had to cope with heavy personal problems.[7]

Jewish background

Marcel Mauss was the grandson of the great liberal rabbi, Moïse Durkheim of Epinal, who was the begetter, through two generations, of scholars who gave French sociology its importance. Unlike his uncle, Mauss was not brought up in the household of a rabbi, but his mother, Rosine, was conformist in her practice of the Jewish religion. His second forename, Israël, meant he could never escape his Jewish identity, for he would have to declare this name in any legal document. Indeed, he was fascinated by the word Israël and studied its origins.[8] Unlike his uncle he never seems to have tried to hide or disregard his Jewish background, even if he may have wished to.[9] On the contrary, he was happy to talk about it. He would declare his rabbinical background, one generation removed of course, even to his students. But overriding this, and therefore much like Durkheim himself, he saw himself as first and foremost a French patriot. He would doubtless call himself a rationalist, and in a loose sense, a free thinker. He was a member of the *Union Rationaliste*, and also, as is well known, a radical socialist with strong interests in the cooperative movement and in Bolshevism.[10] But, on the other hand, he was also a member of the Central Committee of the *Alliance Israëlite Universale* in the 1930s. It appears that he joined it through loyalty to Sylvain Lévi and continued to work for it even after Lévi's death in 1935 (see below). Like many Jewish intellectuals, Mauss was opposed to Zionism on the grounds that the movement detracted from a sense of French patriotism. It is a matter of conjecture why Mauss was not picked up by the Gestapo during the Occupation and sent to a concentration camp. Perhaps the authorities were aware of his mental state. It has also been conjectured that German anthropologists intervened and petitioned that he be left alone. He assiduously wore the required yellow Star of David.[11]

Marcel Mauss's relatively early abandonment of Judaism as a religion followed a similar path to that of his uncle. Both, so far as we know, learned Hebrew and studied the Talmud in the local synagogue, both had bar mitzvahs and both came to abandon religious practices and beliefs around the age of eighteen. However, details about Mauss on this point are not very clear.[12] Interestingly enough, their departure from the faith of their fathers did not bring any serious division within the families, which reflects the families' liberal atttiudes. Both Durkheim and Mauss attended the synagogue at Epinal for religious feasts and both went back to Epinal frequently for holidays. It is clear that Mauss did not really enjoy following the prescribed domestic rituals, although his religiously inclined mother begged him to observe them. Clifford holds that, agnostic though he was, Mauss valued his spiritual heritage.[13]

The tomb of the Mauss family in the Cimetière Parisienne de Bagnaux is in simple white stone, without any symbolic decoration, giving just the names and dates of the people interred, and is in contrast to Durkheim's tomb in Montparnasse and to that of Moïse Durkheim in Epinal, both of which have Hebrew lettering on them. This may seem a symbolic reversal of the conclusion of this paper.

The Dreyfus affair

Pierre Birnbaum sees the Dreyfus affair as an historical event of enormous consequence to France at the end of the nineteenth century, and it was of especial significance to Jews in France.[14] In *Destins juifs* he has documented as no one else has the involvement of Durkheim and his colleagues in their support of the Dreyfus case.[15] Without recapitulating his findings, let one point be made. Durkheim and Mauss were highly active in Bordeaux in the late 1890s in issues relating to the Dreyfus scandal. But they differed in their approach. As is well known Durkheim helped to create a local branch of the *Ligue des Droits de l'Homme*. His article 'L'Individualisme et les intellectuels' came to be seen as one of the best apologias for the moral basis of democratic republicanism at this time of crisis, or indeed at any time.[16]

But he became saddened and isolated by the events in the university, which in some instances were anti-Dreyfus. He even had a desire to withdraw from the faculty.[17] Mauss on the other hand, also deeply affected by the national situation, showed greater hope and enthusiasm. This he found in his membership of the socialist party, which of course was against anti-Semitism. Durkheim never joined a political party. Anti-Semitism in France for Durkheim was an abnormal component of society, a *dérèglement*, which gave rise to suffering: by contrast, for Mauss it was not so much a moral problem as an economic one.[18]

For the general subject on hand, an analysis of the Dreyfus affair is of limited value. The *Dreyfusards* were far more numerous than the Jews who supported the cause; indeed, the whole of France was divided over it. *Dreyfusards* consisted of free thinkers, socialists, Protestants, and a few liberal Catholics. The affair did not necessarily reveal the unique attitudes of Jews, for example, the degree to which they were or were not assimilated.[19] Indeed, there were some Jews who were anti-Dreyfus.

Jews in the *Année sociologique* group: intellectual influences

It is sometimes assumed that Jewish scholars were a predominant influence in the *Année Sociologique* group. But the idea is true in only limited respects. The assertion is probably attributable to the fact that three key figures in the early days were indeed Jewish by birth — Durkheim, Mauss, and Hertz. Of course, such was the influence of Durkheim and his nephew that some observers might easily assume that many others in the group were Jewish. However, this was not the case. Nearly all the others connected with the journal, with minor exceptions[20] — shall we say a group of forty — were Gentiles; of these, many were free thinkers, some of a Catholic background (for example, H. Hubert) and at least one, a firm Protestant (G. Richard).

To understand Durkheim's thought, there are those who, in recent times, would argue that one has to be a Jew or well versed in Jewish thought. Two issues are at stake. The first is that to examine Durkheim's sociology, one has to discover how far it has been moulded by Jewish religious thought. This approach stands within the province of the history of ideas, where the researcher attempts to disentangle particular influences at work on a given thinker. Some have considered it necessary to raise in detail the Jewish background of Durkheim, for instance Greenberg[21] and Filloux.[22] The second problem is that of interpretation. Unless a scholar understands the background, social, religious and political, of the writer, a meaningful exposition of his or her work is virtually impossible.

The controversy that has surrounded the work of Durkheim has been raised by such American writers as Meštrović, Lehmann, and Schoenfeld, who call for a Jewish interpretation of it.[23] I have tried to show in the opening chapter of *Debating Durkheim* the problems involved in pressing the issues of Durkheim's Jewishness too far and the difficulty in holding that his Jewishness is the key to his sociology.[24]

Against such a background I intend to raise similar issues with regard to Durkheim's nephew, Marcel Mauss. It is perfectly legitimate to suggest that if Durkheim is made the subject of the sort of enquiries I have outlined, so should Mauss. Some might think this a trivial exercise. But it seems worth considering, for as I shall show, Mauss's attitude to his Jewish background was different from Durkheim's and this helps one to clarify some contrasts in their thought. It cannot be said of Durkheim as it was of Kafka that 'Jewish traditions supplied him with a repertory of allusions and images ... notably Hasidic images.'[25] But might it be said of Mauss?

In what follows I consider something of the intellectual influences on Mauss, and then offer some reflections on his thought. Many in the *Année sociologique* group were able linguists, but probably none more so than Mauss. With an *agrégation* in philosophy from Bordeaux but calling himself a sociologist, he went to Paris in 1895 to study classical oriental languages. During his student days there he acquired a knowledge of Sanskrit and Hebrew. It has been said he became competent in six spoken languages.

One of those who influenced him most when he was in Paris was Sylvain Lévi, the great Indologist.[26] Mauss said of Sylvain that he was 'toujours et tout de suite mon deuxième oncle'.[27] Of course, Mauss was ready to point to his first uncle as his greatest influence, but not far behind him came Sylvain Lévi. Of him he said that he gave him a completely 'new direction' to his intellectual life. Not only was he his second uncle but his 'guru'.[28] Unlike Durkheim, Mauss had no inhibitions about talking of his mentors. In another passage, close to that just quoted, Mauss reported that he lived his life around three great men to whom he dedicated himself — Durkheim, Jaurès, and Sylvain Lévi .[29] Durkheim gave him 'un idéal moral et pratique'. But there is another important dimension. Sylvain Lévi was not only admired for his learning, but also valued for the warmth of his affection towards Mauss, which apparently exceeded Durkheim's. 'Sylvain Lévi was the most affectionate, the most friendly of men. He was the closest to the "Buddha of the Future", who in his actions was deeply human — something that is rare among saints, even amongst the holiest of them.'[30]

We thus have a direct declaration by Mauss of his indebtedness to these two senior Jewish scholars. This may give some clue about Mauss's interests and work. It was rather different in the case of Durkheim, who had confessed that his outstanding mentor was Renouvier. It is thus not inapposite to look a little more closely at the life and achievements of Sylvain Lévi, who is well known to Indologists and students of Nepal in the English-speaking world, but not perhaps very generally.[31]

Born in 1863 of Alsatian parents, Lévi was slightly younger than Durkheim and nine years senior to Mauss. When he came to Paris, Lévi abandoned the study of Hebrew and Jewish history for a new engagement with India. He quickly became the foremost French Indologist of his time. He followed Bergaigne in the chair of Sanskrit at the Ecole Pratique des Hautes Etudes, where Mauss encountered him, when he was also professor at the Collège de France. He died at the age of seventy-two in 1935. Although he was never an official member of the *Année sociologique* group, he did a great deal to support it in the French academic world. Lévi was far from being a *juif déjudaïcé* and remained closely identified with Jewish organisations. He was, for example, president of the Alliance Israëlite Universelle and wrote from time to time in the *Revue des études juives*. Before taking up his appointment at the Ecole Pratique des Hautes Etudes he taught for some time in Paris in a conservative college for rabbis. May I just insert a human note? It is said that members of the extended Durkheim-Mauss household always found Sylvain Lévi boring! Here were young children speaking of a man whose academic and personal qualities Mauss praised to the skies.[32] It was not just his great learning that attracted Mauss to Sylvain Lévi but, as just noted, a close, warm emotional relationship which developed between him and the Lévi family.

There was a natural resonance between Lévi and the Durkheimians. Strenski holds that by 1892 Lévi began to develop a social approach to the study of religion before knowing much about Durkheim and his followers.[33] Lévi underlined the notion of collectivity as being of great significance in the study of religion. Later on, he encouraged the Durkheimians to develop the idea of the sacred, as well as that of ritual. In the matter of religion Strenski shows convincingly Lévi's importance to the Durkheimians, which, he holds, exceeded that of Robertson Smith.

Incidentally, Mauss was also drawn to the rabbi, Israël Lévi (1856-1939), again a member of the Ecole Pratique des Hautes Etudes, on account of his rigorous method in studying Judaism and his vast knowledge and vision. However, Mauss criticised him for using the comparative method in an undiscriminating way, rather than within a sociological framework.

Mauss and reviews on religious subjects

While Durkheim was alive, Mauss was the chief reviewer for the *Année sociologique* of the section entitled 'la sociologie religeuse'. Either by choice or through the direction of his uncle, he found himself making the scientific study of religion his speciality.[34] In this he had Hertz and Hubert as colleagues. Many of the reviews dealt directly with Jewish subjects. Some of those topics were the sabbath, the feast of Purim, circumcision, the synagogue as a house of prayer, taboos on menstrual blood — subjects which (apart from the last) were seldom, if ever, mentioned by Durkheim.

As is well known, Durkheim received some form of 'revelation' in 1895 through his reading of Robertson Smith and became convinced that religion was the key to the understanding of society, something Mauss does not seem to have openly accepted (see below).[35] Articles and reviews on religious topics appeared in abundance in the *Année sociologique*, some from Durkheim but far more from the triumvirate just mentioned. Mauss contributed most, over two hundred reviews, compared with Durkheim's fifty.[36] If the *Année sociologique* group had, as we noted, few Jewish scholars in it, it was Mauss, Hertz, and Durkheim who spearheaded the contributions in religion.

Mauss accepted the claim that the new human and social sciences were radical in their conclusions, and he himself was radical in his analysis of religious institutions. He identified himself with the 'scientific study of religions' — *la science religieuse*. With his vast knowledge of Biblical and Talmudic subjects, he saw the Bible in terms of history, rather than revelation.[37] Many were excited at the time by the prospect of the new sciences of religion, which were concentrated in the Fifth section of the Ecole Pratique des Hautes Etudes, created in 1886 on the initiative of Louis Liard. Research was the key aim of the new institution, where Mauss was to become such a prominent member and leader. His position matched that of many Jewish intellectuals. For example, James de Rothschild, in creating the *Revue des études juives* in the 1880s, made its policy one of restricting itself exclusively to *la domaine de la science*.[38] That meant viewing religion *sub specie humanitatis*. Above all, it implied impartiality and a refusal to be propagandist: its aim was to be neutralist-agnostic. And so hope was fostered in *la science religieuse* or *les sciences religieuses* — terms unknown and even rejected in English academic circles, then and still today.

Such an approach also proved attractive to French theologians. Many who were formerly traditionalists began to adopt a liberal-scientific position about the origins of their own religion, both theologically and historically. The same was true of thinkers in other countries, not least the United States. However, Mauss had little sympathy with the basic thought of William James.[39] In general this liberal stance contained certain romantic notions about the emergence of religions.

Origin of the Hebrews

In Mauss's eyes one such romantic position involved theories concerning the origin of the Hebrews. By way of introduction to the subject we might say that it is easy to adopt an attractive theory of evolution by visualising the early Jews as a tribe of nomads in the desert contemplating their god, who was eventually called Jahweh (but whose name came never to be pronounced, only written). This tribe, which gave rise to the Israelites, chosen by God for no specific reason, was held to have kept itself isolated, free, and immune from surrounding undesirable influences, notably those of pagan civilisations found in and centred on towns and cities. It was not only devout Jews who held to this position but Christians as well, since Christianity, historically and theologically, is based on the Old Testament. Ernest Renan (1823-92), a liberal Christian, brought up a Catholic, was one such upholder of this theory of nomadic isolation, which was an advantage to those who rejected the notion of some kind of sudden, divine intervention made on behalf of the Israelites.[40] The concept of isolation preserved the notion of a specially selected people who developed their own ideas and practices, later to be the basis of Judaism and then Christianity.

In 1926, in his contribution to a Festschrift for Israël Lévi, Mauss attacked the romantic evolutionary theory of the origin of the Jewish nation.[41] The facts were, he argued, that the nomadic pastoralists were not isolated from sedentary peoples, who were held to be pagan and idolatrous and therefore would undermine the Jahwist religious system. On some occasions the sedentary communities would conquer the nomads and on other occasions the nomads would storm and take over settlements. Another important assertion in the same article was based on the similarities in the social institutions of pastoral nomadic peoples over a wide area, from the Semitic peoples covering a great area of Mesopotamia and Egypt, to the far south, to the Nilotic peoples, such as the Masai and their Bantu-speaking neighbours. Many of these became composite groups, who were nomads as well as cultivators, shepherds, and warriors, using camels and horses. This is but another way of criticising the notion that the Jews emerged from a small group of pure nomads who had as legendary founders Abraham, Isaac, Jacob, and Joseph (compare Wendy James's discussion in chapter 14 below).

That the Masai could be compared with the Semites, Mauss had accepted almost twenty years earlier in a review he wrote of two books on this people.[42] A major issue at stake is the extraordinary parallel between the religious beliefs of the Masai and those of Jews, especially in the matter of monotheism. Merker, a German ethnographer, held that the Masai had an almost purely monotheistic system. Engai is a unique god, a spiritual creator, for whom the Masai are an elect people. According to Merker, each individual among the Masai is overseen by a guardian angel and follows the Ten Commandments. The English ethnographer Hollis, in contrast, held that there were two gods, one black and the other red, the first good and associated with clouds and the other bad, a god of thunder.

In what might be seen as a prelude to the debate that Evans-Pritchard launched on the monotheistic notion of divinity amongst the Nuer,[43] Mauss preferred Merker's position to that of Hollis (though on the grounds of sociological parallel, rather than cultural diffusion). Mauss points out the many other parallels between the ancient Jews and the Masai, such as dietary taboos and the drinking of blood as in sacrifice. Both peoples also have a strongly held taboo against mixing fat and lean meat, and they never cook a lamb in its mother's milk — a theme Mauss was keen to develop. Also, very important were such ritual prohibitions in relation to other peoples, that is to say that they held themselves to be a separate tribe.[44]

Early in his career, in 1896, Mauss had distanced himself from traditional Jewish sympathies in another way, when he classified Judaism as a noncivilised religion since it calls for blood revenge.[45]

Prayer

Mauss's early academic interest in religion was to have provided the subject of his proposed doctorate, directed by his chosen supervisor, Sylvain Lévi. As is well known, it was on the subject of prayer, but never completed, although when he first came to the Ecole Pratique des Hautes Etudes, fired with enthusiasm, he hoped to finish it within three years.[46] In 1909, fourteen years after beginning it, he planned to have the first part, largely introductory, published. But then he withdrew it on the advice of Lévi. A few copies were then circulated only amongst friends. Karady said of the text that it is a work, even in its fragmentary state, which remains one of the most substantial that Marcel Mauss has left us.[47] History has shown a somewhat different judgment: it is *The gift*[48] which scholars today value most highly, as most conferences testify. One wonders why 'La Prière' has received so little attention.

In a more general vein, one might make the mundane observation that Mauss's interest in prayer is derived from his knowledge of the synagogue. With the 'right background', or at least a very good background, he was in a position to appreciate the social setting for prayer. The synagogue appeared relatively late in the development of Judaism and emphasised the notion of people gathering together for reading the scriptures and for prayer.[49] As in his essay on sacrifice, written in conjunction with Hubert, so in the introduction to his study of prayer, the two material sources are Hinduism and Judaism. However, there is also a long section at the end on prayer among the Australian Arunta.

Mauss holds that prayer, as a religious phenomenon, has gone through evolutionary changes. In the course of time it has become increasingly spiritual and has moved from a mechanistic and material phase to being an activity exclusive of images, where consciousness and attitudes of the soul dominate. Ideas are prominent. Further, prayer over the ages has become less a corporate than an individual action. However, all prayer in the end is derived from the social, no matter how individualistic it might appear.[50] Another characteristic of prayer is that it is action — a rite. He said: 'Prayer is, above all, a rite — something that is effective. It produces a certain effect because it has certain powers.'[51] These words are pure Durkheim.

Conclusion (1): Mauss's 'Jewish' approach to religion

Of course it is true, as Fournier says, that Marcel Mauss's interest in and knowledge of Judaism and the Hebrew language were extremely useful in his study of prayer.[52] As has been noted, in many of his articles and lectures Mauss offered examples from Judaism to a far greater extent than did Durkheim. One might recall Durkheim's references to Judaism in *The division of labour* and in *Suicide*, as well as in less important writings.[53] But Mauss could talk and write about Judaism far more freely than his uncle.

Can one go beyond that? It is virtually impossible to prove that Mauss's thought at a conceptual level was in any way influenced by his Jewish origins. As was said at the beginning of this chapter, certain scholars have argued a contrary case with regard to Durkheim. His notions of justice, solidarity, ritual, the sacred, and so on, were, it is argued, drawn from Jewish sources.[54] If this kind of assertion is difficult to substantiate, then it is no easier when applied to Mauss.

A point of considerable significance is that Mauss was opposed to making the concept of the sacred a universal one. Durkheim in *The elementary forms* made the strong assertion that the sacred-profane dichotomy was precisely that and further, it was an ultimate category in understanding, not only religion but society itself, and not only the past but the present, and by implication the future. Mauss never seems to have accepted this. By contrast, he held that its applicability was limited and was best suited to religions of Semitic origin — Judaism, Christianity, and Islam. In the place of the sacred, he would substitute *mana* as a universal category. Apart from any problems raised by this alternative as a universal concept, it was never intended to have the power of explanation and the epistemological status that the sacred had in Durkheim's thinking.[55]

In extending this point of difference between Mauss and Durkheim, I was struck by some words addressed to me by the Cambridge anthropologist, Malcolm Ruel, but I have subsequently modified it and what follows cannot be blamed on him. The daring gambit is this. Durkheim shows something akin to a 'Christian' approach to the study of religion: Mauss a more 'Jewish' one. Of course, I am not making a contrast by referring to the state of the two religions in the early days of Christianity, when the church was little more than a Jewish sect. Rather, the contrast is made in idealised terms between the church in the high Middle Ages and Judaism in the same period. Let me try to support the thesis in the following way.

In a series of lectures given annually between 1926 and 1939 at the Institut d'Ethnologie, Mauss gave the last of his lectures the title 'Phénomènes religieux'.[56] This is parallel to earlier chapters, 'Phénomènes économiques,...juridiques, ...moraux' (a very short chapter). We confine ourselves entirely to the chapter on religious phenomena. Mauss appears to be reluctant to use the word religion. To be sure, on one or two occasions he does use religion as a synonym for religious phenomena. He referred to religious phenomena as being of three kinds. The first is religious phenomena *stricto sensu* which are based on the universal notion of the sacred, more often than not *mana*, and coupled with such a characteristic was that of obligation, which implies the social authority of such phenomena.

In contrast to religious phenomena *stricto sensu*, there are religious phenomena *lato sensu* which consist principally of magic and divination, and (the third heading) there are popular superstitions. Mauss gives less treatment to the latter categories than to the first. I have no intention of arguing about the legitimacy of employing such a division but rather wish to emphasise his use of the phrase 'religious phenomena' rather than the word 'religion'. While he did not in any sense avoid using the word religion, especially when he contrasted it with magic,[57] he had, of course, written an 'Introduction à l'analyse de quelques phénomènes religieux' with Henri Hubert for the book *Mélanges d'histoire des religions* (1909).

However, is this not a case of Mauss staying with early Durkheim, who had written his first systematic analysis of issues relating to religion in the article 'De la définition des phénomènes religieux'?[58] Of course Durkheim later saw the essay as inadequate. He felt forced to abandon some of its ideas and seldom referred to it again at length. Instead, in a more systematic mode, he pointed to religion rather than religious phenomena when he defined 'a religion' in *The elementary forms*, in a way that taken in its entirety has not proved to be popular.[59] The shift in Durkheim's thought in this respect has been treated in detail elsewhere.[60] Mauss, so far as I know, never embraced Durkheim's final definition, and he never defined religion along the same lines as Durkheim did. Further, Durkheim's uncritical use of the word religion, which implies a form of unity, coherence, and system, and which was a feature of his uncle's work, Mauss seemed reluctant to adopt. Perhaps he was wise, as the attempt to define religion has given rise to controversy for a long time and has often ended in sterile debate. There have been those who want to bypass the word since it is essentially a Western concept stemming from the Latin *religio*, which anthropologists have sometimes argued does not apply to preliterate societies.

Christianity, as developed from the middle of the first millennium, reached a peak of systematisation with Thomist theology and philosophy, which attempted to present itself as a logical whole defined in terms of credal statements, with attention to coherent definitions. Whether it achieved the level of rationality that some have claimed is open to debate, but there was a streak in Durkheim which harked back to the high Middle Ages, as to some kind of ideal.[61] Religion in the West was institutionally a social force then at its zenith.

Why is it then that one can dare to hazard the thesis that Mauss's approach to religion, and perhaps to sociology itself, is Jewish in approach rather than Christian? The simple reason is that Mauss never produced a book that dealt systematically with religion in the way that Durkheim attempted in *The elementary forms*. He did not consider the role of religion in society in any formal and generalised way, nor did he consider it functionally. His approach to religious and other phenomena was selective — taking specific themes of social life, for example, prayer, the gift, techniques of the body, and analysing their concrete manifestation, their nature, value, and inner meaning — call it what you will — for society. How can this selective approach to social phenomena, and therefore to religious phenomena, be said to be in any way symbolic of Judaism?

Judaism, as a much older religion than Christianity, has obviously deeper and more diverse roots than the religion it spawned. It never succumbed in a lasting way to the influence of Greek philosophy, save for a short time in the Hellenistic period, and under the limited influence of Maimonides. It is a religion without formal creeds, but if there were creedal statements, as in Maimonides, they did not have the same function as creeds in Christianity. There has never been the demand for individuals and groups to profess verbally 'correct statements' about the saving facts of their faith. Nor does Judaism have a systematic theology, compared say to Calvinism, Thomism, or even Lutheranism. Rabbis are teachers rather than dogmatic theologians. Judaism has not attempted to bring about a unity in itself through rational thought. Indeed, it might be argued that, apart from certain Jewish philosophers such as Spinoza, rational thought, as seen in the Enlightenment, and exemplified by Descartes, is quite foreign to Judaism.

Durkheim is distant from this. He was a philosopher *manqué*. Certainly he wanted to make a contribution to epistemology in *The elementary forms*. Mauss, having studied philosophy at Bordeaux, tended to steer clear of it, except for developing notions of abstract categories, and even here he does not try to solve the basic philosophical problems of their origin, as did Durkheim.

Thus, Durkheim appears to have cut his Jewish roots. He was identified with the Enlightenment, save for its inadequate view of science, hence he called himself a critical rationalist. He held that Descartes was the father of French intellectual life. Above all, he was a systematiser who thought in terms of wholes. His nephew, however, took a slightly different path. Whilst firmly dedicated to a 'scientific approach' to the study of social phenomena, he seems to have preferred themes to systems, while seeking to specify in a distinctive and sensitive way the 'total' nature of connectedness in human life (*l'homme total, prestations totales, le fait social total,* and so forth) as discussed in several contributions to the present volume. Thus, his treatment of subject matter was essentially selective. In all this, he can be said to be in his sociology symbolically more Jewish than Christian.

The approach that Mauss appears to have adopted in the matter of religion meant that he did not find himself caught up in certain controversies which some have felt marred Durkheim's analysis of religion. I have mentioned the problem of defining religion. But there is another issue, that of the cult of the individual, which Durkheim was so keen to propagate. Mauss's commitment to socialism, absent in Durkheim, may be the reason for the lack of his reference to the cult of the individual. Because Durkheim was committed to a 'doctrine' about the persistence of the sacred in society, he was logically forced to posit something akin to the cult of the individual for the present and the future, whether it was empirically justified or not. Mauss was not caught in this trap and could be much more sceptical about the future of religion. The evidence for this is to be seen in the fact that in lectures given late in life he asserted that in the course of history *homo religiosus* has been superseded, not by *homo faber* but by *homo economicus*.[62] Whether one might consider this as stemming from Mauss's radical socialism or not, it is hardly in keeping with Durkheim's position.

Conclusion (2): a wider application

What has just been briefly stated is in part based on numerous observations made by scholars that Mauss's work is typified by no unifying principles, no coherence, a lack of system, and so on. The thesis put forward here is a response to this. But, of course, there are other possibilities. Henri Lévy-Bruhl, the son of Lucien Lévy-Bruhl, thought that the failure of Mauss to finish his thesis was because 'his impulsive spirit was loath to elaborate a "doctrine".... His mind was awash with ideas, some ingenious, some new, others profound', etc.[63] Lévy-Bruhl relates Mauss's abhorrence of doctrine to his character. This conclusion may be more acceptable than the one I have put forward, but I have tried to go further and relate it to an outlook which has certain idealised Jewish components. This has nothing at all to do with Mauss's inability to finish the thesis but, as I have said, his approach and method in dealing with religious phenomena, his preference for themes rather than systems, with certain exceptions already noted, has a symbolic relation to Judaism rather than to Christianity. His subtle and imaginative mind — for that he certainly had — was more like a rabbi arguing, perhaps dialectically, about the meaning of a text than a Christian theologian affirming a dogma.

All that said, Mauss did not *intend* to adopt a particularly Jewish position over against a non-Jewish one, if that were in any way a possibility. He stood essentially for the application of science to social phenomena and here he is in exactly the same mould as his uncle. But the way science is applied practically to social phenomena and more particularly to religious phenomena, brought out disparities between them. Overall, there remains the fact that in their attitudes towards their Jewish background there were significant differences between uncle and nephew. Apart from Mauss's openness towards his roots, which is undeniable, he adopted an intellectual approach to the study of religious phenomena which in aim and methodology was more 'Jewish' and less 'Christian' than that of Durkheim. Above all, I hope I have carried out the simple task of showing the folly of bracketing uncle and nephew together in the matters raised here.

NOTES

1. M. Fournier, *Marcel Mauss*, Paris, 1994.
2. Tartarin de Tarascon is the hero of a series of novels by Alphonse Daudet, published between 1872 and 1890. In the popular mind he represented a bragging southerner. I am grateful to Claudette Kennedy who, as a cousin of Marcel Mauss, has supplied some of these family reminiscences.
3. See Karady's introductory note to 'La prière' [1909], *Oeuvres*, vol. 1, p. 356; and also Mauss's 'An intellectual self-portrait' included as chapter 2 in the present volume.
4. Fournier, *Marcel Mauss*, p. 721.
5. Ibid., p. 729.
6. M. Mauss, 'Sylvain Lévi' [1935], *Oeuvres*, vol. 3, pp. 535-45.
7. Fournier, *Marcel Mauss*, pp. 652-8.
8. Ibid., p. 38.
9. Cf. Durkheim's position; see W.S.F. Pickering, 'The enigma of Durkheim's Jewishness', in W.S.F. Pickering and H. Martins, eds, *Debating Durkheim*, London, 1994.
10. See M. Fournier, 'Introduction' to *Marcel Mauss: écrits politiques*, Paris, 1997.
11. Ibid., p. 53.
12. Fournier, *Marcel Mauss*, p. 38.
13. J. Clifford, *Person and myth: Maurice Leenhardt in the Melanesian world*, Berkeley/Los Angeles, 1982, p. 152.
14. The Dreyfus affair, which was destined to rock France to the core and even split families, began in 1894 when an army officer, Alfred Dreyfus, was falsely accused of treason in betraying military secrets to Germany and was sent to Devil's Island. He was exonerated eight years later, after a great upsurge of public opinion in his favour. The affair quickly raised wide-ranging issues, notably anti-Semitism.
15. P. Birnbaum, *Destins juifs. De la révolution française à Carpentras*, Paris, 1995, p. 71ff.
16. Translated by S. and J. Lukes as 'Individualism and the intellectuals' [1898], *Political studies*, 17, 1969, pp. 14-30. See also S. Lukes, *Emile Durkheim: his life and work. A historical and critical study*, London and New York, 1973, p. 332ff.
17. Birnbaum, *Destins juifs*, p. 88.
18. Ibid., p. 80.
19. See Pickering, 'Enigma of Durkheim's Jewishness'.
20. For example, M. David, E. Lévy, I. Lévy, J. Marx.
21. L. M. Greenberg, 'Bergson and Durkheim as sons and assimilators: the early years', *French historical studies* 9, 1976, pp. 619-34.
22. J.-C. Filloux, 'Il ne faut pas oublier que je suis fils de rabbin', *Revue française de sociologie* 17, 1976, pp. 259-66.
23. For further information and analysis about these American writers, see I. Strenski, *Durkheim and the Jews of France*, Chicago and London, 1997, pp. 1-15.
24. Pickering, 'Enigma of Durkheim's Jewishness'.
25. R. Robertson, *Kafka: Judaism, politics and literature*, Oxford, 1985.
26. Ivan Strenski has recently brought before the English-speaking academic world the work of Sylvain Lévi and his influence on Mauss; see Strenski, *Durkheim and the Jews of France*, chap. 5.
27. Mauss [1935], *Oeuvres*, vol. 3, p. 537.
28. Ibid., p. 535.
29. Ibid., p. 544.
30. Ibid., pp. 544-5. It is interesting to note that Mauss said of his three heroes that each lived a life crowned by *une belle mort* (*Oeuvres*, vol. 3, p. 544).

31. See Strenski, *Durkheim and the Jews of France*, chap. 5.
32. Fournier, *Marcel Mauss*, p. 101.
33. Strenski, *Durkheim and the Jews of France*, chap. 5.
34. Cuin notes that Mauss had a predilection for religion. See C.-H. Cuin, 'Durkheim et Mauss à Bordeaux: naissance de l'ethnologie scientifique française' in *L'ethnologie à Bordeaux*, Université de Bordeaux II, 1995, p. 134. This article contains interesting observations on the influence of Durkheim on Mauss while the latter was in Bordeaux.
35. W.S.F. Pickering, *Durkheim's sociology of religion: themes and theories*, London and Boston, 1984, chap. 4.
36. Ibid., pp. 52-3. See also I. Strenski's review of this volume in *Contemporary Sociology* 14, 1985, pp. 394-5.
37. See D. Lindenberg, 'Marcel Mauss et le "Judaïsme"', *Revue européennes des sciences sociales*, 34, 1996, p. 48.
38. Fournier, *Marcel Mauss*, p. 86.
39. Mauss [1904], *Oeuvres*, vol. 1, pp. 58-65.
40. Joseph-Ernest Renan, having withdrawn from being ordained in 1845, studied Semitic languages and became professor at the Collège de France. He became famous through his book, *Vie de Jésus*, 1863.
41. Mauss, 'Critique interne de la légende d'Abraham' [1926], *Oeuvres*, vol. 2, pp. 527-36.
42. Mauss [1906], *Oeuvres*, vol. 2, pp. 537-43.
43. E.E. Evans-Pritchard, *Nuer Religion*, Oxford, 1956. Cf. D.H. Johnson, *Nuer Prophets*, Oxford, 1994.
44. I should like to note in passing that in Mauss's essay on the origins of the Israelites there appears one of the few references made at the time, or indeed made subsequently, to Durkheim's notion of positive and negative rites. Mauss speaks of the positive rites of the Israelites where flesh and blood of beasts are used in sacrifice. Negative rites are locally powerful interdicts — 'Thou shalt not cook a lamb in the milk of its mother', as mentioned. 'Légende d'Abraham', p. 532.
45. Mauss [1896], *Oeuvres*, vol. 2, p. 687.
46. Mauss [1909], *Oeuvres*, vol. 1, pp. 357-477. See Fournier, *Marcel Mauss*, p. 93. For the plan of the thesis, see Mauss's 'Intellectual self-portrait', chapter 2 in this volume.
47. V. Karady, in *Oeuvres*, vol. 1, p. 356.
48. Mauss, *The gift: the form and reason for exchange in archaic societies* [1925], trans. W.D. Halls, London, 1990.
49. Mauss [1909], *Oeuvres*, vol. 1, p. 364, n. 9.
50. Ibid., p. 361.
51. Ibid., p. 481.
52. Fournier, *Marcel Mauss*, p. 40.
53. E. Durkheim, *The division of labour in society* [1893], trans. G. Simpson, New York, 1984, pp. 138-40; *Suicide: a study in sociology*[1897], trans. J.A. Spaulding and G. Simpson, Glenco, 1951, pp. 155-7, 159-60, 167-8.
54. Pickering, 'Enigma of Durkheim's Jewishness', p. 29ff.
55. For a more thorough exposition of this issue, see S. Martelli, 'Mana ou sacré? La contribution de Marcel Mauss à la fondation de la sociologie religieuse', *Revue européenne des sciences sociales* 34, 1996, pp. 51-66.
56. Mauss, *Manuel d'ethnologie* [1947], 3rd edn, Paris, 1989.
57. For example, Mauss [1909], in *Oeuvres*, vol. 1, p. 411.
58. E. Durkheim, 'De la définition des phénomènes religieux', *Année sociologique* 2, 1899, pp. 1-28. Translated by J. Redding and W.S.F. Pickering, in *Durkheim on religion*, London and Boston, 1975.

59. E. Durkheim, *The elementary forms of religious life* [1912], trans. K.E. Fields, New York, 1995, p. 44.

60. Pickering, *Durkheim's sociology of religion*, chap. 9.

61. Ibid., p. 427ff.

62. Mauss, *Manuel*, Paris, 1989, p. 204.

63. Fournier, *Marcel Mauss*, p. 352.

*Foundations of
Maussian anthropology*

Chapter 4

A VAGUE BUT SUGGESTIVE CONCEPT:

THE 'TOTAL SOCIAL FACT'

Alexander Gofman

It is well known that the Maussian theory of the 'total social fact' is itself far from being total. On the contrary, it is quite fragmentary; moreover, it is not a theory in the true sense of the word. What we are dealing with is more a matter of certain implicit conceptual orientations to be found in his studies and a certain number of opinions or statements scattered through his works. Mauss himself did not claim to be constructing a theory of the 'total social fact'. Doubtless, he was unable (and unwilling) to do without conceptualisations, but, as a 'positivist, who only believes in facts',[1] he scorned general theories. In his eyes, 'facts' in general, and 'total social facts' in particular, have a heuristic rather than a theoretical value; they are the means of discovering other facts previously unknown. He blamed the sociology of his time for being too abstract. In contrast to Durkheim, he considered that to know, explain, and understand certain facts on the one hand, and to construct a theory based on those facts on the other, are quite different things.

Nevertheless, this vague concept of the 'total social fact', whose theoretical status is insufficiently clear and well defined, has aroused a great deal of theoretical interest. It must be added that similar cases have occurred fairly often in the history of the social sciences. Examples are provided by the concepts of alienation, social class, the sacred, gender, mode of life, etc. It may well be that all the key concepts of sociology belong to this same type. As for the theoretical sociology of the present day, its ambiguities and obscurities have almost become a matter of principle and of good taste, having been carried to an extreme. One could even formulate a quasi-law whereby the more a theory or a concept is clear, well defined, and open to unequivocal interpretation, the less are its chances of success within the community of sociologists. And conversely, the more a theory or concept is ambiguous, obscure and confused, the more it is likely to dominate the sociological mind.

In my view, this can be explained partly by the amount of prestige attached to the different occupations and intellectual roles in the profession of sociology. Let us, for example, imagine the appearance of a social theory which is very explanatory, clear, noncontradictory, convincing — in short, a 'beautiful' theory. What would then be left for other specialists to do? They could simply accept this theory and popularise it, or they might be obliged to confirm it with their own findings and, at most, add a little extra to it. Neither of these intellectual functions is held in very high esteem, either by the scientific community or by the public. Of course, one could also attempt to refute the theory, which would bring a little honour and glory, but this would still be in a sense a secondary kind of work and not very prestigious. So, there is not very much to say or to do where clear, exact, and convincing theories are concerned.

Now let us envisage a sociological work which is fundamental and rich in ideas but incomplete; it is fragmentary in character and full of ambiguous judgements and vague concepts. In this case we, the analysts, have a wonderful opportunity for expressing ourselves, for exercising our analytical powers, in short, for putting forward our own ideas in interpreting the work. In this instance its obscurity is wholly favourable to subsequent sociologists, for they no longer have to deal with a ready-made, completed theory, but with ideas and judgements providing ample latitude for the different interpretations of the interpreters themselves.

This is what we have seen, for instance, in the history of Marxist theory. We know that most of the interpretations of Marx are based on his unfinished works, on his manuscripts and letters, sometimes even on the rough drafts of these. The key concepts of Marxist theory are vague and ambiguous. Despite that, or rather because of it, a multitude of interpretations or readings of Marx are available to us today. They can be diverse or contradictory, crude or sensitive, very closely based on his texts or very far removed from them. A great number of commentaries seek to discover the 'authentic' Marx. Moreover, we are faced with many theories purporting to be Marxist or what one might call 'variations on the theme of Marx', which show scant regard for fidelity to the original texts. Thus the example of the Marxist tradition demonstrates that the incomplete and vague nature of a theoretical work in sociology is one of the most effective stimulants to its subsequent development. No doubt there are many others. But, in my opinion, it is precisely this stimulus that today's 'postclassical' and 'postmodern' theoretical sociology often draws on as one of its chief means of development. It is afraid of the clear and univocal and, unlike certain classics of sociology, it attempts to be suggestive and fruitful by relying on the obscurity and ambiguity of its theoretical constructions.

Let us return to Mauss and his famous concept of the 'total social fact'. In contrast with many other similar cases, the ambiguity of this concept does not derive from theoretical construction, but from theoretical nonconstruction; in other words, from Mauss's refusal to theorise. Mauss attached a great deal of importance to the concept. As far as he is concerned, and as has already been indicated, we do not have a theory of 'total' facts, but rather underlying theoretical orientations which are 'hidden' or 'dissolved' in his studies, and some judgements or slogans which arise from them. Thus, our analytical task consists in the attempt to *reconstruct* as adequately as possible the implicit orientations which are embodied in the Maussian concept of the 'total social fact' and which constitute the spirit or the *hau* of this concept, to use Mauss's favourite Maori term.

Mauss's choice of this concept arose from his general fondness for the concepts of 'total' and of 'whole', as well as of 'complete' and 'concrete'. We can see this in the range of related expressions he uses, such as 'total human being', 'total prestations', the 'totality of the body of society' or the 'whole of the social system'. We can find a distant source for this fondness in the philosophical tradition going back to classical antiquity and, subsequently, in the 'universal whole' and the 'totality' of Dom Deschamps,[2] and in the concepts of totality developed by Kant, Schelling, Hegel, Comte, O. Spann, etc. It is probable that the Maussian passion for 'totality' was prompted by certain trends in the psychology of his time, trends which Mauss followed very closely. In particular, we may recall here the 'law of totality' propounded by Harald Höffding, and the work in *Gestaltpsychologie*.[3] The influence of the latter explains, perhaps, the somewhat unexpected appearance of the word 'form' (*Gestalt* in German) in the subtitle of *The gift*.[4] Doubtless, this pursuit of the 'total' resulted from Mauss's dissatisfaction with the traditional intra- and interdisciplinary divisions which partitioned reality in an artificial way. He believed that the most significant and interesting problems in the human and social sciences were to be found on the frontiers of scientific disciplines: therefore, the 'total' vision of objects should contribute to the erosion of disciplinary boundaries. It is especially this theme which he tackles in 'Body techniques';[5] his discussion there of the 'cursed' category of the 'miscellaneous' which we nevertheless have to penetrate recalls the Platonic argument quoted by Henri Bergson, concerning a cook who has to cut up meat according to its natural divisions.[6]

This 'totalising' orientation is apparent in Mauss's general idea of the human being. It differs from the Durkheimian notion of *homo duplex* which considers the human being as an entity in which two forms of existence are separately present — the individual (a bio-psychological organism), and the social. Mauss, in contrast, defended the idea of the 'complete' human being as a reality whose biological, psychological and socio-cultural characteristics make up an indivisible whole. He declared, 'Whether we study special facts or general facts, it is always the complete human being we are primarily dealing with.'[7] From there follows the idea of the 'triple alliance' of biology, psychology, and sociology.

Just as Mauss considers the study of the 'complete human being' to be the main objective of the human sciences, so he considers the study of 'total social facts' to be the supreme cognitive objective of the social sciences. In my view, a reconstruction of the implicit theoretical orientations embodied in the idea of 'total social facts' leads us to distinguish between two meanings of the expression in the works of Mauss.

The first meaning lies in his constant desire to consider social phenomena as integrated objects-and-subjects, in all the fullness and complexity of their properties. In this sense, *all* the facts of social life which are the objects of sociology (and the social sciences in general) must be studied, ideally at least, as total facts. But, in interpreting them as totalities, Mauss does not consider them to be closed and sufficient unto themselves. The entire social system, 'the social system as a whole', is treated as an entity of the most general and fundamental kind; it is to this entity that the particular phenomenon it encompasses must be related: '...each of the special systems is only a part of the whole social system. Therefore, to describe one or other of them, without taking them all into account and especially without taking into account the supreme fact that they form a system, is to render oneself incapable of understanding them.'[8] The 'total' approach to social phenomena, the interpretation of each phenomenon in close relation to the others and to the social system in which they are set, constitutes the specificity of the sociological method, making it distinct from the methods of the other social sciences.[9]

But Mauss's orientation towards the search for the totality of social phenomena is combined with his desire to study the mechanisms of interdependence and interpenetration of the social and the individual. He does not consider social facts as being *pars pro toto* (part for whole):

but nor is his standpoint at the opposite extreme, of *totum pro parte* (whole for part). This is particularly evident in his interpretation of symbols as distinctive characteristics of social facts. According to him, symbols represent social reality as well as mediating individual attitudes and orientations.[10] He always studies in minute detail the particularities and details of social phenomena.

The first meaning of the idea of 'total social facts' we have detected in Mauss is *epistemological and methodological* above all else; it consists in the tendency, as we said above, to study *all social facts as total*. But Mauss also considers 'total social facts' as *specific ontological entities*, which are *sui generis* (to speak in a Durkheimian vein) and distinct from other social facts. In this second sense, these total facts, as he see them, are phenomena which penetrate every aspect of the concrete social system; they concentrate it and constitute its focus, they are the constitutive elements, the generators and motors of the system: 'In certain cases they involve the totality of society and its institutions ... and in other cases only a very large number of institutions.'[11] One can say that these are 'total social facts' in the true sense of the term. Each of them cuts across different institutions, values, and actions; it is at one and the same time legal, economic, religious, political, relating to production and to consumption, etc.[12] The best-known and the most important example of such facts in Mauss's work is, undoubtedly, 'the gift' in archaic societies.

It is obvious that the two meanings of the term that we have distinguished are very close to one another in Mauss's work, but, all the same, they are different and it is useful to distinguish between them if we wish to understand the true role of the concept in the works of its inventor.

It is also obvious that the idea of 'total social facts' was in keeping with the general movement of the birth and and development of the systemic orientation in twentieth-century science. There is no doubt that in this respect Durkheim's influence on Mauss was decisive. But whereas Durkheim took as models for the social system only the biological (primarily) and mechanical systems — the organism and the machine — Mauss also had before him other epistemological patterns, namely those of psychology and linguistics,[13] where the principle of the totality of the objects of study was of paramount importance at that time.

The 'total' in Mauss has many attributes or virtues; it is simultaneously the 'general', the 'universal', the 'real', the 'concrete', the 'dynamic', and so on. The attribution of all these features to the objects of study tended to bring ambiguity and even a certain mysticism into the interpretation of social phenomena. This ambiguity is seen especially in the demand that one consider *all aspects of social phenomena at once, simultaneously,* as in the conception of total phenomena proposed by Georges Gurvitch.[14] Here, the 'totalising' approach to objects of study can only be realised by means of a purely emotional or quasi-mystical process similar to the Diltheyan *Erlebnis* (experienced emotion).[15] The 'total' now obviously extends beyond the limits of the kind of rational knowledge that would be open to any precise interpretation.

The ambiguous and fragmentary character of the idea of 'total social facts' in Mauss gave rise to quite different interpretations of it. The best known, of course, are those of Gurvitch and of Claude Lévi-Strauss.[16] It is very typical that these two contrasting theoreticians should have focused on the same idea. In their analyses of this idea Gurvitch and Lévi-Strauss both wanted to find an intellectual precursor in Mauss. That is why their interpretations of the 'total social fact' were, to a large extent, the projections and reflections of their own points of view: the two theoreticians elaborated their own approaches using Mauss's idea of the 'total social fact' as a pretext.

Despite, and perhaps thanks to, the ambiguity of Mauss's ideas, the theoretical history of the notion of the 'total social fact' is not yet over; its heuristic possibilities have not yet been exhausted. It is possibly with that notion that there began the 'return to the actor' proclaimed by Alain Touraine.[17] Although he was a faithful Durkheimian, Mauss renounced the institutionalist and normative determinism of Durkheim. For the latter, as is well known, sociology was a science of the institutions which represent or embody the social system (he saw even suicide as a kind of institution). Despite the fact that in his early works Mauss was as 'institutionalist' as Durkheim (see, for example, the article he wrote with Fauconnet in 1901[18]), his attention was subsequently increasingly drawn to the actions and actors who created norms, values, and social institutions. Indeed, this concept of the 'total social fact' encompasses not only the 'totality of the system', but also the 'totality of the actor', individual and collective. It is this encompassing concept that corresponds to the deeper aspirations of present-day social science, which is constantly in search of the actors, agents, subjects — in a word, of the creators of social rules and institutions.

In considering social facts as total, Mauss studied societies as a specific number of persons who are linked together by different relationships and bounded by specific spatial and temporal limits. But he pursued his approach to the extent of making a principle of studying social facts as 'totalities-within-totalities'. That is why he attempted to study societies in their relations with other societies, to situate them within the framework of greater totalities. From this there followed his division of phenomena or facts into intrasocietal and intersocietal; but the important thing is that, according to Mauss, *intersocietal facts are also social*.[19] He was not, therefore, assimilating the idea of society to that of the nation-state. In his studies he situated social phenomena among the phenomena of civilisation — the latter being, in his view, 'a sort of hypersocial system of social systems'. From all these orientations was born social anthropology, of which Marcel Mauss is justly considered one of the founders. For the spirit of this discipline indeed consists in the notion that the world community or, at least, a 'hypersocial system of social systems' is the most basic 'total social fact'.

From what we have said, it is obvious that Mauss's ideas rank among those which are to be found at the origin of theories of globalisation. Anthony Giddens returns to Mauss's favourite themes when he emphasises that social totalities exist only within the framework of 'intersocial systems', and that while all societies may have a systematic character, at the same time they are constituted by the intersection of a great number of social systems.[20]

Finally, Mauss's theses remain of prime importance for today's sociology in that they see all social phenomena as falling within the sphere of the human will, of the different options open to it, and of the arbitrary choice between them. But while recognising these features of social reality, as well as the originality of each society, he did not in any sense deny the necessity for nomological judgements in sociology and did not reduce the discipline to everyday knowledge and mere common sense. In my view, in this connection one can find in his work a good warning against that current style of sociology that proclaims itself 'nonpositivist', 'nonclassical', 'postmodern', etc., and which, while quite rightly giving up the determinism and 'laws' of the 'Ancien Régime' in sociology, at the same time is sometimes ready to give up all the principles of social science and reduce the discipline to a solipsistic and ambiguous jumble of commonsensical clichés and confused ratiocinations of excessive abstraction, verging on the mystical and susceptible neither to interpretation, verification, nor refutation.

In contrast to Durkheim, Mauss did not design a unitary theoretical edifice (or more than one of them), possessing global scope and a degree of closure. His concern was to resolve particular problems rather than to elaborate his theoretical views. That is why his views are sometimes a bit vague and fragmentary, and why, in consequence, they can be interpreted in a great variety of ways. On the other hand, his ideas were more subtle and open than those of his teacher. Like Saint-Simon, he knew how to pioneer new paths leaving to others the task of following them in whatever way they chose. It is for us to follow them and to invent others — as indeed always happens with a thinker of classic status.

NOTES

1. Mauss, 'Intellectual self-portrait', chapter 2, this volume.
2. See E. Beaussire, *Antécédents de l'hégélianisme dans la philosophie française: Dom Deschamps, son système et son école*, Paris, 1865, p. 47, etc.
3. H. Höffding, *Psychologie in Umrissen auf Grundlage der Erfahrung* [1882], 2nd edn, Leipzig, 1893, p. 217.
4. See W. Köhler, *Gestalt psychology: an introduction to new concepts in modern psychology* [1929], New York, 1959, p. 189, etc.
5. 'The notion of body techniques' [1934], in *Sociology and psychology: essays by Marcel Mauss*, trans. B. Brewster, London, 1979, pp. 95-123, at pp. 97-8.
6. H. Bergson, *Les deux sources de la morale et de la religion*, Paris, 1932, p. 109, recalling Plato, *Phaedrus* 265E.
7. 'Real and practical relations between psychology and sociology' [1924], in *Sociology and psychology: essays by Marcel Mauss*, trans. B. Brewster, London, 1979, pp. 1-33, at p. 27.
8. 'Fragment d'un plan de sociologie générale descriptive'[1934], in *Oeuvres*, vol. 3, pp. 303-58, at p. 306.
9. 'Divisions et proportions des divisions de la sociologie', ibid., pp. 178-245 at pp. 213-6.
10. 'Real and practical relations', p. 21.
11. M. Mauss,*The gift: the form and reason for exchange in archaic societies*, trans. W.D. Halls, London, 1990, p. 78.
12. Ibid., pp. 5-6, 79.
13. Ibid., p. 80; 'Real and practical relations', p. 20.
14. G. Gurvitch (ed.), *Traité de sociologie*, vol. 1 [1958], 2nd edn, 1962, p. 27, etc.
15. See W. Dilthey, *Selected writings* [1910], trans. and ed. H.P. Rickman, Cambridge, 1976, pp. 168-245, at pp. 226-8. For the significance of the German term 'Erlebnis' see Rickman's Introduction, p. 29.
16. C. Lévi-Strauss, *Introduction to the work of Marcel Mauss*, trans. F. Baker, London, 1987 [1950], pp. 25-33.
17. A. Touraine, *Le retour de l'acteur*, Paris, 1984.
18. M. Mauss and P. Fauconnet, 'Sociologie' [1901] in *Oeuvres*, vol. 3, pp. 139-77.
19. 'Fragment', *Oeuvres*, vol. 3, p. 312.
20. A. Giddens, *The constitution of society: outline of the theory of structuration*, Berkeley/Los Angeles, 1984, p. 164ff.

Chapter 5

THE MAUSSIAN SHIFT:

A SECOND FOUNDATION FOR SOCIOLOGY IN FRANCE?

Bruno Karsenti

The Durkheimian foundation of scientific sociology in France did not really consist in the definitive establishment of an unambiguous theory, henceforth needing only to be applied religiously. It was more a matter of formulating a problematic, of opening up the conceptual space for a group of questions where the social is less a positively determined given than a research horizon under which the very objectification of the social is a project that is constantly renewed. Quite properly, historians of sociology have endeavoured to clarify the internal tensions and the complex composition of what is globally known as the Durkheimian School. The image of this school of thought which emerges from their work is not at all one of scholastic dogma. Indeed, its consolidation as a theoretical current is strikingly accompanied by internal reflexive movement. Thus it makes progress by constantly debating with itself, and consequently by also redefining the particular domain of its own discourse in relation to other domains which are perceived as connected rather than as radically foreign to it.

To come to grips with this dynamic of Durkheimian thought — which, as one must always bear in mind, was a collective dynamic — is to recognise that the closure or completeness of sociological knowledge has never been wholly assured, and *what is more never can be*. In a recent and fundamental work on sociological epistemology, Jean-Claude Passeron puts forward the hypothesis that this lack of cognitive closure, which prohibits any maintenance of disciplinary boundaries and the involution they produce, is characteristic of the specific kind of knowledge that is developed in the field of the social sciences. Now it is exactly by adopting a strongly Maussian tone that Passeron describes this process of opening out, when he discusses the relation between sociology and history:

> The passionate debates provoked by nineteenth-century thought and its sociological and anthropological doctrines have not been resolved, but rather worn down by the very evolution of the operational concepts of the two disciplines. From their long-term mutual association, the disciplines have borrowed from each other, not only arguments, but also ways of softening and forgetting them. Thus they learned to remove the obstacles created by the naivety of their initial theories. The early problems faded away — the only way one ever finds theoretical problems being resolved in the social sciences — as the passionate commitment which gave them life was forgotten and replaced by a new rigidity of formulations deaf to fresh questions. [1]

In many ways, this consideration could serve as an epigraph for a presentation of Mauss's work, focusing on the elements of it that are original and significant for the human sciences as they have developed during the course of this century. Consider the project of breaking out from that static situation in which questions are posed only to close back upon themselves within the space of their formulation, of freeing ourselves to grasp their resonance with other questions which, although posed in other spaces, nonetheless belong to the same horizon of knowledge. Such might be the definition of a *new foundation* of the social sciences in France, one to which the name of Mauss would be much more fittingly attached than that of Durkheim. This foundation is marked less by the emergence *ex nihilo* of a brand new approach, than by a shift introduced within an already existing problematic, or in other words, to adopt Passeron's terminology, through the play of displacements and borrowings whereby disciplinary conflicts are blurred as if by erosion.

In his lecture to the French Psychological Society in 1924 on the 'real and practical' relations between psychology and sociology, Mauss speaks in language less local and more sophisticated than his title may suggest of 'services rendered' in both directions, by psychology to sociology, and conversely. And further, we must remember that even the discipline of historical study is not excluded from the way the sociologist is contemplating a realignment of the human sciences. Thus, it is with explicit reference to historians and to the requirement for synthesis which underpins their approach that Mauss confers on the 'total social fact' one of the most resounding of his formulations in the *Essay on the gift:*

The historians feel and and rightly object to the fact that the sociologists are too ready with abstractions and unduly separate the various elements of societies from one another.[2] We must do as they do: observe what is given. Now, the given is Rome or Athens, the average Frenchman, the Melanesian from this island or another, and not prayer or law by itself. After having of necessity divided things up too much, and abstracted from them, sociologists must strive to reconstitute the whole. By doing so they will discover rewarding facts. They will also find a way to satisfy the psychologists.... All these study or should observe, the behaviour of total beings, not divided according to their faculties. We must imitate them. The study of the concrete, which is the study of completeness, is possible, and more captivating, more explanatory still in sociology.[3]

My aims are to elucidate what I have just called the 'Maussian shift', and to measure the divergence it represents from Durkheim's own work even while it tries to extend the life of that work, and in short to understand the effects of the founding or refounding of the social sciences attributable specifically to the Maussian impetus. With these aims in mind I would like to make the most of this well-known passage and particularly of the epistemological figure it conjures up. The figure is that of *l'homme total* (the total human being), *l'individu complet* (the complete individual), or again, to follow the Maussian formulations literally, *l'homme tout entier* (the human being in his or her entirety).[4] It is by setting up this figure that Mauss's work reveals its strategic aims: the strategy is to take his own sociological heritage and reorient it, to weave new relationships between sociology, biology, psychology, history, linguistics, and psychoanalysis, and to open up anthropology in this new space. In this it succeeds essentially by giving itself a new theme: the total human being, in which the living organism, the psychological, and the social meet together, a being whom it now becomes possible, under certain conditions, to study as a complex and complete whole. To grant the Maussian impetus a decisive significance, is to recognise this: that the figure of the total human being is precisely the object that, over relatively recent times, the human sciences have collectively given themselves, whether implicitly or explicitly, and which in either case constantly underlies their investigations. To put it in another way, in the manner of Foucault,[5] but also (in a sense) running counter to some of his conclusions, the total human being is, I think, 'the mode of being of that which there is to know about' in the human sciences, and provides an objective polarity determining the new coherence of this knowledge and the modalities of its relationship with philosophical knowledge.

This expression, *l'homme total*, has had a strong attraction for commentators. Gurvitch, for example, stressed the comparisons to be made on this subject between the Maussian approach and certain

Marxist themes — the theme of the 'total man' being, as is well known, central to the *1844 Manuscripts* and the *Theses on Feuerbach*. However, as Gurvitch recognised, this comparison comes up against the fact that these texts — which were certainly unknown to Mauss — only use the concept of *l'homme total* in reference to the concept of *praxis*, that is the active taking over by human beings of the social determinations acting on them: it would be very dangerous to seek a corresponding concept in Maussian sociology.[6] Rather than that, one must go back to the sources of French thought at the beginning of the nineteenth century to find the notion in the form taken up by Mauss. In fact, it was forged during this period in the conflictual articulation of spiritualism and materialism, the two tendencies being involved jointly in the project for a '*science de l'homme*' that aimed to embrace humankind in its integrity. Two types of anthropology were then opposing each other: one primarily psychological, as expressed particularly in the work of Maine de Biran, the other primarily physiological, which had its roots in Cabanis and the Ideologues and was to impose itself as the dominant concept of anthropology with Broca. But we must remember that Maine de Biran makes a special appeal in his *Nouveaux essais d'anthropologie* for the foundation of '*une science de l'homme intérieur*' (a science of the inner human being) whose object would be to consider *l'homme tout entier* or *l'homme total*' (both expressions are used[7]). In 1833, these spiritualist arguments were fiercely opposed by Pierre Leroux, although he used some of the same terms, for he pointed to the necessity for a 'wider study', covering the human being as a whole, *l'homme tout entier*. He also added: 'That is what, in their own way, the disciples of Cabanis understood when they championed phrenology and anthropology against psychology alone.'[8]

On reading the Maussian texts, we cannot fail to be struck by the resurgence of these old expressions dating from before the work of Durkheim (in which they had been obscured) — and that despite the fact that they were originally formulated in a wholly different epistemological context. As for the intention to return to the *l'homme total* and to develop a science of humanity whose completeness depended on its capacity to restore the integrity of its object, certainly this is not in itself basically new. What is new, however, is that this restoration was to be made *from the point of view of sociology* — that the complete individual was to be recaptured from the privileged angle of his or her sociality.

How is this intention actually realised? To answer this question while avoiding over-generality and abstraction, we shall consider a concrete study where the concept of the whole human being is fully brought into play along the lines laid down by the lecture on 'Real and practical relations between psychology and sociology'. I am referring to the study of 'The physical effect on the individual of the idea of death suggested by the collectivity' (1926). To begin with, we must consider the title of the lecture. The use of the concept of suggestion may appear a little surprising in the context of a Durkheimian perspective, given that this perspective defined itself by its opposition to the psychology of crowds, but we must not let this distract us. For the concept here has a very specific meaning: by no means does it indicate an obscure causality modelled on magnetic attraction or on contagion. On the contrary, it is deliberately considered *exclusively at the level of its effects*. Now these do not reveal themselves in the vague unity of the crowd, but in that simultaneously very concrete and very complex unity of the individual. Released from its attribution to a force which is by nature supraindividual, suggestion finds expression on the level of individuality itself: that is, the human subject considered in his or her capacity to influence the self by suggestion, in other words to produce, at the absolutely particular level of his or her being, a determination to die.

> Hence we shall consider only those cases where the *subject who dies* does not believe or know himself to be ill, *he only believes, for precise collective causes, that he is in a state close to death.* This state generally coincides with a break in his communion, either by magic or through sin, with the sacred powers and things whose presence normally sustains him. His consciousness is then completely invaded by ideas and sentiments which are entirely of collective origin, which betray no physical disturbance. Analysis is unable to hit on any element of will, choice or even voluntary ideation on the part of the sufferer, or even of individual mental disturbance, other than the collective suggestion itself. This individual believes himself to be bewitched or at fault and dies for this reason.[9]

We must thus try to ask ourselves about a particular psychological condition of the subject — for if collective causes play a part here, it is only via the subjective belief in their efficacy. We must also add that the object of this belief is not physical disorder, real or imagined, which would naturally entail death: it bears only on the imminence of death and its inevitability, in relation — in 'coincidence', says Mauss quite specifically — to a particular collective situation. This is tantamount to saying that on the level of subjective consciousness, it is the efficacy of the social that is completely re-created, invading the whole of psychic space and thereby activating, in the last analysis, physical consequences that are fatal. Now this complete creation certainly constitutes the most mysterious aspect of the Australian and New Zealand evidence, and particularly hinders any attempt to classify these cases as thanatomania or suicide. In the end, what do we see? We see individuals dying by 'witchcraft' — here, it would seem that the term is even more appropriate for the observer than for the subject observed who does indeed appear to die, so far as the ethnographer can see, 'as if enchanted' — but under such strict constraints that death sometimes takes place at a very clearly predetermined time,[10] without it ever being possible to identify a specific cause, either in some deliberate choice made by the subject, or in their particular physiological condition.[11]

We must, therefore, lay stress on what one is tempted to interpret as an obliteration of the personality brought about by individuals themselves. Let us say a man adopts a social attitude because, by suggestion, he acts upon himself, and thus believes himself doomed to die. One could also say that this obliteration in the face of social forces has no other origin than his *auto-affection*, which itself can be studied scientifically as a neuro-psychological phenomenon.[12] But if this means that a solution begins to emerge as far as the psycho-physiological viewpoint is concerned, that is not the case for the sociologist: for here the individual subject seems to move into the foreground. His or her own physiological constitution, and the vital force sustaining it, are like the singular incarnation of a collective force. The social is integrated at the biological level of instinct, considered in its natural primordial form, namely as the instinct for self-preservation: 'And thus it is that the feeble trust in life either founders definitively or is restored to equilibrium by a medicine, magician or protective spirit, itself of a collective nature, like the loss of equilibrium itself.'[13]

So, the ascendancy of the collective force is so great, and yet so subtle, that it takes over even the most essential vital control, and insinuates itself to the extent of threatening or unbalancing the 'instinct for self-preservation' inherent in every living being. Now it is evident that such a force can only merge with life itself if it is aroused in a manner immanent to the individual, and itself, as it were, acts as an instinct.[14] In the light of this it becomes easier to understand Mauss's interest in research on aspects of psychological phenomena pertaining to instincts and drives, and more specifically on various kinds of hysteria.[15] Such research reveals the solidarity of the corporeal and the psychic in an original way, and enables us to conceive it otherwise than as a causal relationship which keeps one outside the other. In other words, the sociologist must seek inspiration from psychology when the latter attempts to think out 'the relation there is between things and the body and above all the instinct, the *Trieb* [drive], of the whole being, of its assembled psycho-physiological mechanisms'.[16]

One can see the reason why an enquiry into the principles on which the human being is 'assembled' turned out to be instructive for the sociologist: for basically it means a reorientation of the very conceptualisation of the social. Not merely internalised, but truly internal, natural in the strong sense of the word, the production of the social must henceforward be envisaged within the structure of the individual subject, conceived as a socialised living being. According to Mauss, the forces active in the cases of what is called thanatomania are indeed social forces: but only in the sense that they are in fact released by a *modification of the equilibrium within the individual*, between his or her social, psychological and bodily dimensions. In other words, we need to conceptualise the total human being, that is to say the complex unity of the subject in himself or herself, in whom is constructed the architecture of these three indissolubly linked dimensions. Only in this way can we interpret the surprising phenomena reported by ethnographers.

We must now draw out the profound theoretical consequences of this type of study. Under the proposed scheme, as is clear, the individual and the social are not distributed between two poles whose postulated reality remains unchanged; instead they are embodied as two structuring axes on the level of the subject himself or herself. Thus when Mauss studies the phenomena of suggestion relating to the idea of death, he cannot take the view that the group as such, and the mental unity that it forms, are the primary cause of psycho-physiological changes. For according to his argument, the social and the individual do not confront each other as two separate orders of reality, capable of reacting upon each other by virtue of this original separation. On the contrary, the collectivity is viewed as a power capable of suggestion only from the angle of its material effect within the belief system of an individual, and within the body that is specifically affected. From the effect, Mauss refuses to go back to the cause; he refuses to follow an explanatory procedure which threatens to bring back an ideal and abstract construction. Instead, he confines himself to following the observable data as closely as he can, and limits himself to describing phenomena of 'coincidence'. All that it is possible to observe objectively is, in his precise terms, a 'physical effect on the individual of the idea of death suggested by the collectivity'. That is to say, to an actually experienced collective situation there corresponds an individual belief in the necessity of dying, to which in turn there corresponds a fatal physical event. The result of the description is just this.

But limiting oneself to indicating phenomenal correspondences — is not this a refusal to explain? We must emphasise the aspiration that motivates this apparent refusal. There is no doubt that Mauss shows, here as elsewhere, a deep mistrust, not so much of the process of explaining, but of what it systematically threatens to introduce: the sovereign and disembodied phantom of social laws. Those social laws

which, revealed by the game of comparative statistics, or by use of the
method of 'concomitant variations' recommended by Durkheim in *The
rules of sociological method*, can have no grip on phenomena whose
social meaning is only to be grasped in a lived context.[17] Paying
attention to the concrete is above all paying attention to lived
experience as such. Consequently, Mauss's studies could not fail to
resonate with the ideas of phenomenology, which, when it relates to
the human sciences, seeks to attain, to use Husserl's own terms, the
'living sociality' (*socialité vivante*) whose meaning is immanent in
individual experience.[18] The kinship between the two perspectives is
certain, and many authors have drawn attention to it.[19]

Yet, does this kinship encompass anything more than a common
general attitude? One might well doubt it on reading 'The physical
effect ... of the idea of death'. Indeed, this text inclines one to take up a
prudent position on the point. As may have been noted, the behaviour
in question is not interpreted as a unitary vector, related to the effect
exercised by a meaning still conceived of abstractly; it is envisaged,
rather, as a given state of equilibrium and interaction between three
orders of determination. In these conditions, to describe simply means
to reveal the connections, without going behind the web they weave
and looking for some fundamental basis which would allow one to
render a systematic account of them. Now if this is the way Mauss's
epistemology was really developing, it seems to me that it should be
compared with the thought of Wittgenstein rather than that of
Husserl. It will be remembered that Wittgenstein was writing a critical
commentary on Frazer's *Golden Bough* at more or less the same period,
and presenting the idea of anthropological understanding as resolutely
nonexplanatory and based on 'arranging the factual material so that
we can easily pass from one part to another and have a clear view of it
— showing it in a "*perspicuous*" ["*übersichtlichen*"] way'. Wittgenstein
then says : 'This perspicuous presentation makes possible that
understanding which consists just in the fact that we "see the
connections". Hence the importance of finding *intermediate links*'.[20]

The figure of the total human being, in Mauss's vocabulary,
constitutes exactly the epistemological location for the fulfilment of
this 'perspicuous' or synoptic vision, essentially understood as a vision
of the correlations in the systematic ensemble that they define. In it
the social is theorised, not as some original and substantial foundation
keeping itself in the background in relation to individuals, but simply
as a constellation of events whose regulated connections we must
strive to reveal at the level of what is really given, that is to say, at the
level of the socialised behaviour of the individual. The object of study
neither resides in some transcendental force nor can it be reduced
to an irremediably particularised psychological datum. The true

object here is the whole human being, seen as a complex structure in three dimensions:

> ...these facts are also among the 'total' facts of the type I think should be studied. Not even a consideration of the psychic or rather of the psycho-organic is enough here, even to describe the complex as a whole. The social also has to be considered. Conversely, the study of only that fragment of our life which is our life in society is not enough. Here we see how to place Durkheim's *homo duplex* into a more precise setting, and how its double nature is to be envisaged.[21]

This general remark concludes the concrete study of the physical effects of the idea of death. Let us emphasise the point of these lines, namely that the 'total fact' expressly signifies a human phenomenon: that of the subject carried along in the movement whereby the individual being perfectly expresses the social being, to the extent that the fatal destiny of the latter is entirely assumed by the former. In this case, the concept of the 'complex as a whole' certainly relies on the Durkheimian figure of the *homo duplex*; but it does more than simply specifying its form. Beyond the explicit fidelity of the disciple, we need to recognise here that the change in approach is in fact the sign of a much more radical upheaval. Its results can be seen with regard to two fundamental points.

Whereas Durkheim's human being is double only in relation to what is basically situated externally and only secondarily imposes its imprint on the individual, Mauss's human being, on the other hand, constitutes a fully-fledged object all by itself, one that coheres simply by reference to itself and to the unity it materially embodies. Its social being is not a more or less concealed borrowing: it belongs to the human being himself or herself, and reveals itself in the dynamic form of an immanent process of socialisation. The task of the sociologist now becomes that of describing how this process works, and this will require reference to discoveries developed within the framework of the sciences of the individual. Far from being erroneous explanations, as was perhaps believed when the tendency was to hypostasise social causality as a specific regime, these discoveries provide the necessary insights for an approach which hopes to capture the social in action and hence in relation to behaviour that is always determined on the level of the individual.

If these particular approaches are to be taken, the sociologist will be obliged also to make a better attempt at distinguishing them; they can no longer be merged under the broad heading of sciences dealing with the individual. That is the second point on which the 'total human being' diverges fundamentally from Durkheim's *homo duplex*. Organo-psychic factors are organic *and* psychic. It is not possible to take them together as a block, under the simple category-label of the individual, and conceive them as opposed to factors that are properly social, for they make up together the social being of humankind, a complex totality which merits differential consideration under each of its aspects. Maussian humanity has three dimensions, rather than the two which result from a split between the individual and the social. Totally individual, the human being is also totally social, and this unitary totality is open to readings on three registers as distinct as they are solidary.

In the light of the new object, material and complete, of the total human being, the link between psychology, biology, and sociology has to be completely reformulated. A fundamental change of interdisciplinary relations is involved here whose innovatory impact needs to be assessed. Two lectures Mauss gave to the French Psychological Society have a direct bearing on the matter: that of 1924 on the 'Real and practical relations between psychology and sociology' referred to above and that of 1934 on 'The notion of body techniques'.[22] In common with the lecture we have just discussed, these two texts put forward the idea of the total human being, and sketch the outline of this figure. In so doing they allow us to take the measure of the meltdown and recasting effect that is inherent in the Maussian moment in the history of sociology. Relations are formed, connections established, and passages introduced which lead to a redistribution of knowledge. The latter, insofar as it no longer suffers from a foundational split, can now be seen from a unitary viewpoint and can take back the name of anthropology — although the old term has now acquired a new meaning. To the extent that it has freed itself from the abstractions necessarily engendered by the Durkheimian cleavages and can now construct a total and concrete understanding of human phenomena, sociology has the imperative duty to fulfil itself on this basis and rediscover its place within anthropology.

NOTES

1. J.-C. Passeron, *Le raisonnement sociologique*, Paris, 1991, p. 59. From this, Passeron infers the impossibility of a 'stable paradigm' in the social sciences. This impossibility is connected with the need for an exchange of perspectives between undertakings which share a common, empirical base, referred to as the 'historical course of the world'.

2. Here, Mauss seems to be alluding to the criticisms Henri Berr had directed at Durkheimian sociology, notably in his *La synthèse en histoire*, Paris, 1911.

3. Marcel Mauss, *The gift: the form and reason for exchange in archaic societies* [1925], trans. W.D. Halls, London, 1990, p. 80.

4. For a discussion of the problems involved in translating *l'homme total* into current English, see chapter 1 in this volume, at pp. 15-16.

5. See the conclusion of Michel Foucault, *The order of things* [1966], trans. A. Sheridan, London and New York, 1970.

6. G. Gurvitch, *La vocation actuelle de la sociologie*, vol. II, Paris, 1963, pp. 254-5.

7. F. P. Maine de Biran, *Oeuvres* vol. X-2, Paris, 1989, p. 19.

8. P. Leroux, *Réfutation de l'eclectisme*, Paris, 1979, p. 121.

9. Marcel Mauss, 'The physical effect on the individual of the idea of death suggested by the collectivity' [1926], in *Sociology and psychology: essays by Marcel Mauss*, trans. B. Brewster, London, 1979, pp. 35-56, at p. 38. Mauss's italics.

10. An Australian example: 'A writer who made his observations around 1870 saw a man who stated that he would die at a certain time and who died at that moment "by the power of [his] imagination".' Mauss, 'Physical effect', p. 43-4. In this passage Mauss attaches a good deal of importance to the rite of the 'bone of death' among the Wonkanguru of Australia. For a variant of this rite see the fine descriptions and ethnological interpretations that form part of a police enquiry in the novel by Arthur Upfield *L'os est pointé*, Paris, 1994, p. 213.

11. Polynesian examples: 'Dr (later Sir) Barry Tuke knew an individual in good health and with a Herculean frame. He died in less than three days from this "melancholia". Another man was to all appearances well and ... became chagrined at life; he said he was going to die, and die he did, within ten days. In most of the cases studied by this doctor, the interval was three or four days' (Mauss, 'Physical effect', p. 49).

12. From this point of view, these phenomena do seem to be remarkable when viewed from our perspective as outsiders, but not inexplicable. Mauss wholly admits this by calling for a neuro-pathological and psycho-pathological discussion of the subject. He affirms, however, that the point of view of the sociologist remains pertinent even if a solution were to be found, since the point is to evaluate the mode of determination of a social force in its connection with psycho-physiological structures. See 'Physical effect', p. 53.

13. Mauss, 'Physical effect', p. 46 (translation slightly amended).

14. 'I could go on for ever about the importance of instinct where collective psychology is concerned. In one aspect — and you [psychologists] have always known this — social life is only the gregarious instinct hypertrophied, adulterated, transformed and corrected. Here too my experiences as a normal man in the war made me violently aware of the physical and moral force, simultaneousıy both segregational and aggregational, of instinct, both expressive and inhibitory, which inspires the whole being or discourages the whole being, according to whether our personality is or is not threatened' (Mauss, 'Real and practical relations between psychology and sociology' [1924], in *Sociology and psychology: essays by Marcel Mauss*, trans. B. Brewster, London, 1979, pp. 1-33, at. p. 18). Here, the recourse to instinct does not correspond to an emergence of the social from the individual: it is a question of showing how the instinct in itself already operates as a socialising force. Thus, the case studies of the suggestion of the idea of death show by themselves 'to what degree [the instinct for self-preservation] is dependent on society and can be denied by the individual himself for an extra-individual reason' (Mauss, 'Real and practical relations', p. 24).

15. On this point Mauss mentions Babinksi, Monakow, and especially W.H.R. Rivers, who specifically emphasises, in his last works (*Dream and primitive culture*, 1917; *Instinct and unconscious*, 1920; *Psychology and ethnology*, 1926) the innovative character of Freudian theories (cf. B. Pullman, 'Aux origines du debat ethnologie-psychanalyse: W.H.R. Rivers', *L'Homme* 100, 1986, pp. 119-42). This interest makes him one of the precursors of American cultural anthropology.

16. Mauss, 'Real and practical relations', p. 17.

17. It is from this point of view, I think, that we should interpret the quasi-absence of statistical methods in the studies of Mauss, when these methods were used by a number of Durkheimians — not to mention Durkheim himself, at least in his *Suicide*.

18. Letter from Husserl to Lucien Lévy-Bruhl, 11th March 1935, cited by M. Merleau-Ponty in *Signes*, Paris, 1960, p. 135. The text of this letter was published in French translation in the article by P. Soulez, 'Sur la mythologie primitive', *Gradhiva* 4, 1988, pp. 63-72.

19. Merleau-Ponty was the first to stress the interest of Mauss's work for the phenomenologists; see his *Sens et non-sens*, Paris, 1947, pp. 155-8; and *Signes*, pp. 143-57. On this point, cf. C. Lefort, 'L'echange et la lutte des hommes', in *Les temps modernes*, vol. 6, 1940, pp. 1400-17, reprinted in his *Les formes de l'histoire*, Paris, 1978, pp. 15-29, and in J. P. Lyotard, *La phénoménologie*, Paris, 1986, Part 2.

20. Ludwig Wittgenstein, *Remarks on Frazer's* Golden Bough [1967], trans. A. C. Miles, ed. R. Rhees, Harleston, 1979, pp. 8e-9e. Original italics and quotation marks.

21. Mauss, 'Physical effect', pp. 53-4. Translation slightly amended.

22. Mauss, 'The notion of body techniques' [1934], in *Sociology and psychology: essays by Marcel Mauss*, trans. B. Brewster, London, 1979, pp. 95-123.

Chapter 6

DERRIDA'S READING OF MAUSS

Tim Jenkins

Derrida published a set of lectures in 1991 entitled *Donner le temps*, later translated as *Given time*, and devoted in part to Mauss's essay *The gift*. In the Foreword Derrida states that these lectures take up a seminar he first gave in 1977-8, and that this seminar had a particular significance for his own work, for in it he attempted to give a systematic shape (*une figure plus thématique*) to a series of questions that emerged in his early writings and that shaped his subsequent work.[1] This organising theme, at first implicit, but to which the later works are 'all...devoted (is) the question of the gift'.[2]

Derrida's relation to Mauss is then not straightforward. Not only does Derrida put forward a reading of Mauss's *The gift*, but also his organising theme can be interpreted as a transformation of ideas refined by Mauss, answering questions of the kind posed by the *Année sociologique* school. It is legitimate to ask whether and to what extent Derrida's 'question of the gift' corresponds to Mauss's 'gift' and also, in pursuing these matters, not to confine ourselves solely to the lectures in question, but to invoke as well Derrida's earlier writings, for he himself has drawn these into the reading of Mauss and this question of the gift. There are two essays of particular interest to us among these early writings, which are devoted to the work of Lévi-Strauss, and which draw heavily upon the latter's introduction to the work of Mauss.[3] As shall emerge — although in barest outline and in provisional form — the influence of Durkheimian ideas is more pervasive than any simple filiation would permit.

In order to present the argument, I employ two organising themes: first, Derrida's notion of *an economy*, and second, his *critique of empiricism*, and I seek to show the convergences and divergences of

these themes with, on the one hand, the *Maussian gift* and, on the
other, a set of Durkheimian preoccupations that I shall call the
vocation of sociology.

Derrida's notion of an economy

Derrida begins his critique in *Given time* conventionally enough by
opposing the categories 'economy' and 'gift'. The gift, he suggests,
cannot fit with the regular returns, distributions and orderliness of
economic calculation and, the other way about, in the circle of
economic exchanges, the gift represents the figure of the impossible.[4]
Further, he ties the economic to a certain notion of time: 'wherever
time as a circle...is predominant [he writes], the gift is impossible.'[5]
There could only be a gift, he continues, on condition that circulation
has been interrupted. Moreover, this instant of interruption must not
be part of time, if time is the regular ordering of successive instants; it
has a logical rather than a chronological status, it concerns time but
does not belong to it. A gift, he concludes, is not thinkable as a
temporal present, a moment in time, but only as the paradoxical
instant where time tears apart.[6] The gift is notable for its disruptive
properties,[7] its impossibility, and paradoxical relation to time: it seems
to dissolve certainties of an economic order.

Derrida then proceeds to a phenomenological analysis of the gift,
exploiting this contrast with the economic circle or the notion of
return, to draw out this sense of impossibility. The notion of the gift, he
says, in ordinary language, shows a fourfold incoherence.[8] First, there
can be no reciprocity, for any return whatsoever immediately enters
into an economic circle of calculation, interest, use, measurement,
and so forth (compare the argument of Alain Testart's chapter in this
volume).[9] Second, for similar reasons, there can be no consciousness
of having received on the part of the recipient, for even recognition of
the gift as such is some kind of return.[10] Likewise, the donor should
not recognise the gift as such, for self-gratification in multiple forms is
also a return on the gift.[11] Lastly, not only are reciprocity, the recipient,
and the donor impossibilities, but so is the gift itself:[12] since the gift
cannot appear as a gift, either to donor or recipient, and as soon as it
does appear, it constitutes both as part of an economic cycle,[13] it is
impossible to speak consistently of the gift, for it disappears upon its
appearance. Derrida therefore describes the gift under this aspect as a
'radical forgetting'.[14]

In this analysis, therefore, the gift has two distinct aspects, or works
at two levels,[15] the one negative, the other positive: on the one hand, in
contrast to the phenomena of common sense, or the economic cycle, it

is marked by a certain excess, impossibility, or paradox. On the other hand, the phenomena of common sense are given or permitted by this elusive excess. As Derrida says: 'what is given is time'[16] and, elsewhere, forgetting is 'another name for being'.[17] In short, the structure of the impossible gift is also that of Being and Time.[18]

This analysis in fact precedes the appearance in the text of Mauss's 'monumental book on the Gift',[19] about which Derrida makes two major claims. The first is that it talks about everything except the gift,[20] and the second, that Mauss's essay is concerned less with the phenomenon of the gift and more with the word 'gift', and how it can be used.[21] These two claims structure the approach of this paper: we may come to agree — with reservations — with the first, but — equally with reservations — to distance ourselves from the second. Concerning the first claim, I shall make two remarks.

First, this 'structure of the impossible gift' bears strong similarities to one of Durkheim's central preoccupations. Throughout his work, Durkheim is concerned to define what one might call the 'compulsions that order the social', the forces which precede and are given form in social life, which in his later work he terms 'the sacred'. Through this concept he approaches the givenness or force of a particular world view, the brute fact that certain things are thus and not otherwise. By so doing, he renews what is perhaps the basic question of sociology, which is: since people create things with their hands and construe the world, both natural and social, with their minds, why then do their products, whether they be notions of impurity, commodities, idols, totemic beasts, priests, kings and princes, or gods, compel them, rather than vice versa? By this single move, Durkheim links questions of political and religious authority, showing them to be comparable phenomena, and hints at parallels between economic facts and the orderings of primitive classifications, with their prohibitions and obligations. Mauss and Derrida both take up this hint, in different styles.

Durkheim's broad claim is that the question of force or compulsion unlocks an understanding of human practices; a subsequent claim is that among these practices is philosophy. This latter aspect is crucial, and yet has been underplayed in recent discussions. One of the topics brought into play, corresponding to the order and coherence of the social, is the order and coherence of the forms language takes. Force, in the sense Durkheim gives it, is prior to social forms, such as law and politics; it is also prior to intellectual forms including philosophy and science. It is worth remarking, then, that the distinction between 'sacred' and 'profane' is not so much between empirical facts — the claim that some things are sacred while others are profane — but rather a logical distinction of a different kind, one that is apprehended in the contrast between obscurity and self-evidence: some facts can be

grasped at sight, but others cause you to think, for they order the field
of the everyday; they are the prior obligations that distribute the order
of the probable. Durkheim is therefore concerned, on the one hand, to
question the status of categories and distinctions that we take as
fundamental or given and, on the other hand, to develop some way of
talking about the movement of difference that underlies language and
our possibility of speaking. Both are the work of 'the sacred'.

It is possible to match these concerns with those of Derrida in *Given
time*, for example, with his identification of the 'impossible gift' on the
one hand, and with what he refers to as 'the problem of language
before linguistics'[22] on the other. Equally important — and this is my
second observation — Derrida's early work is devoted to similar
questions, especially in the essays collected in *L'écriture et la différence*.
His principal target there is structuralism, and his main criticism is
that the concern with geometric figures and their recombinations
tends to exclude questions of force and time. The metaphor of
structure can explain neither the compulsions of meaning nor the
scansions of history. Derrida proposes therefore an 'energetics' to add
to or supplement the 'mechanics' or formal working of the structure,[23]
whose object might correspond to 'the sacred' or to the 'impossible
gift'. In these essays, he mobilises two series of terms that correspond
respectively to the categories of 'force' and 'durée', the first including
notions such as excess, hyperbole, beyond measure, noneconomic
expenditure, and violence,[24] the second notions such as delay, deferral,
supplementarity, saving, inscription, and repetition. And he undertakes
to relate the two series in what he calls — confusingly, perhaps — an
economy: a distribution of force and time that underwrites meaning
and history.

Confusingly, because of course this 'economy' is not reducible to
the economy of a cycle of exchanges. We might, following Bataille,
call the one 'general' economy, and the other 'restricted'.[25] The
relation between the two is summed up in the undecidable question of
whether 'the gift' is an economic question; as Derrida writes in his
essay on Foucault: 'uneconomic expenditure is always caught up and
surprised by saving'.[26] Derrida explores this notion of an economy
(that is a 'general' economy) through these two unequal moments of
expenditure and saving, which closely match terms mobilised by
Mauss in his approach to economic questions.

In the broadest terms, Mauss aims to get beyond the commonly told
story of human origins and the connected origin of the division of
labour. In this rejected story, human individuals are united by their
biological needs, initially in natural families. The first anticipations of
the division of labour, and therefore of 'the social', may appear in these
groups, between the sexes and between generations. Society only truly

begins, however, with barter between families, where certain products may upon occasion of need be exchanged against others, the products of hunting (say) against those of simple manufacture. Hence the division of labour is associated with barter and the satisfaction of simple needs, and the basis of social intelligibility is the figure of the individual man, his needs, and scarcity. For the meeting of scarcity drives production and exchange, which in turn accelerates the division of labour and the development of society, the progress of civilisation, which in turn creates new needs to be met. This is a genetic or evolutionary account. As Marx pointed out, questions of the calculation of equivalence become central to understanding this process.

Mauss, however, denies the validity of this account of the intelligibility of the social order. He suggests that it is the speculative and unverifiable projection back of contemporary categories, an unreflective claim as to the universality of our understanding. Instead, in *The gift*, he proposes that we might see as 'basic' excess rather than scarcity, expenditure rather than saving, consumption rather than production, the group rather than the individual, desire for honour rather than biological need, deferred obligation rather than an instant striking of accounts. In short, the generous gift — rather than calculated exchange — provides a better clue to the intelligibility of human societies, and therefore points to different resources available to human beings, to a different ethics and a different politics, and also a different relation between the terms of the two series, less an evolutionary or genetic one, rather a balance or distribution: indeed, what Derrida calls an 'economy'.

In *Given time* Derrida claims — as we have noted — that Mauss talks of everything except the gift. There is rather, he says, a series of displacements: 'potlatch, transgressions and excesses, surplus values, the necessity to give or to give back more, returns with interest — in short, the whole sacrificial bidding war.... All the gift supplements (which) ... are destined to bring about once again the circle in which they are annulled'.[27] He suggests, later in the analysis, that the essay itself shares the structure of the gift, pointing out that Mauss more or less concludes by cancelling out what has gone before, and citing him to this effect:

> However, we can go even farther than we have gone up to now. One can dissolve, jumble up together, colour and define differently the principal notions that we have used. The terms that we have used — present and gift — are not themselves entirely exact. We shall, however, find no others. These concepts of law and economics that it pleases us to contrast: liberty and obligation; liberality, generosity, and luxury, as against savings, interest, and utility — it would be good to put them into the melting pot once more.[28]

It is on these grounds in particular that Derrida makes his second claim, that the *Essay* on the gift looks increasingly like an essay on the word 'gift', to see how it can be used.[29]

Derrida's critique of empiricism

Derrida's employment of the term 'economy' then bears upon much the same set of issues as Mauss's discussion of the gift. That being said, let us pursue no further the delicate analyses Derrida makes in *Given time* of the way the gift disturbs the circle of economic exchange, save to list the topics he selects from Mauss: the circularity of the *kula* ring; the 'madness' of the potlatch; the ambiguities of charity; the apparent equivalence in certain languages of the terms for 'giving' and 'receiving' (which, he points out, provides both Lévi-Strauss and Benveniste[30] with the basis of their analyses of Mauss's text); the nature of money; and the symbolic uses of tobacco. Instead, to question the adequacy of Derrida's second claim (which he makes in tentative terms), I shall raise the matter of the difference in style, or tone of voice, between the two texts. What is at stake is Mauss's recourse to ethnography, or the inertia of the ethnographic text and the demands it imposes, which we will approach through Derrida's criticism of empiricism.

The general economy consists, we have seen, in the relation of two countervailing moments, of expenditure and saving, or excess and inscription, that is experienced in a structure of time as repetition, rather than as the present. The general economy then precedes and conditions any local, actual, or particular distribution of differences, such as an economy in our common language sense, the latter kind however taking itself on its own terms, as self-evident, or given. If a restricted economy seeks to explain its own ground, it does so according to its own categories — of time, space, causality, and so forth — tending to resort to essences rather than relations, and unable to focus upon questions of force and deferral. As Derrida says, there is a formal blindness to conditioning forces.[31]

When he addresses particular authors, it is these formal blindnesses — and their incoherencies — that he seeks. So, in his reading of Lévi-Strauss, published in *L'écriture et la différence*, despite his approval of the project, Derrida identifies three symptomatic points at which closure is effected. Each point concerns the 'Introduction' to Mauss, and each focuses upon the recourse to empiricism. First, and most straightforward, there is Lévi-Strauss's claim that further empirical studies will add to or invalidate his analyses.[32] Derrida suggests that to make such an appeal to the empirical is always to fall back into the categories with which Lévi-Strauss wishes to break, depending upon a notion of an accessible truth 'out there'. In a somewhat similar fashion, he points out, Lévi-Strauss's notion that the inexhaustible empirical wealth of myth is related to the generative power of the underlying structures also implicates a creative source, rather than an endless play of substitutions.[33] He therefore approves, as subverting this empiricist tendency, Lévi-Strauss's appropriation of Mauss's use of terms such as *mana* to the conscious expression of a semantic function, a zero symbolic value that permits signification.[34]

The second criticism concerns the difficulty Lévi-Strauss has in accounting for time, change, and history: he deals on the one hand with transformations of structures, and on the other, with the intrusion of the real in notions of chance and discontinuity. Again, the focus for this criticism is the 'Introduction' to Mauss, in which Lévi-Strauss refers to language being born 'at a stroke', an instantaneous move from a state of there being no signification to one of an excess of it, to be mapped progressively, with the excess to be experienced as such. Derrida repeats this criticism in discussing *Tristes tropiques* in *De la grammatologie*: this pattern of contingent change and the sequential unfolding it provokes at once ignores the realities of the actors (the ethnographic facts) and developments over time. In his discussion of the action or 'gesture' in the 'Introduction', Derrida says of Lévi-Strauss that he has to 'set aside the facts' at the moment he wants to grasp the essential specificity of a structure;[35] historical change is always conceived on the model of a catastrophe, a natural deviation from nature.

The third criticism concerns the place of violence. Lévi-Strauss's suppression of history has implicit in it a distribution of values between 'historical' and 'ethnographic' populations, which permits him, according to Derrida, to display a nostalgia for the original state of man, taken to be natural, innocent, and without violence, a nostalgia that is expressed in the vocation of the ethnographic project.[36] Yet, Derrida points out, violence not only appears in the empirical accounts, at the level of events, but is also there as the violence of excess and the violence of inscription, as the condition of the possibility of difference, permitting classification, prohibitions, and the contravention of rules.[37] Lévi-Strauss, he says, writes only at the level of laws and their transgressions[38] which, symptomatically, he treats as contingent or accidental.

Whatever the force of these reservations with respect to Lévi-Strauss, they do not hold for Mauss. Mauss appreciates the complexities of violence: for example, he points out both that the gift is a form of warfare and a substitute for warfare; he also — in an ambiguous fashion — both underlines the secondary, excessive nature of the potlatch, and begins the essay with it. Further, as Sahlins has pointed out, Mauss is concerned not only with the elementary forms of economic life but also with those of political life too, and sovereignty may be defined as a relation to violence, the right to risk life and to resist death, a strategic deferral of death. In Sahlins's interpretation, Mauss proposes a third form of sovereignty, avoiding both the state of nature and Leviathan, the sovereignty of the individual and that of the State, suggesting that groups may retain their right of recourse to violence, and yet relate through the gift, and so posing another basis for sociality and the progress of civilisation.[39]

On the other hand, Mauss clearly has recourse to the empirical, in the sense Derrida identifies. I wish to elaborate this claim, for Mauss uses several techniques or procedures, three of which in particular are already present in Durkheim's writings. He begins by identifying native terms and categories, and explicating them in the total context of the social institutions of that people. The example is tightly located, in terms of place, date, and the sources of information. On this basis, he builds up comparisons, drawing first upon like phenomena among neighbouring peoples, and then expanding the geographical range further in a similarly controlled fashion, in this case, from the North-west Coast American Indians to other peoples around the Pacific rim. Only then does he bring in possible parallels from other geographical areas, and historical materials, including European examples. At one level, this 'empirical' approach is simply the controlled application of scholarly protocols, but it is extremely difficult to use ethnographic materials so scrupulously. It took Mauss twenty-five years to perfect, and the achievement in *The gift* stands as a counter to critical claims that he lacks clarity or is confused. It is worth remarking, too, that Lévi-Strauss is a master of these protocols, and in this respect at least a true disciple of Mauss.

Instead then of discussing the general, theoretical preconditions for the distribution of difference, Mauss offers us examples to enable us to pursue the matters at issue. Alternative ways of thinking are not imagined, but demonstrated. There is a polemical element in this: in elaborating his object, Mauss rejects, reverses or transforms a number of theories and principles, as well as distinctions, that tend to be taken as self-evident, and even as fundamental, in many arguments in the social sciences. Notably, as we have seen, he rejects the model of a 'primitive economy' based upon barter, and the political opposition between the state of nature and Leviathan. He also transforms some of our basic categories and distinctions, by situating them as local to our time and place, rather than allowing them to be fundamental and universal; in the course of *The gift*, oppositions between persons and things, concrete and abstract, public and private, pragmatic and spiritual, are shown to be secondary and derived. At a deeper level, he refuses the organisation of the world by binary oppositions, for his subject matter is the pre-categorical forces that lie behind and are expressed in the compulsions that order the social, in the enduring cohesion of polities and in the glimpsed excesses that underwrite particular forms, words, and actions.

Mauss makes one further move, also to be found in Durkheim. He not only describes ethnographic examples which enable our thinking to develop along certain lines, but also identifies a number of indigenous concepts that appear to name and discuss aspects of the problem being defined. This is the importance of the introduction of the words *hau, wakan, orenda,* and *mana.* This aspect of the recourse to native thinking is perhaps the most intensely discussed feature of Mauss's work — the whole debate about the 'spirit of the thing'; but I do not think it need carry the weight that is sometimes placed upon it. Its interest lies in the claim that not only do indigenous cultures offer us some kind of laboratory for the development of our ideas, they also offer us collaborators or partners.

In the Maussian project, one cannot completely separate spheres, which is why, in the end, one is concerned with questions having an ethical component. This approach may undermine a positivist account of the possibility of disinterested sociological description, but at the same time, it frees what we may call sociology's vocation, which becomes that of recasting the possibilities of human orderings, through gaining an understanding of the compulsions at work and the resources available.

This vocation, then, is also part of Durkheim's complex bequest to Mauss, and derives from the fact that the task of sociology shares, in certain important respects, in the character of its object. As we have seen, the subject matter of sociology is the forces that appear in values and obligations, and thereby underwrite the specific categories and forms of a given social body. The business of the sociologist therefore both describes and expresses these forces, for it too consists in more or less compelling interpretations. Since it participates in these forces, it may contribute to them: the sociological vocation is inescapably political and ethical, because it is a human practice.

Durkheim pursued the reciprocal relation between the sociological vocation and the sociological object through the concept of 'the sacred', which he investigated using empirical accounts of the inscription of the force of obligation in the mental and institutional categories of the social. Mauss developed this approach through the 'total social fact', a term which marks the same complexity, obscurity, and reflexivity of the object in question. While critics have noted the apparent disorganisation of Mauss's work, and the wide range of his reference, they rarely interrogate these features further.[40] Karsenti is an exception: he connects the apparent disorganisation of the argument both to the central concept and to the method of elaboration adopted;[41] the type of sociological understanding Mauss seeks and the type of phenomenon he wishes to describe both demand a certain kind of practice, one that we have called 'empirical'.

Concluding discussion

In conclusion, both the ambiguity of the status of the gift, and the recourse to the empirical, equally derive from Durkheim. Once 'the sacred' has been identified as a 'pre-category', underwriting the whole social order, there emerges the problem of how to find sure ground from which to speak. Mauss reformulated this insight in terms of the 'total social fact', and claimed to find specific ethnographic instances to assist our thinking, beginning from the North American potlatch. At the same time he developed a method adequate to the task of handling these 'philosophical experiments'.

To revert to Derrida: corresponding to Derrida's notion of 'an economy', the concept of the 'total social fact' (of which the gift is a privileged example) touches upon matters of necessary being, problems of epistemology and language, and ethics. In both Derrida and Mauss, a philosophical handling of the question of compulsion is placed back at the centre of practical concerns of the utmost importance in our own society. It is not clear, however, that in Mauss this move is reducible to a question of words, for it is achieved by an interrogation of philosophy by ethnography, a process whereby the demands of the empirical (= the given) give life to the categories of philosophy. This then may be the sense of the recourse to the empirical: the empiricism or humanism evoked by Lévi-Strauss and criticised by Derrida may be markers of the end to be achieved.

This recourse links a number of well recognised problems. For example, if the subject matter is the particular force in things, one cannot move to a general level of explanation that abandons entirely the actor's sense of meaning. This is a recurrent problem for Durkheim, as well as Derrida: for the informant, categories, orderings, institutions *are* sacred, true, self-evident, and so forth; it is not simply 'as if' that were the case. The resort to 'as if' conjures away the matter at issue. This paradox of explanation, indeed, is one of the forms resistance to reordering takes — and Mauss's appeal to the empirical, and to native categories, marks this distinction. To put it another way, it may be that in discussing the force of the particular, notions such as intention, purpose, personality and so on cannot be bracketed out. We are concerned with human facts, and quasi-biological formalism will endlessly fail in the task it sets itself, to grasp 'life' in a non-reductive way. In short, Mauss's recourse to empiricism marks the irreducibly moral nature of ethnography.

NOTES

1. J. Derrida, *Given time* [1991], Chicago, 1994, p. x.
2. Ibid.
3. J. Derrida, 'La structure, le signe et le jeu dans le discours des sciences humaines', in *L'écriture et la différence*, Paris, 1967. J. Derrida, 'La violence de la lettre: de Lévi-Strauss à Rousseau', in *De la grammatologie*, Paris, 1967. C. Lévi-Strauss, *Introduction to the work of Marcel Mauss* [1950], trans. F. Baker, London, 1987.
4. Derrida, *Given time*, p. 7.
5. Ibid., p. 9.
6. Ibid.
7. Ibid., p. 3.
8. J. L. Marion, 'Esquisse d'un concept phénoménologique du don', *Archivio di filosofia*, 62, p. 76ff.
9. Derrida, *Given time*, p. 12.
10. Ibid., p. 13.
11. Ibid., pp. 14; 23.
12. Ibid., p. 14.
13. Ibid., p. 24.
14. Ibid., p. 18.
15. Marion, 'Esquisse', p. 75.
16. Derrida, *Given time*, p. 3.
17. Ibid., p. 23.
18. Cf. ibid., p. 27.
19. Ibid., p. 24.
20. Ibid.
21. Ibid., p. 55.
22. Ibid., p. 18.
23. Derrida, *L'écriture et la différence*, p. 29.
24. Ibid., pp. 93-6.
25. See the essays on Bataille in Derrida, *L'écriture et la différence*.
26. Ibid., p. 95.
27. Derrida, *Given time*, p. 24.
28. Mauss, *The gift*, cited in Derrida, *Given time*, p. 55. See trans. by W.D. Halls, pp. 72-3.
29. Derrida, *Given time*, p. 24.
30. See Lévi-Strauss, 'Introduction', E. Benveniste, 'Don et échange dans le vocabulaire indo-européen', in *Problèmes de linguistique generale* 1, Paris, 1979.
31. Derrida, *L'écriture et la différence*, p. 44.
32. Ibid., p. 421.
33. Ibid., p. 423.
34. Ibid., p. 425. Derrida distinguishes far more clearly on this matter between the positions of Mauss and Lévi-Strauss in *Given time*, p. 73.
35. Derrida, *L'écriture et la différence*, p. 426.
36. Ibid., p. 427.

37. This passage concerns the argument about proper nouns, invoked by both M. Bazin and M. Colas during the discussions at the conference 'Marcel Mauss Today' in Oxford, September 1996. See the analysis in JDerrida, *De la grammatologie*, p. 159ff.
38. Ibid., pp. 164-5.
39. Marshall Sahlins, 'The spirit of the gift', chap. 4 of *Stone age economics*, Chicago, 1972, p. 142.
40. Ibid.; J. Parry, '*The gift*, the Indian gift and "The Indian gift"', *Man* 21, 1986, p. 455.
41. B. Karsenti, *Marcel Mauss. Le fait social total*, Paris, 1994, pp. 4-5. See also Karsenti's contribution to this volume, chapter 5 above.

Critiques of exchange and power

Chapter 7

UNCERTAINTIES OF THE 'OBLIGATION TO RECIPROCATE':

A CRITIQUE OF MAUSS

Alain Testart

The first paradox of Mauss's well-known essay *The gift*[1] is that, despite its title, the author never tells us what a gift is. He never gives us a definition. Nor does he explain wherein lies the specificity of the gift.

True, everyone is deemed to know. To give, is to hand over something to somebody *free of charge*. To give, is not to seek payment, it is even more or less the opposite. I am only drawing attention to the obvious here, but it is precisely this sort of obviousness that I should like us to reflect on. We find in the dictionary that to give is to hand over something without any return.[2] Once again, it is the opposite of an exchange, in which each party yields some possession *only against a corresponding return*.[3] There is a natural antinomy between the fact of giving and that of exchanging. For if to exchange is always to let someone have something against a corresponding return, to give can never consist in yielding one thing against another: it would no longer be a gift. Here we have some of the factors which enable us to define a gift, that is, to explain what its actual specificity is in relation to the many ways in which we can transfer something in our possession to someone else.[4]

But let us return to Mauss. Not only does he fail to tell us what is specific about a gift, but he gives us to understand that in the archaic forms of social life to which he devotes much of the *Essay*, it is inappropriate to distinguish between a gift and an exchange. Often indeed, he seems to hesitate, employing one or other term to indicate the same reality. Our categories, he says, do not apply. Why do they not apply? Because the primitive world confuses what we try to differentiate. This argument inevitably brings to mind the thesis linked with the name of Lévy-Bruhl. Personally, I believe that when ethnologists invoke confusion of ideas in the heads of primitive people, they are only betraying the confusion to be found in their own. But it would take me too long to justify this point.

Finally Mauss goes further: he tells us that everywhere, in every transfer, in an exchange as with a gift, there is an 'obligation to reciprocate'.

I am astonished by such a statement. It is manifestly false. A short while ago, I gave a franc to somebody who was begging in the street. Obviously, he will never give it back to me since there is very little chance that we shall meet each other again; I even think that if this were to happen, he would not try to give me back my coin but would more probably ask me for another. Besides, there is no obligation of any kind for him to give me back anything at all. Nor is it evident that he feels 'under an obligation' to me, according to a somewhat old-fashioned expression. He did not even say to me: 'The good Lord will repay you.' In short, in this entire affair there is no question either of reciprocation or of obligation. Nor is there any such question in the whole domain of what might be called charitable donation: this is relevant to a whole chapter of our social history, given that it was an important practice for the upper classes and the nobility in particular. It was a practice which in certain periods brought into play an impressive amount of wealth when the donations were destined for the Church, a practice, indeed, which was almost institutionalised. That was the case in the Christian West. The charitable donation is certainly even more important in the lands of Islam and Buddhism. We must also mention ancient philanthropy whereby a powerful man could make a donation to a city or a political entity and, in consequence, be honoured as a public benefactor. Veyne has shown that this practice differed significantly from Christian charity, being a distinct category both in its motivation and in the social forms it assumed.[5] But, no more than with the charitable donation, is there the least obligation to reciprocate, or anything like it.

Therefore we cannot speak, as Mauss does, of a *universal* obligation to reciprocate: we know of gift-giving practices, historically important and ideologically different, from which this obligation is absent. That is my first point. It is straightforward and easy to understand. My second will be less so. It will consist in showing that the term 'obligation' has a multitude of very different meanings covering quite distinct social realities. The simplest thing will be to proceed by giving a series of examples.

Let us imagine that a colleague invited me to dinner several months ago, and I have not yet returned the invitation. In this second example, there is something akin to an obligation to reciprocate, for 'I feel under an obligation' to invite this colleague in return. Let us emphasise that the question is only one of a feeling, a feeling of obligation. In what way does this obligation oblige me? What will happen if I do not return the invitation? Probably not much. Obviously, the colleague is not going to haul me up before the courts to assert his right to be invited; his case would be dismissed, for I have no legal obligation to reciprocate him anything whatever. Equally obviously, I shall not lose my job because I do not invite him; perhaps he is not even expecting such an invitation. I *feel* obliged but I am not really obliged. There is nothing obligatory in all this; *there is no sanction* attached to this 'obligation to reciprocate', which is merely a feeling. Allow me to emphasise the difference between feelings of obligation and what is obligatory: we shall have to return to it later.

Let us now imagine that I am a Kwakiutl chief living in the North-west Coast region of America in the nineteenth century — if you like, this can be our third example — and that I have, as in the previous example, been invited by a colleague, that is to say, in this society, by another Kwakiutl chief. The given facts of the problem are slightly different from those of the preceding case. For in not reciprocating the invitation, I run the real risk of losing my honour, of losing 'face', and at the same time my position as chief. Of course, we must not overestimate the extent to which societies of the North-west Coast could reorganise their hierarchies according to the capacity (or otherwise) of chiefs to match the sumptuousness of the potlatch feasts to which they had been invited. One should not overestimate the agonistic character of the potlatch.[6] Be that as it may: it is indeed the honour and the prestige of the chiefs that is at stake in the obligation to reciprocate. It is not merely a feeling, as it was in the previous case. The difference is that the whole of society has its eyes fixed on the chiefs who, with their people and their followers, spend months preparing the feast which will demonstrate that they are capable of holding their rank. The difference is that the potlatch is a major, even crucial, institution of this type of society — whereas the invitation from one colleague to another, in our society, is not. The difference is that there is now a *social sanction*, a sanction implemented by society and which revolves around these questions of honour, rank, and prestige. A sanction, we need to add, imposed by the whole of society. If the chief is not capable of reciprocating, those who should have been repaid feel contempt, but he also suffers a fall from grace, a loss of prestige in the eyes of his own people. It is a *public sanction*, whilst the feeling we were speaking of earlier remained in the private domain.

The obligation to reciprocate, then, in the case of the potlatch, is stronger and more serious, more pressing than the obligation to reciprocate invitations among colleagues. It is more than a feeling, since it is a matter of the reputation of the person this obligation weighs upon. Does that make it obligatory? Not at all.

In this context I should like to quote extensively from a text by Curtis which is often cited but whose lessons have not yet all been learned: 'A man can never receive through the potlatch as much as he disburses, for the simple reason that many to whom he gives will die before they have a potlatch, and *others are too poor to return what he gives them.*'[7] The poor will reciprocate nothing, let us emphasise that again, *contra* the universality of reciprocation claimed by Mauss. And there are several reasons for that: in the first place, because they are too poor to reciprocate, but also because considerations of prestige only concern chiefs. The sanction whose existence we recognised above is relevant only to people who have honour to lose, a 'face' to save, a rank to maintain. The poor will return nothing: are we even justified in speaking of them in terms of an obligation to reciprocate, even, as in our previous example, of a feeling of obligation? Nothing allows us to think so. Let us now move on to the dead. Our laws have accustomed us to the idea that debts are transmissible, in the same way as assets. This is not exactly true of the Kwakiutl: 'As for those who die, it may be said that *theoretically* a man's heir assumes his obligations, but *he cannot be forced to do so, and if they far exceed the credits he is likely to repudiate them.*'[8] The obligation to reciprocate is 'theoretically' transmissible but one remains free not to honour it. Even more explicitly, Curtis writes: 'Property distributed in a potlatch ... need not be repaid at all if the one who received it does not for any reason wish to requite the gift.'[9] There is an obligation to reciprocate, but it is not obligatory to fulfil it; for all the contrast with regard to the 'obligation' we indicated in the preceding case, this resembles it closely.

What is the sanction for this obligation? For the poor, there does not appear to be one. And it is no doubt only with regard to chiefs that Curtis envisages the case where what is returned is less than what was initially given:

> Not infrequently at a potlatch a guest calls attention to the fact that he is not receiving as much as he in his last potlatch gave the present host; and he refuses to accept anything less than the proper amount. Even this action is likened to 'cutting off one's own head' and results in loss of prestige; for the exhibition of the greed for property is not the part of a chief: on the contrary he must show his utter disregard for it.[10]

All of which signifies that it is not easy to apply the sanction, for by demanding one's due, one loses as much prestige as by failing to pay one's debts.

Let us say at once that, so far as I can see, in the case of the North-west Coast there is no other form of sanction on the obligation to reciprocate. In particular, there is no enslavement for debt, contrary to what Mauss says, in the whole of that part of the coast which practises the potlatch, that is to say the northern part (whereas this type of slavery did exist in the south, in the northern part of the state of California). This point is further developed in the Annex below.

We now see how we can speak of a sanction and how this sanction differs from the kind prevailing in our societies. The obligation to reciprocate on the North-west Coast is rather more than a feeling that one ought to make a return, but it is rather less than a legal obligation. A legal obligation would allow us to use constraint against the person who did not reciprocate, either by seizing his property, or by reducing him to slavery for debt. Nothing like this seems to obtain on the North-west Coast (I am still speaking only of the northern part), and although there is a sort of obligation to reciprocate, the person to whom this obligation is owed cannot oblige the other to fulfil it. Permit me to emphasise this point which is perhaps the most difficult of my argument: *the fact that I recognise myself to be obliged to someone for whom I ought to do something, and the fact that this person might oblige me to do it, constitute two social situations that are quite different.* The difference is that in the second case, but only in that case, this person can *require* me to discharge the obligation. The difference is that in the second case this person, personally or through the intermediary of a public authority, can *compel* me to discharge this obligation. So we can speak of a *legal* obligation, and we can do so to the extent that this person has a right *vis-à-vis* the other, a right which can be put into effect by resorting to constraint.

The *kula* will provide our fourth example. I think we have been over-eager to classify the *kula* with the potlatch and to see in them two classic examples of the 'gift'. I believe, on the contrary, that we have here a question of two quite different institutions.

In the first place, a counterpart is asked for in the *kula*. The person who offers the *vaga* (initial gift) in fact pronounces, according to Malinowski, a few words such as: 'This is a *vaga* (opening gift) — in due time, thou returnest to me a big *soulava* (necklace) for it!'[11] The demand for a counter-gift is explicitly made. This is what Malinowski underlines in saying that the *kula* is 'a gift repaid after an interval of time by a counter-gift'.[12] In any case, even if the person providing the *vaga* did not demand the counter-gift in advance, the whole institution, the whole spirit of the institution one might say, clamours for this return.

Not only is a counterpart asked for in the *kula*, but more than that, it is required. It can be taken by force. Here is what Malinowski says:

> If I have given a *vaga* (opening gift of valuable) to a partner of mine, let us say a year ago, and now, when on a visit, I find that he has an equivalent *vaygu'a* [*kula* object], I shall consider it his duty to give it to me. If he does not do so, I am angry with him, and justified in being so. Not only that, if I can by any chance lay my hand on his *vaygu'a* and carry [it] off by force (*lebu*), I am entitled by custom to do this, although my partner in that case may become very irate. The quarrel over that would again be half histrionic, half real.[13]

This fundamental passage calls for a lot of commentary, but I shall content myself with one: the procedure described is exactly like a seizure of goods, in the sense in which our judicial system proceeds to the seizure of a debtor's goods. There is literally a 'forced discharge' of the debt, with use of force. We are now confronted with what I have called above a legal obligation.

One point, however, needs to be clarified. In our societies, a seizure of goods is carried out on the property of a recalcitrant or insolvent debtor. According to French law, it is the worldly wealth as a whole that guarantees the debt: we seize moveable property or fixed real estate, valuables, or odds and ends. The reason for the debt is of little importance; it does not matter whether the debt was incurred by marrying off a daughter, by living a life of luxury, or by providing for an aged mother. The same is not true of the Trobriand Islanders: *only kula-type goods can be seized for a kula debt.* It is also necessary to point out: not any type of *kula* object may be taken, but the specific type which the one-way direction of the *kula* cycle allows the creditor to take, a necklace for a bracelet or a bracelet for a necklace. But it is totally out of the question to take yams in reimbursement for a necklace. In other words it is not, contrary to the case with us, the whole of a person's wealth which guarantees the debt, it is only *kula* goods. And, as these goods circulate, the person with the claim has to wait until the debtor has acquired the appropriate object. The contrast with our institutions does not lie in the kind of transfer; it is not that there we have a gift and here we have an exchange, for in both cases we have exchange with the obligation to return, in both cases we have debt and credit, debtors and creditors. The difference lies in the *different rules governing the liability for debt*: roughly speaking, in the Trobriands it is a matter of liability limited both by rules relating to the direction of circulation, and by the type of goods in question (*kula* goods are of the two kinds only, necklaces or bracelets). In Melanesia debt is only claimable on specific goods of a well-defined type. Putting this another way, the repayment of a debt can only be demanded if and when the debtor has actually obtained an appropriate object.[14] It is a conditional debt, which represents a significant difference from our institutions.

Our fifth example is that of the debtor in our societies. We have already said everything necessary about this and must pass on to our sixth and final example: the debtor in certain precolonial societies in Africa, as, for example, those of the lower Congo. In these societies, a non-return exposes one to something quite different from what takes place in ours: one may be put in pawn to the creditor and perhaps eventually become his slave. I do not know why this phenomenon is never considered in discussions on the obligation to reciprocate: it is clearly attested in many societies in Africa and Asia. What is the difference from our previous cases? Now the debt is not only claimable on the property but also on the very person of the debtor. If, in the case of Melanesia, we could speak of a limited liability which never involved the general property of the debtor, in the case of Africa we must speak of the unlimited liability of the debtor, extending even beyond a person's property in the ordinary sense.

Let us sum up and conclude. We have put forward six cases. In five of them we have been able to speak of the 'obligation to reciprocate', but the expression covered very different realities. Let us consider only the sanction on the obligation: from one case to the other, it runs the gamut of variations from a purely moral sanction to the most severe kind of constraint on the person. And there is very little in common between, at the one extreme, self-reproach along with the vague feeling of having failed in one's duty and, at the other, the sanction of slavery for debt. It is not, however, a question of an infinite scale of minute gradations, a continuum which cannot be broken up. The six cases we have discussed fall into two groups.

First Group:
1. In the charitable donation, there is no question of an obligation to reciprocate.
2. In invitations among friends, there is only a feeling of obligation but no sanction.
3. In the potlatch, there is a social sanction but not a legal one.

In none of these three cases can a return be demanded; the donor has given and cannot require reciprocation. We are justified in speaking of 'gift': a gift is the act of someone who provides something without demanding a return. That does not mean that the donor might not hope for one; but none is requested and there is no recourse against the ungrateful recipient who returns nothing. *It is a question of rights*: according to what everyone understands by a gift, the donor has no right to claim a return. The donor cannot oblige the recipient to reciprocate.

Second group:

1. In the *kula*, the donor (I am only using this term out of respect for anthropological tradition as I consider that 'creditor' would be a more appropriate term) can seize from the donee (whom I would prefer to call the 'debtor') a *kula* object.
2. In credit as it is practised in our society, the creditor can proceed to a seizure of the debtor's goods.
3. In numerous precolonial African societies, the creditor can seize the person of the insolvent debtor and make that person a slave.

These three cases differ only in the extent of the liability brought into play by the obligation. In all three an individual has provided something which entails the right to claim a return; there is a right, the person can demand it and, to exercise this right, can have recourse to certain forms of constraint. We are no longer in the area of the gift but in that of the exchange, of debt and credit.

If we do not see that, if we do not ask ourselves about the modes of sanction associated with the idea of obligation, we blur all the difference between gift and exchange.[15] This is precisely where Mauss's famous thesis on the obligation to reciprocate leads. If it simply applied uniformly to every kind of transfer, there would no longer be a difference between giving and selling, between parting with something free of charge or explicitly against a significant charge, between giving for a consideration or for nothing. It is not the smallest paradox of the *Essay on the gift* that after reading it, if we embrace the theses of its author, we can no longer see what a gift is.

A final comment. I have put forward these six cases simply to demonstrate the inadequacies of Mauss's reflections on the notion of obligation and correlatively on that of sanction. The range of variations one could construct from ethnographic examples is obviously much wider. And just as obviously, there is much more one could say on the notion of obligation. I would emphasise that the essential distinction proposed in this chapter is a jural distinction, and it is only in this way that we can distinguish gift and exchange: the exchanger (seller, creditor) has a jural right to a return, the donor does not. On this point we need to beware of the current mistaken tendency to assimilate obligation, what is obligatory and the person under an obligation, on the one hand, with necessity, what necessarily ensues, and what a person cannot escape, on the other. Spoken French uses the expression *bien obligé* to signify that one cannot do otherwise. Now a jural obligation does not entail an ineluctable consequence. In our societies, the creditor may well have a claim sanctioned by public authority and the full force of state control, the debtor may well have a legal and absolute obligation to repay, but if the debtor owns nothing the seizure of goods will have no effect: there will have been an obligation to reciprocate and yet nothing will be repaid for the good reason that nothing can be repaid. Cases of failure or bankruptcy are common: the legal obligation to reciprocate does not mean complete regularity in exchanges. Conversely the lack of a legal obligation to repay does not mean irregularity in exchanges. I do not have enough data on the frequency of default regarding return in the potlatch — I do not believe that anyone else has either — but I do not see why obligations to reciprocate should be less honoured by Kwakiutl chiefs than their debts are by capitalist entrepreneurs.

ANNEX: Was the obligation to reciprocate in the potlatch sanctioned by slavery for debt?

This is what Mauss writes on the subject of the potlatch:

> The punishment for failure to reciprocate is slavery for debt. At least, this functions among the Kwakiutl, the Haïda and the Tsimshian. It is an institution really comparable in nature and function to the Roman *nexum*. The individual unable to repay the loan or reciprocate the potlatch loses his rank and even his status as a free man. Among the Kwakiutl, when an individual whose credit is poor borrows, he is said to 'sell a slave'. There is no need to point out the identical nature of this and the Roman expression.[16]

Here is attached a footnote which reads: 'When an individual so lacking in credit in this way [translation slightly amended] borrows something in order "to make a distribution" or "to make an obligatory redistribution", he "pledges his name", and the synonymous expression is "he sells a slave"' ; the reference is directly to Boas.[17]

We will now briefly examine the question of the Roman *nexum*. It was already very controversial at the time of Mauss,[18] and was to become even more so afterwards.[19] We know practically nothing about this ancient institution from the beginnings of the Republic, which was modified by the law of Poetelius in 326 B.C.: Roman specialists continue to dispute the contents of this law and construct in its connection increasingly cautious hypotheses, which nonetheless remain flimsy ones.[20] All we know is that the ancients called a man *nexus* who was bound by the *nexum* (these terms derive from *nectare*, to bind, which can be taken in the legal sense of a bond as well as in the literal sense), that these people were chained before the law of Poetelius and no longer were afterwards. We know of a few formulaic scraps of wording relating to the *nexum*, but modern authors who have had anything to say on the question have not been able to specify exactly what was the legal status of the *nexus*, any more than the Roman authors could (they were all late). This material will certainly not help us to understand what happened on the North-west Coast. More than that, it can only confuse us. And in any case Mauss is wrong in presenting the *nexus* as an enslaved debtor: to our knowledge, no historian of Rome has ever upheld this thesis. It is directly contradicted by the ancients who stated and emphasised that the *nexus* is a man of free status.[21] Slavery for debt in Rome, at least according to the specialists' view of it, resulted from a legal procedure described in the Twelve Tables, and affects a man who is *addictus* (taken away by the creditor following a judgment), not *nexus.* The institution of *nexum* was indeed related to debt, but there is no proof that the creditor could seize the debtor to make a *nexus* of him. One of the rare historical examples we have of this question comes from Livy's *History* (though even this case is far from certain, since Livy was writing three centuries after the event). It concerns a son who proposes himself, that is to say voluntarily offers himself, as a *nexus* to a creditor on account of his father's debts.[22]

Today these questions of Roman law are neglected and largely out of fashion. Nonetheless, I wanted to put them forward for otherwise one might imagine that Mauss had at his disposal some argument, barely comprehensible to the present-day reader, drawn from his knowledge of Roman law. I do not believe that he had, and I do believe that ancient Roman law is no easier to reconstruct than Kwakiutl law. But let us move on to the heart of the subject.

On what sources does Mauss base his statement that the obligation to reciprocate in the potlatch was sanctioned by slavery for debt? Solely on the Kwakiutl expression quoted by Boas in *Secret Societies* and translated as 'selling a slave'.[23] From this expression Mauss draws the conclusion that slavery for debt sanctions the obligation to reciprocate in the potlatch. But he is making several mistakes.

First, there is an error of interpretation regarding the meaning of the expression, which is also a logical error. *To have to 'sell a slave' to settle a debt is not, in fact, the same thing as being reduced to slavery for debt.* If the Kwakiutl say that an individual man (whose 'credit is poor', to use Mauss's term) who borrows is 'selling a slave', they are not saying that he is selling *himself* or ought to sell himself into slavery. The expression implies nothing of the kind, and all this evidence makes the interpretation of the expression in terms of slavery for debt seem improbable. Along the whole of the North-west Coast, chiefs had many slaves at their disposal; copper discs were exchanged for slaves and nothing could be more ordinary than to pledge a slave to guarantee a loan. If the loan cannot be returned, the slave is forfeit, naturally, and it is just as if his owner had sold him.

Second, Mauss makes a mistake in his reading, having failed to put Boas's phrase into context. *Boas, in fact, does not deal with the potlatch,* nor the obligation to reciprocate in the potlatch, on the page quoted nor in the subsequent pages. He refers only to the way in which one acquires potlatch goods outside potlatch ceremonies, and this is through a purchase, a purchase on credit.[24] At this point indeed Boas presents very precise data on the credit and rates of interest operating at the time of his observations: but these data relate only to a way of purchasing potlatch goods in advance of a potlatch ceremony, not to the potlatch itself. Nothing is easier to understand than that two different forms of transfer should exist side by side in these societies:[25] the same is true in our own, for when I buy something on credit from a retailer in order to give a present to my children, the same object is successively involved in a sale and a gift. From all this we must conclude, with complete confidence, that even if the Kwakiutl expression 'selling a slave' indicated the existence of slavery for debt, it would in no sense prove that this form of sanction applied in the potlatch.

Third, and finally, Mauss takes the Kwakiutl expression literally without asking himself if it might not simply be a metaphor. After all, it is perhaps only a manner of speaking: the existence of a verbal expression and the reality of an institution are two separate things. Indeed, doubts may perhaps have already entered our mind when we read in Mauss's note (cited above, at the start of the Annex) that 'selling a slave' is, according to Mauss, synonymous with 'pledging one's name'. How can pledging one's name be the same thing as slavery for debt, that is to say, the same as pledging one's liberty, or one's person? We may well pledge our name, and even our honour, in our own societies (one can be 'on one's honour' to reciprocate a loan), but there is no slavery for debt.

If Mauss had reproduced Boas's text completely, he could have answered the question we have asked. Here is the text:

> When a person has a poor credit, he may pawn his name
> for a year. Then the name must not be used during that
> period, and for 30 blankets which he has borrowed he
> must pay 100 in order to redeem his name. This is called
> q'a'q'oaxo (selling a slave).[26]

This text could not be clearer; it is the name that is pledged, that one pawns. We know how important names are on the North-west Coast, of similar importance to titles, heraldic emblems, etc. A man who borrows pledges his name, which is already a great deal, but he does not pledge his person or his liberty. There is no slavery for debt, nor does the borrower sell one of his slaves to guarantee or to pay back a debt. The expression 'selling a slave' is pure metaphor. This is also the conclusion that one can draw from Curtis's text — a text which Mauss could have known since it was published some years before the *Essay on the gift*. In it Curtis deals with exactly the same phenomenon of borrowing, the same procedure (with an interest rate of 200 percent, analogous to the hundred blankets which in Boas's account had to be repaid for the thirty borrowed), the same expression. But he gives more detail than Boas. The borrower can introduce his daughter into the bargain and express himself in these terms: 'I wish you to take hold of the foot of my daughter' or ' I wish you to buy my daughter's name to be your slave'. It is the daughter's name which is put into slavery, not the daughter. It is a metaphor in the same way as 'taking hold of the foot' of the daughter.[27] Curtis describes the ceremony: a model hand is publicly fashioned from the bark of a cedar tree. Nothing happens to the girl. What consequences follow from this solemn and particularly weighty form of loan? Curtis does not say; and doubtless Codere, commenting on Boas's text, is right to interpret this 'slavery of the name' by saying that a person who has pawned a name in this way cannot take part in the potlatch for the entire duration of the pledge,[28] a year according to Boas. This seems to me the most probable meaning of the Kwakiutl expression.[29]

However, we have not yet quite finished with our critique of the Maussian text we are calling into question. For a text sins by omission as well as commission. And so we need to add what Mauss does not tell us: no ethnologist has ever claimed that the person who did not reciprocate goods received during a potlatch could be reduced to slavery. The silence of sources is certainly a weak argument, but in the end, if other ethnologists have seen and spoken of slavery for debt elsewhere in the world, in Africa, in Asia, and even in northern California, why, if it had existed among the Kwakiutl, Haida, or Tsimshian, did nobody notice it? Indeed the sources are not totally silent. Earlier I quoted Curtis, who explicitly denies any form of constraint in the potlatch: it follows that he would even more strongly have denied debt slavery. In fact he does deal with debt (which arises not from the potlatches, but from loans, phenomena which he never confuses[30]) and he explicitly says that the creditor has little recourse against an insolvent debtor. A creditor's cause will only be considered a just one if he pledges himself to make some public distribution, and the debts are in fact reimbursed on the very same day, so that the creditor immediately loses what he has just regained. Who could believe that a society imposing such an unenviable fate on a creditor would at the same time practise slavery for debt?

NOTES

1. M. Mauss, *The gift: the form and reason for exchange in archaic societies* [1925], trans. W.D. Halls, London, 1990.
2. *Dictionnaire historique de la langue française*, ed. A. Rey, Paris, 1992.

3. This is something which has been emphasised by a multitude of researchers, the latest to my knowledge being Temple and Chabal, the first part of whose recent book bears the heading: 'A gift is the opposite of an exchange' (D. Temple and M. Chabal, *La réciprocité et la naissance des valeurs humaines*, Paris, 1995). These authors, however, do not necessarily draw the same critical conclusions as I do concerning Mauss.

4. A more complete definition appears in a separate work (A. Testart, 'Les trois modes de transfert', *Gradhiva* 21, 1997, pp. 39-58.

5. P. Veyne, *Le pain et le cirque*, Paris, 1976.

6. This point has been sufficiently clarified by the research of Codere and of Mauzé. The agonistic character of the potlatch probably only developed after 1850, because of the influx of quantities of goods of considerable value, and also by reason of the appearance of a class of the newly rich, etc. We should mention, of course, that we do not reproach Mauss for describing the potlatch under the erroneous label of agonistic giftgiving, as the research allowing this to be corrected is quite recent and could not have been known to him. (H. Codere, *Fighting with property: a study of Kwakiutl potlatching and warfare, 1792-1930*, New York, 1950; M. Mauzé, 'Boas, les Kwagul et le potlatch: éléments pour une réévaluation', *L'Homme* 26, 1986, pp. 21-63.)

7. E.S. Curtis, *The Kwakiutl*, vol. 10 of *The North American Indians*, Norwood, 1915, p. 143 (my emphasis).

8. Ibid., my emphasis.

9. Ibid.

10. Ibid.

11. B. Malinowski, *Argonauts of the Western Pacific*, London, 1922, p. 98.

12. Ibid.

13. Ibid., pp. 353-4.

14. In my opinion this remark accounts for what has been called 'the enigma of the third person' in the *hau* of the Maori (D. Casajus, 'L'énigme de la troisième personne', in *Différences, valeurs, hiérarchie: textes offerts à Louis Dumont*, ed. J.-C. Galey, Paris, 1984). The person who has received an object must not and cannot reciprocate until this item has been passed on to a third person, who responds with an appropriate, and different, object, usually as a counter-prestation, which can then be used in making a return to the original donor.

15. This argument has already been capably put forward by D. Vidal, in 'Les trois Grâces ou l'allégorie du don', *Gradhiva* 9, 1991, pp. 30-47, at p. 41.

16. This paragraph appears in Mauss's famous argument on the 'three obligations to reciprocate', more precisely in that part of the argument on the obligation to reciprocate which begins thus: 'The obligation to reciprocate is the essence of the potlatch.' Mauss, *The gift*, p. 42.

17. Ibid., footnote 204, p. 122. This refers to F. Boas, 'Secret societies and social organization of the Kwakiutl Indians', *Rep. Amer. Nat. Mus.*, 1895, p. 341; F. Boas and G. Hunt, 'Ethnology of the Kwakiutl', *35th Annual Report of the Bureau of American Ethnology*, 1921, pp. 1424, 1451, under the heading *kelgelgend*. Cf. p. 1420.

18. Mauss deals with the *nexum* a few pages further on in *The gift*, but only in accordance with his view of the confusion of things and persons in archaic forms of law and from the point of view of 'magic' which prevailed at the time (closely following Huvelin's interpretation, which he quotes; see p. 48ff).

19. The matter has recently been settled by specialists in Roman law. See A. Watson, *Rome of the XII Tables*, Princeton, 1975, pp. 111-23; or R. Villers, *Rome et le droit privé*, Paris, 1977, pp. 69-71. A simple and sensible account of the question is offered in the latter, as well as a reasoned selection of references taken from a particularly abundant bibliography.

20. For example, G. MacCormack, 'The "Lex Poetelia"', *Labeo* 19, 1973, pp. 306-17; or
A. Magdelain, 'La loi *Poetelia Papiria* et la loi *Julia de pecuniis mutuis*', in *Jus imperium
auctoritas, Etudes de droit romain*, 1990, Ecole française de Rome, pp. 707-11. The
latter confines himself to a more critical point of view.

21. According to the often quoted text of Varro, 'Liber qui suas operas pro pecunia
quam debet dat, dum solveret, nexus vocatur' (a free man who gives his labour in
exchange for the money he owes until he has discharged the debt is called a *nexus*).
(*De lingua latina*, 7.105.)

22. See Livy 8.28.

23. The other two references given in his note (see no. 17 above) are to vocabulary lists,
which in themselves could not possibly establish that slavery for debt existed.

24. Codere saw this clearly, when in commenting on this same text of Boas, she speaks
of these loans or sales as being 'preparatory' to the holding of a potlatch (*Fighting
with property*, p. 70ff and figure 5).

25. This is precisely Mauss's problem, in that he does not distinguish, either for the
Kwakiutl or in his own general analysis, between the different forms of transfer.
Thus, when he writes in the paragraph quoted, 'L'individu qui n'a pu rendre *le prêt
ou le potlatch* perd son rang' (my emphasis) he simply puts loan and potlatch into the
same category, and he does not seem to feel the need to ask himself whether they
refer to the same form of transfer, whether the first does not refer to an exchange
and the second to a gift.

   [*Editors' note*: In the translation by W.D. Halls which we have used above, the
very wide sense of the French *rendre* has been separated into two for purposes of
conveying the sense better in English: 'The individual unable to *repay the loan or
reciprocate the potlatch* loses his rank' (our emphasis; see above). This distinction
between *repay* and *reciprocate* matches Testart's point.]

26. Boas, 'Secret societies', p. 341.

27. Curtis, *The Kwakiutl*, p. 144.

28. Codere, *Fighting with property*, p. 70, note 23.

29. I am grateful to my friend Marie Mauzé for drawing my attention to a passage in
Drucker and Heizer's book relative to this same institution, '*q!aqakwa* ("buying a
slave"), in which a chief's son was nominally purchased, to be redeemed by at least
three times the original amount of wealth goods plus various privileges' (P. Drucker
and R. Heizer, *To make my name good: a reexamination of the southern Kwakiutl
potlatch*, Berkeley and Los Angeles, 1967, p. 73). Although the description is short,
it is in agreement with what we already know: it is a *nominal* purchase, more a case
of putting into pawn or a fiduciary loan than a firm sale (given that buying back is
an explicit possibility). The interest of the text lies elsewhere: the informants of
Drucker and Heizer compared this phenomenon to fictive or 'mock' marriages
whereby a girl could marry the arm or the foot of a chief or even one of the piles
supporting the house. The interest of these marriages lay in the distributions and
redistributions for which they, like other marriages, provided the occasion. It really
was a legal fiction, one that entailed the movement of goods, but not of rights over
people, neither over the daughter in the mock marriage, nor over the son of the
chief supposedly 'sold as a slave'.

30. 'The potlatch and the lending of property at interest are two entirely distinct
proceedings' (Curtis, *The Kwakiutl*, p. 144).

Chapter 8

MUTUAL DECEPTION:

TOTALITY, EXCHANGE, AND ISLAM IN THE MIDDLE EAST

Paul Dresch

Mauss seldom focused on the Middle East. Like Durkheim he acknowledged a debt to William Robertson Smith for suggestions in the study of sacrifice and of what Mauss, like Durkheim, identified as generically religion.[1] Other aspects of the region were left aside. In Mauss's work no picture emerges of the region's people, only of their formal religious practice. Even Smith's concerns with what Mauss called morphology were not pursued (the references we have are mainly asides in reviews on Africa; compare Wendy James's discussion in chapter 14). One reason the Middle East is treated marginally may be its lack of 'total' societies. Exploring the implications of totality, albeit in what I take to be negative cases, helps locate some of Mauss's assumptions but also some of our own when, drawing on Mauss, we debate exchange.

These debates, especially for English readers, are coloured by later writing, and Mauss himself drew on literary texts rather than field experience. On the first score, I shall take one of Jonathan Parry's essays, now deservedly a staple of undergraduate teaching, as the main point of reference. On the second, we must look before going further at a Qur'ānic passage which Mauss himself cites and at English versions of his French rendition of the Arabic, for a surprising amount slips otherwise between the lines. The relation between action and totalising models is then examined. Then the rhetoric of close-range marriage so prominent in parts of the Middle East, and so at odds with ideologies of communality through total prestation, is addressed before summarising a more general distrust of face-to-face exchange that occurs quite widely. The ideal in many cases would seem to be of moral autonomy in the face of a practical dependence on others as unavoidable as in the bourgeois societies to which Mauss counterposed his image of totality.

Monotheism, secular traditions, and generosity

Not all the implications of the sources Mauss used in *The gift* were explicitly worked out by him. Attention to such omissions enlivens work on India (that of Parry and Raheja, notably),[2] where the 'poisoned gift' touched on by Mauss in Germanic form as well as from Vedic law displaces assumptions of social harmony. The Middle East is as interesting. But the 'poison', as it were, is all relational rather than substantial, and this distrust of exchange *per se* deserves pursuing. There are cases, famously, where marriage and revenge are closely linked and revenge is the only 'exchange' depicted locally with diagrammatic neatness.[3] In many places traditions of unrestricted giving cross-cut with niggardly calculations of equivalence, apparent in marriage and tort alike, to give a picture of great complexity.[4] And generosity associates with a formal idea of alms. (This is an important part of Parry's exposition, where rhetorical contrasts of freedom against obligation are underlined as typical of societies concerned with commerce and salvation: alms, so to speak, are contract's complement.)[5] Mauss's own reading of '*Déception mutuelle*' (Qur'ān LXIV) is not straightforward, for the sacred text fits neither of his type forms, the (European) modern or the archaic.

Near the end of *The gift* Mauss cites the Qur'ān to draw 'a conclusion both sociological and practical' from all that has come before. 'Mutual Deception':

15. Your possessions and children are only a trial and Allah it is with whom is a great reward.
16. Therefore be careful (of your duty to) Allah as much as you can, and hear and obey and spend (*ṣadaqa*), it is better for your souls; and whoever is saved from the greediness of his soul, these it is that are successful.
17. If you set apart from Allah a goodly portion, He will double it for you and forgive you; and Allah is the multiplier of rewards, forebearing.[6]

Cunnison's version is perhaps drawing here on English translations of the Qur'ān and perhaps on his own Arabic. Halls's translation follows

Mauss more closely and therefore deals with the passage differently. 'Mutual Disappointment':

15. Your wealth and your children are your temptation, whilst God holds in reserve a magnificent reward.
16. Fear God with all your might; listen and obey, give alms (*ṣadaqa*) in your own interest [*dans votre propre intérêt*]. He who is on his guard against his avarice will be happy.
17. If you make a generous loan to God, he will pay you back double.[7]

The French text and Halls's raise their own problems, for Mauss has just said, two pages earlier, that 'only with difficulty and the use of periphrasis' can the phrase 'individual interest' (*intérêt individuel*) be translated into Latin, Greek or Arabic. The difference between *propre intérêt* and *intérêt individuel* is unclear. Actually one doubts whether a construction around the Arabic term *naf'*, for instance, is any more periphrasis than one around the English 'interest';[8] but the terms in the passage cited are even more direct — 'for your own good', *khayran li-anfusikum*. The term *ṣadaqa*, meanwhile, which can indeed mean 'give alms' (in the imperative, *faites l'aumône*), is not in the Arabic. *Ṣadaqa* is not a gloss here but an explanatory interpolation on Mauss's part. The idea of a free yet somehow sacred gift, which Parry teases out as part of the rhetorical difference between mercantile and small-scale societies, seems already to be haunting Mauss.

The very title of the passage, *al-taghābun*, is problematic. *Taghābun*, as Mauss suggests, can mean judgement — 'On the day He gathers you for the day of gathering that is the day of *taghābun*' (verse nine of the same *sūrah*)— though why that should be so is disputed. Perhaps 'mutual defects' are brought to light; perhaps the saved will attribute defects to the damned; perhaps they will 'over-reach' (*taghbun*) the damned.[9] God is the best of knowers. Were it not for sheer lack of context, however, 'mutual deception' would be a fair interpretation. It is true to the world in which the Qur'ān was revealed and to several contexts where since then it has been adored. Let us take the phrase as at least a metaphor.

The Arabic text is immutable and available. A cautious, literal translation, adding one preceding verse, might run like this:

14. O you who believe. Among your wives and children is an enemy for you, so be cautious of them. If you pardon and forbear and forgive, Allah is merciful and forgiving.
15. Your wealth and your children are a temptation [*fitnah*, also 'a source of discord'], and Allah it is with whom is a great reward.
16. So fear Allah as you can [as in 'fear God': pay attention, take note]. Hear and obey and spend [*infaqū*; a common word, noun-form *nafaqah*,

not limited to sacred contexts] for the good of your souls [or your selves, *anfusikum*]. Whoever is saved [passive contruction] from the greed of his soul [or self], they are the successful ones (*al-mufliḥūn*).

17. Make Allah a good loan and he will pay it you again [all the commentaries say 'pay double', suggesting more than just 'paying back'] and forgive you. He is thankful and wise.

18. He knows the hidden and the visible.

Ample passages can be found in the Qur'ān, let alone in works of commentary, that put clearer stress on the family. But verse 16 suggests the difficulties of close interpretation, and verse 14 is worth adding. It affects the tenor of the whole passage. The sociological conclusion drawn by Mauss for modern times is open to question, and several steps, even after the interpolation of *ṣadaqa*, are needed to arrive there. 'Substitute for the name of Allah that of society and the occupational grouping, or put together all three names if you are religious. Replace the concept of alms with that of co-operation.... You will then have a fairly good idea of the kind of economy that is at present laboriously in gestation'.[10] Self-interest and the common interest are indissoluble, runs Mauss's argument. Once this is recognised sociability will triumph. Yet the message of God is in places otherwise. It seems more what Jesus was suggesting in the parable of the rich man and the camel or in asking his followers to throw away their means of livelihood — quite at odds with the vision that many would associate with Mauss.

The Qur'ān, in different terms, presents as radical a possibility as does the Bible: your possessions and children are a trial or temptation (a source of discord indeed), however phrased in a foreign language; release from such connections, perhaps from family connections, is a means to godliness or happiness, to 'success' of some kind (*mufliḥūn* is clear enough), but not reliably to a vision of sociability. Wealth in goods or in children comes vertically, as it were, from God (even wealth in children may be greater than one's agnates'), not from horizontal transactions and interdependence among persons. It is utterly divisive. The circulation anthropologists so often stress, exemplified nicely in South-east Asian 'flows of life', is conspicuously absent. Nothing corresponds to the image of a needle weaving to and fro, knitting things together.[11] Nothing obvious corresponds to 'society'.[12]

Attempts to recuperate monotheistic morals as deferred reciprocity are often weak. To see sacrifice in the Abrahamic religions, for instance, as *dadāmi te dehi me* (I give to you, so you give me) — the *se* in Mauss's text makes no sense to Sanskritist colleagues — would strictly speaking be blasphemy. The circle never closes, although your own generosity may be supplemented by God's and your ability to give thus sustained indefinitely: to give in secret brings recompense seventy-fold, to give in Kufa a thousand-fold (as a Shiʿite tradition has it), in Medina ten-thousand-fold and in Mecca a hundred-thousand-fold.[13] Much of this (in Sunni tradition too) takes part in the aesthetic of excess so common in Semitic piety. Consider the Old Testament: Job did not 'live happily ever after', but rather, by the end, 'had fourteen thousand sheep, and six thousand camels, and a thousand yoke of oxen, and a thousand she asses. He had also seven sons and three daughters; ... and Job saw his sons, and his sons' sons, even four generations'. The flow of life goes on and out and ever downward, always in one direction. God's bounty is then replicated in the world of politics (generosity is of *khayrāt*, good things from the Almighty), so as recipient one praises God for one's fortune; one is not closely bound to the person giving. 'Political' payments seldom add up.[14] The poor and indigent give too, and proportionally often give far more, without clear prospect of reward in this world or the next.

Hospitality is problematic. There are cases where generosity to strangers brings great prestige, but in a world of 'undifferentiated exchange' (Pitt-Rivers' important phrase) this often seems too long a shot for even sophisters and economists to treat as deferred reciprocity. Unlike the models of alliance made popular by kinship studies (restricted exchange, generalised exchange), there is no determinate set in which to calculate loss and profit as participant or analyst. A stranger may come from anywhere. As with alms there is often a certain privacy. These two points, indeed, are complementary. In examining 'the problem of how to deal with strangers', Pitt-Rivers puts his stress far more on the strangeness they share with gods than on the gods who may support them individually or make their hosts recompense.[15] He is right to do so. The patterns occur where no God and no afterlife are recognised.

If there is one pre-Islamic Arab name that remains widely known and quoted (more than that of ʿAntara ibn Shaddād the warrior of slave descent, more than Asʿad al-Kāmil the warrior king) it must surely be Ḥātim Ṭayy, famed for his generosity. Ḥātim gave everything.[16] If a guest came to Ḥātim's tent, every animal in reach was slaughtered for the feast: his relatives, whom he impoverished time and again, were appalled by him, but his name lives for evermore. In the world of Ḥātim's youth there was no One God, thus no means for an anthropologist to depict the straight line of giving as the arc of a moral circle. Nor was there for generous heroes who came before him.

In secular (colloquial) tradition, particularly in certain kinds of Middle Eastern setting, the theme runs on. Here is Thesiger's account from Arabia in the 1940s.

Two days later an old man came into our camp. He was limping, and even by Bedu standards he looked poor. He wore a torn loin-cloth, thin and grey with age, and carried an ancient rifle.... In his belt were two full and six empty cartridge-cases and a dagger in a broken sheath.... I thought 'He looks a proper old beggar. I bet he asks for something.' Later in the evening he did and I gave him five *riyals*, but by then I had changed my opinion. Bin Kabina said to me: 'He is of the Bait Imani and famous.... He hasn't got a single camel. He hasn't even got a wife. His son, a fine boy, was killed two years ago by the Dahm. Once he was one of the richest men in the tribe, now he has nothing except a few goats.' I asked: 'What happened to his camels? Did raiders take them, or did they die of disease?' and bin Kabina answered, 'No. His generosity ruined him. No one ever came to his tents but he killed a camel to feed them. By God, he is generous!' I could hear the envy in his voice.[17]

Unless prestige is everything, which only lunatics believe, the wasted old man and his admirer are mired in paradox. The generous man even takes five *riyals* from the misfit foreigner. And if this is in some way an ideal (bin Kabina envies him), then the exemplar is in an odd position: his son, 'a fine boy', was killed by raiders, which no one would wish on any but a hated enemy. He is free to be generous? If that were all the logic, then even a very young man, as bin Kabina was fifty years ago, would have tempered his admiration.

In formal stories the pressures of circumstance are absent. The same admiration shows up of generosity to the point of political self-immolation. Nor is it 'just the Arabs'. Here is a tale from Baluchistan, *The Lay of Nadhbandagh* : 'I had the wealth of Muhammad! Seven or eight hundred herds of cattle, innumerable herds of grazing camels; nor have I ever gambled, nor is their tale told by the coloured knuckle-bones [i.e. the dice].... I have given it away in God's name to pious men, reciters of the Qur'ān, and to the poor dwelling in the wilderness.' The reasons extend to generations following. The Prophet himself, one remembers, left his kin no material inheritance, and neither does the Baluchi hero: 'I will let nothing be kept back; for then my younger brothers, my nephews and my mourning brethren would quarrel among themselves over the wealth of Nadhbandagh.'[18]

We have moved here from the Qur'ān to the 'age of ignorance', to Arabia a millennium and a half later, and from there to stories of nineteenth-century Baluchistan. There may be a real coherence. That point I shall not argue (not here at least). But such parallels and overlaps within the region are of interest in locating Mauss; for his work, like all these traditions, stands at odds with anthropology's later habit of privileging the explicit and categorical. *The gift* is about compulsion. Compulsion does not reduce to rules or to forms of argument. The complexities of later jurisprudence on gifts and alms, like those of much anthropology, thus obscure the simplicity one sees in giving.

Action and totality

Action is pre-exegetical. Mauss's 'body techniques' (*techniques du corps*) are an obvious case. One can know that a ball is well hit before one sees where it went, and what is said of the action is distinct from the feeling of it being right. More elaborate matters — concluding a marriage, say, over many months — can also 'feel right'. Ṣadaqah (the term usually translated alms) seems often to refer to this. It is 'true', not in the sense of being correct — being judged such by oneself or others — but rather in the sense of being true to itself, not subject to division, perhaps as Arab lexicographers said ṣadq meant a 'true' sword blade. Even in the famous passage 'kind speech and forgiveness is better than ṣadaqah followed by injury' (Qur'ān II, 263, which deals very much with possessions), ṣadaqah reads well as 'a true deed'. Later jurists, one notes, thought ṣadaqah need not be a material object or convertible to cash.[19] 'Things' as such, an important part both of Mauss's work and of many approaches to *The gift* later, are really neither here nor there.

In our own traditions an important objection to self-interest is precisely, not paradoxically, that one is untrue to oneself in acting thus, for awareness of calculation divides the action. (Casuistics in most religions turn on pure intention as though thought were compromise.) Certain deeds are simply right. Mauss caught a truth other than philology — the philology indeed may be too simple — when he sketched a history of *zedaqah* in Hebrew and ṣadaqah in Arabic, saying once they meant 'justice' and only later 'alms'.[20] Generosity is right action. The theory of alms *per se* might be only part of this, for giving as ṣadaqah was known and generosity to the poor a virtue before the revelation (Zaynab bint Khuzaymah, famously, was 'mother of the poor'; her lifetime, like that of Ḥātim, spans the two dispensations), and the extraordinary stress placed by the Qur'ān on the lot of orphans suggests a world that knew the terms but whose practice left something to be desired. Later we get the splitting in ideology that Parry might predict. In jurisprudence the idea of a free gift seems as paradoxical to traditional Muslim scholars as it does to some anthropologists; thus separating even alms and gifts becomes an issue. The idea can occur without the term, of course, and it may be the term itself does not always reduce to the jurists' idea of alms. The passage quoted above which deals explictly with these matters (Qur'ān II, 261-6) can use *nafaqah* — the same term as Mauss explained, but could scarcely translate, as 'alms' — alongside ṣadaqah for what seems nuance. Elsewhere we are told more than once (e.g., Qur'ān CII, CIV) not to hoard but give to avoid hell fire. But ṣaduqāt (later, ṣadāq) meant wealth given a woman at marriage (Qur'ān IV, 4). If early commentators could give *ṣaduqah*, *ṣudqah*, and *ṣuduqah* as dialect variants of *ṣadāq* and imagine *ṣadaqah* itself as another such,[21] then identifying formal 'alms' is work for lexicographers and lawyers.

In Thesiger's story, above, one might call the Imani's generosity to guests *ṣadaqah* (one can argue either way; 'intention' is the issue for theologians), but people in rural Yemen will describe as *ṣadaqah* putting crumbs out for the birds on a grave. This scarcely seems 'alms' except in jurists' theory. As 'sacrifice' (*dadāmi te ...*) it is feeble. Exegesis fails to do it justice. A parallel is more effective: Raymond Chandler's hero, when he hears that a friend is dead, pours two coffees, lights a cigarette for the missing friend and lets the cigarette burn down.[22] Leaving crumbs on a grave is like that. Extravagant giving, the domain of the powerful and the favoured by God, can apparently have the same compulsion, where giving is in some sense piacular, exculpatory, done to avoid entanglement. One remembers Mauss citing van Ossenbruggen to the effect that giving rids one of evil influence even when the evil itself is not 'personalised'.[23] In different places worldliness (entanglement with others; perhaps dependence on them) is coded differently.

The religious 'gift' in Hindu traditions, the *dāna*, must be passed on to those able to neutralise its corrupting essence: 'A Brahmana who neither performs austerities nor studies the Veda, yet delights in accepting gifts, sinks with the (donor into hell)'. Parry spells out how dreadful a necessity that can pose.[24] He also spells out how only in certain kinds of world, whether modern Europe or classical India, are self-interest and generosity opposed in ideology, the necessity of one matching that of the other. The Islamic world fits the argument well. But it makes rather little of objects' spiritual substance (any more than Indian tradition, to take another axis, makes an issue of wealth *per se*), while nonetheless retaining complexity and moral problems. Indeed, reciprocity itself is found problematic, as seems not to be the case in recent reports of India. Across the free gifts of heroes and pious men run the entanglements of others' lives, such as marriage payment (notoriously the site of struggle). Feud is exchange, colloquially. Around commerce of all sorts hovers usury (*ribā*). Muslim theorists have even tangled the gift of alms; for if made to persons, some treat it as Western law treats contract.

Islam itself emerged in a world of trade, and the Qur'ān, in a remarkable passage (II, 282), treats debt in nonarchaic fashion: 'When you contract among yourselves a debt for a named period, then write it down. Have a scribe write it down between you fairly. .. And if you barter among yourselves have witnesses'.[25] There is no sign here of identity of thing and person through spirit or shared substance. It is all relations among persons. Those relations themselves are problematic;

and were they not so, why give unreservedly? Colloquial and learned traditions alike are sparsely phrased and to the point, not displacing the wickedness of persons to the nature of their worldly goods.

Lévi-Strauss objected to a seeming mysticism in Mauss's work. In doing so he dismissed as error the compulsions on which Mauss focused — 'the expression of social sentiments', whether as *hau* or *mana*, the need to act.[26] Mauss's argument is tight, however. His 'theory', as some would have it, therefore splits apart: 'Where we have the "spirit", reciprocity is denied,' says Parry, writing critically of *The gift*; 'where there is reciprocity, there is not much evidence of "spirit".'[27] That division is internal to Indian material in Parry's argument. It might also divide the modern from the archaic, ethnography from ethnography. Middle Eastern cases underline, through their contrast with both, the resemblance between 'primitive' and 'modern' cases which animates *The gift*, while at the same time they pose certain other contrasts without which Mauss seems too easily a muddle, for reciprocity itself is at issue here, not only the means to speak of it. Spirit is merely part of our problem. Apart from the *hau* (the famous Maori spirit), things everywhere have power and value. *Kula* valuables, for instance, have a life of their own, but so do commodities. Marx and Mauss are neighbours:

> A commodity is .. a mysterious thing, simply because in it the social character of men's labour appears to them as an objective character stamped upon the product of that labour; because the relation of the producers to the sum total of their own labour is presented to them as a social relation, existing not between themselves, but between the products of their labour... a definite social relation between men .. assumes, in their eyes, the fantastic form of a relation between things. In order, therefore, to find an analogy, we must have recourse to the mist-enveloped regions of the religious world.[28]

This may be true of any 'thing', hence the difficulty of appealing to objects as the measure of different types of economy. The difference between *kula* and capitalism is not in what each trades but in the relations informing them, neither being free of an 'expression of social sentiments'.

The 'sum total' of labour is a key phrase. As Marx goes on to explain, the anonymity of relations among persons and groups within a systematic division of labour is what produces the mystery of generalised exchange-value. Mauss's 'total relations', by contrast, are not anonymous. The identity of *taonga* (Polynesia) or *res mancipi* (archaic Rome) with groups and families is central to his argument, and he stresses repeatedly the importance of names and heraldry. Such total relations are also standing relations. Counter-prestations are made later without asking. Hence logically the sequence does not run from barter to sale to credit, but rather in barter or sale alike two 'moments in time' (giving and giving back) are brought together,[29] pinching out, as it were, all explicit relations among groups or persons.

Timeless (or in practice delayed) exchange defines relations among known groups. Instantaneous exchange expresses anonymity. (The symbolism of placing goods on the counter from one side, cash from the other, and picking each up together is clear.) Modern credit, with amounts and the dates all specified, is thus the correlate of an atomised society. Where persons and things are radically divorced there is no natural relation among groups or persons and credit must produce one *ad hoc* — hence the documents and formal witness: 'If you contract among yourselves a debt ... write it down'. One alternative in Islamic thought is instantaneous transaction. All else, it appears, becomes entangled with the fear of usury, where the permanence of relations made so much of by Mauss threatens mutual deception of man by man. Early Islam and our later cases are in this respect closer to the modern world than to 'total' societies, yet few ethnographic areas show such stress upon names and prominence.

What Mauss means by total is not transparent. At least two ideas are at issue. First, 'everything intermingles',[30] or perhaps better put, such typologies of social fact as economic, religious, juridical do not apply. That we can agree on. Second, the parties to transactions are not primarily individuals but groups or moral persons, so categories of another sort are dominant — for instance, clans all different from each other but all of the same kind. The argument is evolutionary.[31] Social divisions may once have been elaborate, but the complexity of circumstance stressed in modern discourse would have been less conspicuous; coherence has been lost, replaced by forms of complexity the simplicity of whose terms — 'individual', 'choice' and so forth — is illusory. Some societies are more total, or more totally inclined, than others in Mauss's scheme. Exchanges of everything, clan to clan, are supposedly the most basic, and mutually defined moieties most basic of all. 'Exchange through gift' presumes that base. It lies between totality and contract.[32] The *kula* is somehow further on than *potlatch*, and we in the modern world have moved off the end of the scale and should take a step back to consider implications obscured by modern ideology. To ask how evolution corresponds with chronology may miss the point. But the Middle East, here as elsewhere in Mauss's work, presents a problem. It provides more ancient records than most places, yet Mauss speaks of the Semitic as 'modern' and Babylonian records as at best 'archaic'.[33]

The reasons for discomfort may not be far to seek. 'Morphology' needs to be remembered. Consider Mauss's generalising vision of the past, one of the few points in his work where too clear a distinction is drawn between 'us' and 'them':

> All the societies we have described above, except for our European societies, are segmented. Even Indo-European societies — Roman society before the Twelve tables, Germanic societies even very late on, up to the writing down of the *Edda* saga, and Irish society up to the creation of its main literature — were still based on the clan and, at the very least the large families, which formed internally a more or less undivided block, being more or less externally isolated from one another.[34]

Middle Eastern groups are not so isolated (few perhaps ever were). Nor are many of them now segmented in the sense that Mauss intends: they are not corporate, as the literature on kinship and marriage shows, and at no level is there usually totality of the kind needed. The other meaning of 'total' —not divided among economic, political, religious and the like— acquires heightened significance. In modern cases the same patterns run through what lesser styles of sociology divide among 'institutions'. The wariness of exchange apparent in the Qur'ān's prescriptions on debt (and on usury, correspondingly, were there room to explore this) recurs widely, and there are ample cases where both *commercium* and *connubium* seem, as it were, un-Maussian.

Kinship

By contrast with Central Asia, non-Muslim Africa and India alike, the Middle East lacks an interest in formal exogamy and thus in clear definition of social blocks.[35] Formal restrictions on marriage are usually reduced to the personal degrees forbidden in Islamic Law — siblings, parents, nephews and nieces primarily, plus the range of milk kinship to which Françoise Héritier and Edouard Conte have again drawn attention recently.[36] (On the latter score the complexities of learned tradition are just as difficult as they are with gifts.[37]) There is no formal endogamy, but there is a general unwillingness that women marry down;[38] and localised endogamy, in local terms, thus derives from the presence of people 'without genealogy'. Even then, however, one finds compulsions that anthropologists and locals alike gloss as marriage 'with the closest'. There is equally a tendency to stress agnation. Almost any form of marriage is depicted in these terms as somehow endogamous whether with actual kin or not — and with whatever form of kin as anthropologists count them,[39] so local arguments seem constantly to turn on who is really an agnate, thus really an equal and properly a partner in marriage or dispute.

In a paper of great originality and verve, Lindholm connects kinship regimes with different histories of power.[40] Arabs (his type-case for the Middle East) gave power away, for no brother had the right to rule another; Central Asia, with its ranking by birth order and of collaterals, provided rulers for the Middle East and established its own great empires. Like any sound structural apperception, one can turn this several ways. Lindholm's argument requires turning backwards, for kinship proves to be the dependent variable. Groups who move into the Middle East from the Central Asian world of exogamic rules do not transform the Middle East but themselves come to look 'Arab':[41] the limit of close-range marriage is shrunk to the Islamic minimum, the rhetoric of closeness shifts from 'wife-givers' to fellow agnates. Yet this remains, still, a world of kinship. The starting point of arguments is seldom atomised individuals: 'the Persians in general attach great importance to finding some kinship link (however distant) with anyone they may be brought into contact with',[42] and so do many people of other language groups. The friend, as in the Persian case, is ideally made kin and friends are addressed as sons of brothers. But as Khuri notes for Arabic, affinal terms are not 'extended'. Pakhtu identifies affines with 'friends' as *dostiy*; in practice, however, friends are scarce and affinal kin-terms are avoided in address.[43] Although everyone who might matter is potentially an agnate (we are all Sons of Adam; in Arabic, we might all be *awlād 'amm*), the circle of effective kin is carved out through marriage as encystment.

Structurally different 'types' of marriage are judged to have identical implications. Emrys Peters thus argued for Libya that matrilateral marriage would divide the agnatic group; Jon Anderson for Afghanistan described patriparallel marriage being seen as doing just the same. In Afghanistan what generalists think of as 'Arab marriage' (between the children of two paternal brothers) is the preserve of the destitute and the mighty — either noone will marry with your family, or you will not marry with other people's — and often the same is true in the Arab world (Fuad Khuri, in mischievous mood, takes this as a key to politics). The image is conspicuous, for better or for worse, nearly everywhere. Elisabeth Copet-Rougier points out that, whatever its frequency or local value, this marrying the parallel cousin is an interesting representation: it is not 'global' (in one of Mauss's senses, it is not 'total'),[44] for each alternate generation, formally speaking, requires the introduction of something from outside. The image is not self-sufficient. Nor is identity in these worlds at any level. The interest in a marriage between brothers' children matches that in material autonomy, neither being fully realised any more than one can make a fresh start in life: 'Marrying a stranger would be as impossible as enjoying free and unrestricted access to land.'[45]

Endogamous rhetoric coincides, as Pitt-Rivers argues, with ideals not of alliance but of hospitality and refuge whereby women are *sacra* identified with the household's moral worth.[46] His sketch of 'women and sanctuary' can easily be filled out. The sacred objects of anthropologists' models are mythically the subjects in several story-forms. Here is an Arabian tale:

> O long of life, this man al-Ḥithrubī was away on a journey and was not with his family and a fugitive came and sought refuge at his tent. And another Shammari, Mufawwaz al-Tajghīf, turned him away. .. The mother grasped hold of the tent and ripped the tent cloth apart down the middle seam. And when al-Ḥithrubī arrived, there was his tent ripped apart down the middle seam. He said, 'Why Mother?' She said: 'The tent that cannot harbour a fugitive, let anyone who comes to it sit in the heat of the sun!' She aroused him against Mufawwaz. 'What is the matter?' he said. 'This is the matter!' she said.[47]

Or again from Nadhbandagh's Baluch world,

> The good woman Sammi came with her cows to Doda for protection ..; the Children of Miral raided them and wickedly drove them away. .. Doda was lying on his bed when his wise mother came and roused him, saying ; 'I bore you for nine months in my womb and for three years I suckled you. Now go forth in pursuit of the cattle.' And his wife's mother .. said, 'Men who promise to give protection do not lie asleep in the daytime.'[48]

Al-Ḥithrubī righted the wrong and flourished. Doda galloped off as his mother ordered but was struck down 'and fell from his mare's saddle .. and died there, with red boots on his feet and glittering rings on his hands'. As the tale goes on to say, 'the women go to earn their bread in dreams', the family is destroyed; but so it would have been morally had the senior women let Doda sleep. Identity depends on the ability to protect, primarily against one's fellows. The urge and the need for protection are identified in turn with women.

Although to give wealth can be a splendid thing (even to leave one's kin no material inheritance), women are not 'given'. Nor really are they ever 'swapped'. The Western eye fixes on such things as veiling and seclusion and presumes that women are in men's eyes a kind of chattel, but nothing could be more misleading. To 'sell' a woman would be social death.[49] Rather women are implicated in the fact that, within this scheme of refuge and hospitality, again to use Pitt-Rivers' phrasing, 'reciprocity resides not in identity, but in an alternation of roles'. Women's movement at marriage collapses in identity what usually is finessed as alternation. Always they demand accounting for. An exchange of brides poses radically the question of whether 'kinsmen' are really equal or whether one family encompasses the other as subordinates or dependants — as guests and never hosts, so to speak, within the larger 'house'. Sister-exchange, where the bride-price is small, is an obvious instance.

Marriage by direct exchange is not 'formally condemned by Islam'.[50] Nancy Tapper (now Lindisfarne) has constructed much of a distinguished book around the subject in a Pakhtun case where such exchange describes 20 percent of marriages.[51] There are plentiful examples from the Arab world also where exchange-marriage runs at about this rate, a little above what usually one finds for marriage with the father's brouther's child. In the fullest account we have of Arab marriage, Hilma Granqvist describes a village in the 1920s where 26.5 percent of marriages were by direct exchange, rather more than the percentage of parallel cousin marriages overall and twice that of marriage to the FBC.[52] Exchange, one gathers, is well thought of in Iran and parts of Turkey.[53] Yet direct exchange (in other terms restricted exchange) keeps failing to encompass difference: 'Families sometimes approached symmetrical relationships', says Keyser of a Turkish case, 'but they were not maintained consistently and there was certainly no overall symmetry.... The struggle against diachrony had been abandoned long ago'.[54] In Tapper's northerly Pakhtun example a struggle against diachrony is in part what each exchange comprises.[55] But the struggle is lost before one starts — noone can agree who is equal to whom (is this really symmetrical or is it a form of debt, thus of subordination?) and appeal is made by all to a history of transaction which is indeterminate. Exchange is common. Yet such marriages, people say, result in divided loyalty; they were practicable once, they are not any more because people are self-interested.[56] In Swat, at the south of the Pakhtun area, the very form was abandoned, supposedly for the same reason. Marriage by direct exchange 'implies a continuing and friendly relation between the two families, a relationship that the Pakhtun of Shin Bagh find impossible to maintain in reality'.[57]

Sister-exchange and patriparallel marriage often come together because bride-price in each tends to zero. Both imply equality. Yet equality is something to be sought, not assumed, and marriage by exchange therefore never emerges as ideology while the (seemingly empty) claim to equality through some vague degree of shared descent reemerges constantly. Unwillingness to marry others implies they are somehow not really agnates; marriage often generates an assumption of shared descent. Marriage to the FBC becomes the image of marriage generally, wherein disputes about equivalence are annulled in the nominal identity of a shared ancestor. The meaning of parallel cousin marriage is remarkably close in a range of otherwise very disparate examples. In all of them a rhetoric of endogamy exists that envelops almost any circumstance. Often claims to shared descent cannot be documented, and rhetoric in any case has its own autonomy, as it does in cases that in certain respects define the region's limits: 'However skeptical the ethnographer, my Tuareg friends were quite content that they had indeed married a cross-cousin, and not just any cross-cousin but a mother's brother's daughter of not too remote a degree of kinship... [This] intraverted social system ... speaks in the language of extraversion'.[58] Within the Middle East, by contrast, and, whatever ethnographers may think from their diagrams, many people are content that they have married patri-parallel cousins 'of not too remote a degree'. 'Extraverted systems' speak a language of introversion.

Exchange and independence

Nancy Tapper distinguishes in a Pakhtun case among four domains of exchange, the highest being identified with men (feud and formal alliance), the next with women (marriage contracts), the next with land and animals, and the last with produce, a type of exchange associated with the poor. Finally, off the end of her formal scale in the manner of persons with no *varna*, comes exchange of cash. As in the Baluch *Lay of Nadhbandagh* (above, in the first section 'Monotheism...' of this chapter), so in the Pakhtun world gambling is a despised way of losing money, and exchanges of cash are suspect.[59] Anderson, Lindholm, and many others report this prejudice. To reproduce the argument from elsewhere in the rural Middle East (Berbers, the Arab world, Kurdistan, even Turkey) would not be difficult. But anthropology's image of 'spheres of exchange' is less the issue than the problem of direct equivalence — and thus of mutual deception, if you wish.

Someone, it seems, must always lose. All relations of direct exchange are suspect if conducted with potential equals, for the equality of shared descent is fragile and exchange poses questions of rank divisively; so 'barter' (*adal-badal*) is conducted in Swat exclusively with non-kin, often radio for radio, watch for watch. More than that, 'all barter is strictly dyadic and non-recurrent'. Marriage by exchange was avoided in Swat precisely as *adal-badal*.[60] The general point is made by Anderson in the context of feud and marriage: in 'exchange' (*badal*) one swaps 'things that cannot be equated to anything other than themselves'.[61] In exchanges of humanity, equivalence denotes high seriousness. In lesser cases, as of cash, direct exchange can only mean inequality — either with strangers or to endow one's kin with rank *vis-à-vis* oneself. To cross terms in such a way that a brother or sister appears to have a cash equivalent is to end all pretence of shared sentiment.

There are many things in Pakhtun life that are not in the Qur'ān, goes the saying, and many things in the Qur'ān are not found in Pakhtun life. People elsewhere in the Muslim world might echo that perception for themselves. To a foreigner all we have sketched will anyway seem far removed from Islamic trade, where a system of law derived from the Qur'ān (as most patterns of marriage are plainly not) came to govern an extraordinary range of commerce across the known world. Around that law, however, hovers always a fear of usury and thus a literature of legal 'tricks' (*ḥiyal*). Around it also turns a wish for order. One of the few threads running through different Islamic views of statecraft is the role of the *muḥtasib*, one who guarantees fair trade, for instance by monitoring weights and measures. At the heart of commercial law lies, besides this, an idea of equivalence no anthropologist can ignore. Here is a tradition of the Prophet from which much jurisprudence is derived: 'Gold for gold, silver for silver, wheat for wheat, barley for barley, dates for dates, salt for salt, like for like, the same for the same, hand by hand [measure for measure?]. But if these kinds differ, then sell them, as long as it is hand for hand'.[62] Equivalence of substance requires in later law a balanced and instantaneous exchange, a denial of relationship (compare the section above on 'Action and totality').

A subset of these concerns underpins law on money-changing. But anthropologists will note the concern for pure equivalence and the difference from standard cases usually offered to undergraduates. In the Trobriands half one's yams went to in-laws, and their yams went on again as *urigubu* ; here, if it were yams instead of dates and salt, the exchange would be direct, instantaneous, and problematic. Like the Pakhtun *adal-badal*. Exchanges of strict equivalence (of substance, perhaps) would require one be neither friends nor kin. Otherwise, with unlike things, it is Roman *traditio*, hand it over as you wish for cash. Urban law responds in one way (assuming, even glorifying, the state's presence as the arbiter of equivalence and morality), rural practice on occasion turns in quite another, denying the state a moral purpose and treating sale with deep suspicion.

Wariness of trading produce is found (or was) quite widely. The produce specified can seem arbitrary: parts of Yemen, Afghanistan, and Baluchistan picked out green vegetables as shameful; the Arabs of Karka, on the other hand, who were herders, would not sell butter in the early nineteenth century, and those near Mecca would not sell milk.[63] Typically there was once a wariness of markets. 'Peasants' in Kurdistan went to market, but their feudal lords did not. Throughout the region, in those cases where all men were minor lords ('arms-bearing farmers' as some would say; 'tribesmen' for the more direct) transactions at markets were conducted through middle-men whom no one of worth would either marry or feud with.[64] This heroic disdain for commerce among people with few resources was typical of tribesfolk, the same contingent routinely accused of disinheriting women, abusing the law of dowry and often, at least in Arab cases, enforcing patriparallel marriage within a rhetoric of widely shared descent.

Typical explanations of close-range marriage appeal to 'honour'. So do explanations of disdain for trade. Though such language may be applied to anything and describes with ease either precedence or equality, it is not a mass of only 'floating signifiers'. It refers to an ideal autonomy. Direct exchange of produce, like exchange of brides, is problematic in so far as someone's assessment of worth must prevail over someone else's. Equality is a term to debate this; autonomy is the contested principle. And in systems making much of equality as their ideology (defining themselves in such terms, it seems in fieldwork) one finds exceptions to the rule accorded arbitrary and extreme deference. Persons acquire a magical value, much like that of commodities in Marx's scheme. Relations among men take on the fantastic form of a quality of particular men, not the *hau* but *mana* as 'the expression of social sentiment'. Certain families are large and prosperous. Certain families are hypergamous without exception. Honour then derives for others from inclusion in their realm (as always guests, never hosts, to echo the third section above on 'Kinship') where a little before, or in other contexts, everything appeared to rest on pure equality. Individual people simply *are* superior. Around this, in the same terms of rhetoric, turns the contrary tradition of sheer avoidance.

Social philosophers claim noone ever prospered in isolation. The ambition to do so recurs widely. This is early nineteenth-century Afghanistan: 'Their highest praise of a well-governed country is, that 'every man eats the produce of his own field' and that 'nobody has any concern with his neighbour'.[65] Each household would eat of its own food and provide all the mothers of its next generation or, failing that, absorb them unilaterally from elsewhere. But even hypergamy is not a full solution. The tale is told of a Yemeni tribe, long ago when values were paid more than lip-service, whose pride of lineage was such they married no-one — and died out. Others, faced with economic dependence, so the story runs, sat in a circle and starved to death.

The people famous for extravagant claims to autonomy, for rhetorics of exclusive marriage, for wariness of trade, for unrestricted giving — those in short with an heroic style — are often economic specialists. Arabian bedouin with their camel herds are an obvious case. They could not exist at all without the settled folk who 'lack genealogies' and are thus prevented from marrying 'our' women; their feasts are often of rice (not a desert crop) and their pride was in weapons no society like theirs could manufacture. Ghilzai Pakhtun are as famous, many of them hill-farmers but scarcely subsistence farmers; as Anderson underlines, they are specialist producers of wheat and hay. More generally we are dealing with areas of the world that, for as long as one knows, have been characterised by the presence of states, of coinage, of writing, of religion beyond local domains, and of complexities no bounded cosmology exhausts. With none of the famous cases is *Elementary structures of kinship* of help. With all of them it is hard not to remember chapter 4 of *The savage mind*, where practical dependence and supposed ontology stand at right angles.[66] Claims to autonomy, as Mauss foresaw, are not simply 'economics'. Mutual deception affects everything one might do or say.

Negative cases and Marcel Mauss

Mauss was seldom a structuralist. The consubstantiality of persons and things, not relations among relations, is the theme running through *The gift*. 'What rule of legality and self-interest ... compels the gift that has been received to be ... reciprocated? What power resides in the object ... ?'[67] For Mauss this was one question. A seeming lack of system in his answer makes him hard to read; but the formality of Lévi-Strauss's approach, for instance, (brilliant though it was in its day and remains) is alien to Mauss's project, for the whole of *The gift* is about compulsion and therefore about what precedes systematic forms. Systematicity for Mauss is coldness. Warmth has the colour of heroic life. There is an element of self-delusion in accountancy, he argues, but the illusions that inform modern markets are devoid of magic precisely in so far as consubstantiality of persons and things is lacking — and thus, in *The gift*, are devoid of compulsions linking persons. Nor is Mauss as much the theorist of harmony as some might wish. The potlatch — the agonistic form of total prestation — runs through the work from start to finish. And at the end rank and honour reassert themselves, as if the Parisian bourgeois should appear with a spear-thrower to announce his quality among would-be peers.

Mauss tried throughout to take ethnographies on their own terms. We should pass on the compliment. From our standpoint his world is only one of many, but his method — take the case on its terms, find simpler terms in which to move to the next, show the cases as alternative workings out of principle — remains ours; and we retain an ideal of comparison that might relativise all categorical distinctions whatever, person against thing, substance against relation, reciprocity against free gifts. The evolutionary scheme Mauss himself used need not make a vast difference. At the middle of his project is a 'total' world, with respect to which all distinctions everywhere can be compared but which itself is not addressed and perhaps can never be.[68] Even in *The gift* comparison is free-floating. It is anchored only in awareness of dependence on systems larger than ourselves, on that experience of 'social sentiments' which an intermediate anthropology rejected.

The Middle Eastern topics I have tried to highlight have the attraction of denying totality and not making much of substance — an alternative solution, if you like, to the problem of social beings claiming independence of the worlds that form them. Certain of these traditions stress how in convoluted settings there comes a wish for simplicity. In 'complex' worlds the idolatry of the person can displace that of things on which Mauss focused. And there is more to this than differential treatments of gift and contract in ideology — the compulsions are as real as the categories, the forms of life as distinctive as the local theories, the different forms being linked by the raw fact of people's dependence on one another. None of us is free of 'social sentiment'. Go to a department store and look around. But consider also forms of politics, for increasingly one sees the limited prehistory of contract which Mauss attempted as a path into other matters.

NOTES

1. Some idea (rather modern, one suspects) of transcendence and solidarity colours all their writing. Bichr Farès, writing on pre-Islamic Arabia in *Année sociologique* terms, was forced to conclude that honour for the Arabs 'was' religion. B. Farès, *L'Honneur chez les arabes avant l'islame*, Paris, 1932, p. 165ff. What religion was (the veneration of idols and so forth) he does not say.

2. J. Parry, '*The gift*, the Indian gift and the "Indian gift"', *Man* n.s. 21, 1986, pp. 543-73; G. Raheja, *The poison in the gift: ritual, prestation, and the dominant caste in a North Indian village*, Chicago, 1988. Going back to Mauss's notes, one is surprised by how many of Parry's concerns are marked there.

3. Peters' work on Libya is an obvious case: 'Aspects of the feud', and 'Family and marriage' reprinted in E.L. Peters, *The Bedouin of Cyrenaica*, Cambridge, 1990. Nancy Tapper (*Bartered brides: politics, gender, and marriage in an Afghan tribal society*, Cambridge, 1991) discusses exchange-marriage (*badal*) in great detail, and has much of interest to say on other Pakhtun exchanges (also *badal*), but always gives 'feud' as *badi*. A vowelised or Persianised version of the same term? Other works leave little doubt that feud is *badal* too. On Pakhtun concerns with exchange more generally see the excellent chapter 4 in C. Lindholm, *Generosity and jealousy: the Swat Pakhtun of Northern Pakistan*, New York, 1982.

4. P. Dresch, *Tribes, government, and history in Yemen*, Oxford, 1989, pp. 373-7. Obviously in each local case there are different sorts of exchange. But I cannot think of a fieldwork example where substance is the key, or for that matter religion. Where reciprocity might identify with solidarity, as in gifts at a village wedding, one sees scrupulous accounting stressed as sheer politeness. For a treatment of such issues in a non-tribal setting see A. Meneley, *Tournaments of value: sociability and hierarchy in a Yemeni town*, Toronto, 1996.

5. Parry, '*The gift*', p. 456.
6. M. Mauss, 'Essai sur le don: forme et raison de l'échange dans les sociétés archaïques', *L'Année sociologique* n.s. 1 (1925), p. 178; trans. I. Cunnison, *The gift: forms and functions of exchange in archaic societies*, London, 1970, pp. 75-6. Cunnison's inaccuracies in translating Mauss have often been noted. His thought for the sense of Mauss's argument deserves more consideration. Many a student returned to Mauss directly or through Halls's translation (below) finds themself stuck without as intrusive an explanation as Cunnison imposed. We shall try to suggest why as we go along.
7. W.D. Halls trans., *The gift: the form and reason for exchange in archaic societies*, London, 1990, pp. 77-8.
8. To call a man *naf'ī* in Arabic is to say precisely that he is over-concerned with self-interest, that he is too much out for number one. For a Pakhtu expression of the same idea see Anderson's report of FBC marriage as 'self love' or 'self-centred'. Jon Anderson, 'Cousin marriage in context: constructing social relations in Afghanistan', *Folk* 24, 1982, p. 11.
9. See E.W. Lane, *Arabic-English lexicon* under *ghabana*. Unfortunately one cannot riddle this out by amateur philology, for the term occurs in the Qur'ān just once. The root and the form do suggest 'mutual deception,' however. French *déception* provides two possibilities in English. Cunnison has made the better choice.
10. Halls trans., p. 78.
11. This is one of many points at which Cunnison's notoriously loose translation (Cunnison trans. p. 19) is more accessible than Mauss's image (here of something like a crochet-hook binding straw roofing). Note that Islamic law contrasts 'increase' from transactions among men (*ribā*, which later means clearly usury and may drag one to hell) with increase from God — the key to much anthropology is depicted as a path to damnation. See the entry on *ribā* in *Encyclopaedia of Islam*.
12. Islam set up an *ummah*, which is often translated 'community'. It was not at first the togetherness one associates now with use of the English term, but rather an agreement that bound its signatories to identity of practice: hence 'there is no alliance in Islam and no kinship'. Preexisting relations among the members of the new pact should not produce divisions in dealing with outsiders, or perhaps (though this is less clear) with one another. To interpret this in terms of personal kinship, shared substance and the like may prove misleading.
13. For a discussion of the jurists' idea of *ṣadaqah* see T.H. Weir and A. Zysow, *ṣadaka* in the current *Encyclopaedia of Islam*. Zysow's scholarship is extraordinary and comprehensive. I shall cite the piece several times below. Mauss's own first citation of Islamic alms comes immediately between two references to 'contract sacrifice' (Halls trans. pp. 17-18). Parry's argument follows the same course, aligning alms with deferred reciprocity. Islamic tradition argues quite the opposite.
14. Farès, *L'Honneur*, pp. 119-20, tries to recuperate hospitality in political terms. But see for example Dresch, *Tribes*, pp. 101-2, 207-9.
15. J. Pitt-Rivers, *The fate of Shechem*, Cambridge, 1977, pp. 94, 100, 101, 107.
16. So did Ḥātim's mother before him, and her relatives tried to have her declared *non compos mentis*. This only emphasises the problem. Pre-Islamic Arabia seems from the poetry to have been a chilly world where even the hope of posthumous fame was thought illusory; when you died that was likely the end of it. For a mention of Ḥātim see Farès, *L'Honneur*, p. 94.
17. W. Thesiger, *Arabian sands* [1959], Harmondsworth, 1964, p. 71.
18. M. Longworth Dames, *Popular poetry of the Baloches*, London, 1907, pp. 29-30. Learned Islam elaborates several traditions whereby *ṣadaqah* to kin and neighbours is worth more than *ṣadaqah* at large; but I am not sure any comes close to recuperating this theme of dissolution which Nadhbandagh shares with the Prophet and with many others.

19. Weir and Zysow, *ṣadaka*, p. 708.
20. Halls trans., p. 18.
21. Weir and Zysow, *ṣadaka*, pp. 708-9; Lane, *Lexicon*. People without Arabic should be told that the root *ṣ-d-q* gives such terms as 'honesty', 'truth', and 'friendship'. This is not to say Arabic produces a cloud of unknowing, as Geertz seems to argue elsewhere; it is to say, however, that lawyers in a case like this have ample room in which to work.
22. Marlowe's gesture makes perfect sense (*The long goodbye*, of course). But noone assumes Chandler conceived it as constraining gods by reciprocity or as a mystic communion of substance.
23. Halls trans., p. 17.
24. Parry, '*The gift*', p. 460. Also, in more restricted comparative perspective, Parry, 'On the moral perils of exchange', in J. Parry and M. Bloch, eds, *Money and the morality of exchange*, Cambridge, 1989. As in India, so in the Middle East there are several types of prestation — but none that I can think of offers an easy way out in terms of substance.
25. Dresch, *Tribes*, pp. 374-5, and B. Messick, *The calligraphic state: textual domination and history in a Muslim society*, Berkeley, 1993, p. 203. For the logic see Lindholm, *Generosity*, chap. 4. The world in which Muhammad received his revelation was of course much bound up with commerce. It may be of interest to note how wide is usage of the term *tijārah*, the usual term for commercial trading: 'Shall I lead you to a commerce that delivers you from painful chastisement?' (LXI, 10), or 'Do not consume your wealth among you save as commerce by consent' (IV, 29).
26. The phrase 'expression of social sentiments' is from the essay on magic, cited by C. Lévi-Strauss, *Introduction to the work of Marcel Mauss* [1950], trans. F. Baker, London, 1987, p. 56. To meet Lévi-Strauss head on one might say there is more than 'thought' at issue, which is what makes Mauss's work so interesting.
27. Parry, '*The gift*', p. 463.
28. K. Marx, *Capital* vol. 1, London, 1970, p. 77.
29. Halls trans., p. 36.
30. Halls trans., p. 3.
31. See N.J. Allen, '*Primitive Classification*: the argument and its validity', in W.S.F. Pickering and H. Martins, eds, *Debating Durkheim*, London and New York, 1994. The essay on the person and that on the gift work the same way. But the essay on sacrifice (H. Hubert and M. Mauss, *Sacrifice: its nature and function* [1897], trans. W.D. Halls, London, 1964) — which interestingly gives more space than the others to the Middle East — explicitly does not. It is far more in tune with modern forms of caution over dating evidence.
32. Halls trans., pp. 35, 42, 46, 47, 70.
33. Halls trans., pp. 4, 54, 76.
34. Halls trans., p. 81.
35. Exogamy can mean different things. One can specify groups or sets; one can have terminologies turning kin into affines, affines into kin. By any of these standards the region from Morocco to Afghanistan stands out.
36. F. Héritier-Augé, 'Identité de substance et parenté de lait dans le monde arabe' and E. Conte, 'Choisir ses parents dans la société arabe', in P. Bonte, ed., *Epouser au plus proche*, Paris, 1994. People unfamiliar with Islam and the Middle East should be told that nearly all the Islamic prescriptions are contained in a single *sūrah*, Qur'ān IV. Translations differ, but one can look up the rules easily. Héritier (p. 150) summarises them well.
37. Héritier's analysis ('Identité de substance') thus comes adrift in reading the Qur'ān and *ḥadīth* literature as one. Qur'ān IV, 23 refers to the mothers who suckled you and your milk sisters, which jurists read in a broad sense to implicate ascendants

and descendants. Part of Qur'ān IV, 22 might read, 'And marry not what your fathers married of women'. If one read this as jurists did for milk-kinship it would mean at least African-style exogamy. The rhetoric of substance needs a history. That of relations seems to need far less.

38. P. Bonte, 'Manière de dire ou manière de faire: peut-on parler d'un mariage 'Arabe'?', in Bonte, ed., *Epouser*, p. 378. One might call this a 'rule' — with the proviso that uxorilocal marriages occur everywhere and hypogamy is recuperated by making the affine some sort of agnate, thus nominally an equal. For a tidy example see G. Bédoucha, 'Le cercle des proches: la consanguinité et ses détours', in Bonte, ed., *Epouser*, p. 206.

39. J.M. Keyser, 'The Middle Eastern case: is there a marriage rule?', *Ethnology* 13, 1974, p. 302.

40. C. Lindholm, 'Kinship structure and political authority: the Middle East and Central Asia', *Comparative studies in society and history* 28, 1986. Obviously within the Middle East there are major differences. In the Arab world, for example, brides remain for a long time the responsiblity of their natal male kin, while in Turkey responsibility shifts at once to the marital kin (M. Meeker, 'Meaning and society in the Near East: examples from the Black Sea Turks and the Levantine Arabs', *International journal of Middle East studies* 7, 1976.) This matters greatly in divorce. But for the present purpose one is reminded of the Jinghpaw and Lakher (in E.R. Leach, *Rethinking anthropology*, London, 1961, chap. 5), where one tradition gave away the bride, the other never did so, and the value of affinity was much the same for both.

41. One thinks, for instance, of Turkman cases where the form and content of terminology suggest the steppe world of exogamy and rank, but proverb and practice run the other way. Turkish perhaps is the most intriguing case of all, where even an ideology of matrilateral substance persists (the blood and the bone), yet the rhetoric is not exogamous.

42. B. Spooner, 'Kinship and marriage in Eastern Persia', *Sociologus* 15, 1965, p. 28.

43. Lindholm, *Generosity*, p. 60; F. I. Khuri, *Tents and pyramids: games and ideology in Arab culture*, London, 1990, p. 46.

44. E. Copet-Rougier, 'Le mariage "Arabe": une approche théorique', in Bonte, ed., *Epouser*, p. 453. She points out, most importantly and perceptively, that parallel cousin marriage implies sister-exchange in the next generation but that no-one sees it that way; ibid. p. 458.

45. Keyser, 'Marriage rule', p. 305.

46. Pitt-Rivers, *Shechem*, pp. 102, 120-1, 123. For the local concepts underlying this in an ancient case see Farès, *L'Honneur*, pp. 36-8, 40, 69-70. For a nineteenth-century Arabian case, J. Burckhardt, *Notes on the Bedouins and Wahabys collected during travels in the East*, London, 1830, pp. 100, 166, 191 and *passim*. For Mauretania, Bonte, 'Manière de dire', p. 387. Personal and family identity depend everywhere on an exclusive 'peace', see Dresch, *Tribes*, pp. 62-3 and *passim*. Everywhere the defended centre is identified with women.

47. B. Ingham, *Bedouin of Northern Arabia: traditions of the Āl Dhafīr*, London, New York, and Sidney, 1986, p. 58.

48. Dames, *Baloches*, p. 43.

49. To 'buy' a woman, on the other hand, might seem attractive. The role of concubinage deserves more thought, not least in cases where ruling dynasties avoided the problems of affinity by their men not marrying: from an early date all Ottoman Sultans were sons of concubines, and Ottoman princesses only took husbands who were members of the ruling house or belonged to it by purchase. See L. Peirce, *The imperial harem: women and sovereignty in the Ottoman Empire*, New York and Oxford, 1993.

50. Bonte, 'Manière de dire', p. 377, which I assume is almost a slip of the pen (all Islamic law requires is that women receive their dowry). Colouring this recent French literature as a whole, however, is a distrust of matrilateral links, which does not accord closely with what one hears in fieldwork. The best of such work (see Conte, 'Choisir') now pursues substance, very prominent in the work of jurists but again not conspicuous in fieldwork in the Arab world or the Pakhtu. In (matrilateral) Central Asia, of course, the distinction between blood and bone was a feature of the first ethnographies and required no teasing out at all.

51. Tapper, *Brides*.

52. H. Granqvist, *Marriage conditions in a Palestinian village*, Commentationes Humanarum Litterarum, Helsingfors, 3, no. 8, 1931, pp. 81, 11. 'The figures … can tell us nothing of the political significance of marriages' (Tapper, *Brides*, p. 96). True in that averages tell one nothing of each constituent element; but then neither do individual phenomena explain social facts. For the social facts in a wide range of cases see Bonte, 'Manière de parler'.

53. Spooner, 'Kinship and marriage', p. 27; Keyser, 'Marriage rule', p. 299.

54. Keyser, 'Marriage rule', p. 299.

55. Tapper, *Brides*; Anderson, 'Cousin marriage', pp. 10, 25.

56. The different Pakhtun ethnographies between them cover a useful range. In Swat, tribal families have been there a long time and are anchored in land worked by sharecroppers. In northern Afghanistan, where Tapper worked, they are recent arrivals still carving out space among non-Pakhtun. A full account of the relation of marriage to land would be worth elaborating.

57. Lindholm, *Generosity*, p. 142ff

58. R. Murphy, 'Tuareg kinship', *American Anthropologist* 69, 1967, pp. 167, 170.

59. Tapper, *Brides*, p. 403.

60. Lindholm, *Generosity*, p. 116. Presumably *adal*, like its Arabic cognate, means 'just' or 'fair' and a reasonable translation of the phrase might therefore be 'a straight swap'. Noone with daughters could admit such a possibility. Brides are never 'poisonous' in the Indian sense.

61. Anderson, 'Cousin marriage', p. 8.

62. Muslim, Ṣaḥīḥ, sections 81-3, 85. Also Muslim, *Musāqāt*. I am grateful to Bernie Haykel for the references, which came up in Zaydi arguments about 'analogy'. See Ibn Miftāḥ, *Sharḥ al-azhār*, vol. 3, Cairo, 1938, p. 69ff. The part of the question involving gold and silver (ṣarf for the lawyers) will be dealt with by Aaron Zysow in the *Encyclopaedia of Islam*. Unfortunately at the time of writing that fascicule is still not published.

63. Burckhardt, *Bedouins*, p. 137. For the wider economic context, referred to below, see ibid. pp. 37, 136, 339.

64. Tribal systems in the region have consistently around or within them what Yemeni tradition called 'weak' people, often in tiny numbers. This deserves something more than talk of 'exploitation'. Central Asia and Black Africa alike had blacksmiths to whom were attributed important supernatural value; the Middle East instead had tinkers to whom was attributed at best (and intermittently) a certain skill with love magic.

65. M. Elphinstone, *An account of the Kingdom of Caubul* [1815], Karachi, 1972, vol. 1, p. 327.

66. C. Lévi-Strauss, *The savage mind* [1962], London, 1966.

67. Halls trans., pp. 3, 7, 43.

68. Halls trans., p. 36 — a key passage of which few anthropologists take note.

Chapter 9

MODERN PHILANTHROPY:

REASSESSING THE VIABILITY OF A MAUSSIAN PERSPECTIVE

Ilana Silber

Introduction

Philanthropic giving has recently given rise to a significant surge of research, heavily dominated by studies of philanthropy in North America but now also rapidly extending to other parts of the world. Not accidentally, this rise of interest coincides with the dramatic expansion of the 'nonprofit sector' (financed in part by philanthropic donations and itself including philanthropic organisations) and with a widespread sense of disappointment with the welfare state, whether in its liberal or socialist versions.

On a more conceptual plane, one consequence of the current interest in philanthropy — understood here in the restricted sense of voluntary contribution of private wealth for the public good — is that it calls for renewed attention to the study of gift giving. Long perceived as a privileged subject of anthropological research largely confined to 'primitive', small-scale societies, the study of gift processes has by now generated a rich stream of literature, encompassing the most diverse types of society, from the most ancient to the very contemporary, and yet seldom failing to refer (briefly or extensively, critically or approvingly) to Mauss's pioneering and ever-inspiring contribution, his *Essay on the gift*, (*The gift* for short).[1]

Surprisingly, however, little attempt has been made to assess contemporary philanthropy, specifically, from the point of view of a

Maussian perspective on gift analysis. A number of reasons may help explain this lacuna. First, much of the literature on philanthropy has lain within the purview of philanthropy practitioners or consultants with greater interest in questions of ethics, practical organisation and social policy than in issues of basic empirical or theoretical research in the social sciences. Moreover, to the extent that basic social-scientific research on philanthropy did begin to emerge, it has tended to be conducted by scholars such as economists, rational-choice theorists, or institutional sociologists, with little disciplinary interest in the Maussian legacy of gift analysis. Finally, those scholars who are now most actively involved in working out the implications of Mauss's work for the investigation of gift processes in modern settings, tend to be concentrated in Western Europe, especially France, or in Canada,[2] that is, in countries where philanthropic giving has remained, at least compared to the United States and notwithstanding some recent signs of growth, a phenomenon of relatively minor scope and importance.

More fundamentally, however, Mauss's approach is felt to be much more applicable to gift processes in the primary sphere of family and friends, where face-to-face, direct, and enduring relationships obtain,[3] than to the kind of highly indirect and impersonal forms of gift giving which are believed to be a distinctive feature of modern society, and which modern philanthropy is understood to exemplify. This is, of course, the line of thinking famously inaugurated in Richard Tittmus's 1971 work on blood donations,[4] but also reiterated, more recently, even by studies that have otherwise forcefully argued (as Tittmus himself had done) the lasting relevance of many of Mauss's insights for the analysis of gift processes in modern settings.[5] In this paper, though, and basing my argument solely on the case of North American philanthropy, I shall take the position that the potential contribution of a Maussian perspective to the study of modern philanthropic giving has been only partially tapped. I certainly do not mean to claim, however, that Mauss provides us with all the necessary tools for the understanding of philanthropic giving. In fact, I will also briefly suggest some of the ways in which we need to go beyond Mauss, albeit always with him, to reach for a fuller understanding of modern philanthropy.

The Maussian model: where does it fail?

On the face of it, Mauss seems to have little to teach us concerning modern philanthropy. Following upon a rather extensive discussion of gift processes in the context of archaic societies (of Melanesia, Polynesia, Alaska, and British Columbia), and a somewhat briefer treatment of the gift in the legal systems of ancient (Roman, Hindu,

Germanic, Celtic, and Chinese) civilisations, his observations on the gift in the modern context are confined to his twenty-page conclusion which constitutes a relatively minor part of *The gift*. Moreover, the half-nostalgic, half-utopian tone of these pages may seem to indicate a departure from the more detached, descriptive aim of the previous chapters, rather than their logical, 'scientific' continuation.

Nevertheless, Mauss does pursue in the conclusion the basic argument which he had developed in the previous chapters. Having argued in these chapters that the gift is a fundamental bedrock of human civilisation, displaying impressive continuity throughout very diverse historical periods and cultures, he remains intent on projecting the very same argument onto the gift in modern society. Gift processes, he readily admits, have become marginalised in the modern context as a result of the primacy of utilitarian, market economic behaviour. But they are nevertheless still operative and even regaining strength. Not everything, even in modern societies, is governed by cold, utilitarian calculation of individual profit;[6] and many aspects of our lives, as he sees it, are still steeped in the atmosphere of the gift, mixing interest and disinterest, freedom and constraint, persons and things.

Switching from the descriptive to the prescriptive, Mauss also advocates returning to customs of generosity and mutuality, and to the pleasures and aesthetics of 'noble spending'. Concretely, however, the kind of practices he seems to advocate most clearly, and which he considers to be gaining ground already in his own time, are either various systems of financial sharing within the framework of workers' unions or professional associations, or some form of centralised redistribution of wealth and social insurance through the provision of the state. And although he also commends various kinds of semi-voluntary, semi-obligatory patterns of charity or other modes of contributing to the public good of the kind that operated in many antique civilisations,[7] he does not give any indication as to what their equivalents could be in a modern context . Most significantly for our present purposes, it is only in passing that he has a few words of praise for what he calls (in French) the pattern of the 'Anglo-Saxon countries', with its insistence on the special duties and role of the wealthy as 'treasurers', or stewards of wealth: 'As is happening in English-speaking countries and so many other contemporary societies, whether made up of savages or the highly civilised, the rich must come back to considering themselves — freely and also by obligation — as the financial guardians of their fellow citizens.'[8]

At any rate, these various practices are mentioned by Mauss just as many different expressions of essentially similar gift processes. He draws no distinction between them, nor does he try to distinguish their dynamics from those of the kind of gift exchange he had explored in previous chapters of *The gift* dealing with archaic or ancient civilisations. This is in agreement, again, with the essay's heavy emphasis on the underlying evolutionary continuity of the gift as a 'necessary form of exchange, namely, the division of labour in society itself', as a 'permanent form of contractual morality' and as 'one of the human foundations on which our societies are built'.[9] He thus sees the gift as a universal, generic phenomenon displaying an essentially similar underlying nature across the most diverse social and cultural settings.

True, the conclusion does hint at a possible alternative perception, one that would perhaps emphasise not so much similarities and continuities, but also differences between gift processes in archaic or ancient contexts and modern ones. After all, Mauss is well aware of the much diminished importance of gift giving in the context of modern societies that are characteristically dominated by market exchange. And, as rightly pointed out by Jonathan Parry, there remains a basic (and perhaps a potentially fertile) ambiguity in Mauss's conception of modern gift giving, due to the uneasy coexistence in *The gift* of two very different, and even contradictory arguments: one pleading a basic continuity between the gift in modern and premodern contexts, the other upholding the modern *contract* as the contemporary equivalent of archaic gift exchange. I shall come back later to Parry's own conclusions, implying that gifts have come to represent something entirely different in the modern context where they are defined as distinct from and even *opposed* to exchange (compare Testart's chapter in this volume), and finding much in Mauss's text alluding to such a transformation.[10] Yet even granting the validity of such conclusions,[11] the fact remains that Mauss himself in *The gift* did not explicate the relation between modern forms of giving and the modern contract (nor, for that matter, between the modern contract and market exchange).[12]

While it does have the immense merit of drawing attention to the persistence of gift giving in many, either private, professional, or public, aspects of modern life, Mauss's brief discussion of the gift in modern context thus does not seem to contribute much that is *distinctive* to the understanding of modern giving in general, or modern philanthropic giving in particular. Given the fact that he does argue for an underlying continuity and similarity of gift processes cross-cutting historical periods and cultures, however, we may still want to consider modern philanthropic giving in light of his basic conception of the gift, as it emerges especially from the first chapters of *The gift* that deal with archaic or 'primitive' societies.

I shall not sum up here once again the main lines of Mauss's general conception of the gift in archaic settings, since this has been done so often by others. I will only briefly point out those aspects that are usually singled out as inapplicable to modern giving even by thinkers otherwise most sympathetic to Mauss's work and general intent. I find it useful here to take Tittmus's discussion of blood donations as a sort of springboard, because it constitutes an important landmark in the interpretation of modern gift giving (its many methodological and conceptual weaknesses notwithstanding), and happens to exemplify well that line of thought.[13]

Not unlike Mauss in the conclusion of the *The gift*, Tittmus makes the argument that voluntary giving (of which blood giving is only an example) is not only morally superior, and eventually even practically more efficient than the market in the provision of public goods and services, but is also generally beneficial for the social fabric and constitutive of a higher level of social solidarity. However, he also throws into relief two main features of what he calls modern 'altruistic' giving that he finds hardly compatible with the Maussian approach: one, that it is an anonymous gift typically made to strangers and thus creating no personal bond between donor and recipient (since they do not know each other, or even more precisely, know that they do not know and in all likelihood never will know each other); and second, that such giving entails no expectation of a return gift from the recipient to the donor.

The increasingly anonymous and nonreciprocal character of giving in modern societies, if one accepts Tittmus, would seemingly rule out many of the main features of gift giving identified by Mauss. These would include, for example, the deep intermingling of the donor's identity with the gift that is transferred, what Mauss calls the *mélange* of persons and things in gift exchange; the related capacity of the gift to create, consolidate, or otherwise modulate (including in conflictual or 'nasty' ways) a personal relationship between donor and donee; and, of course, the three-fold sequence of obligations (the obligation to give, accept, and return) which Mauss saw as constitutive of gift exchange. Not only is there no obligation for the gift to be returned to the donor, but there is also obviously no obligation to accept, and at least in what Tittmus categorises as the free, voluntary donation of blood, even the obligation to give becomes radically undermined.

Automatically, other important features of archaic forms of gift exchange dependent upon Mauss's axiom of a highly personalised, particularistic three-fold movement of obligations become then inapplicable as well — such as the effect of incremental return, the tendency to stretch and postpone the return in time, the imposition of unequal prestige and power, and the dramatic effects and self-destructive compulsions of potlatch-like agonistic exchange, display, and competition.

Strangely enough, since it could have been easily harnessed to buttress his argument, Tittmus does not refer at all to the impressive efflorescence of philanthropic giving in the United States, which rather provides him in his comparative scheme with the example of the evils of a highly commercialised system of blood supply. Yet many of his assessments do readily apply to the highly organised and rational world of American philanthropy; a world in which the relationship between donor and recipient has become increasingly indirect and impersonal, because usually mediated by increasingly professional and bureaucratic nonprofit organisations; and where the gift is usually made in the abstract and anonymous form of money, and does not involve, typically, any expectation of a return gift to the donor on the part of the recipient. For better or for worse, such are the patterns of giving that were deemed increasingly necessary and appropriate to modern societies that have typically become, in Tittmus's suggestive phrase, 'communities of strangers'. And such were also the patterns of giving which were enlisted to the systematic and rational advancement of the public good in the heyday of the first great American foundations (such as Carnegie, Rockefeller, Ford) and the emerging so-called 'scientific philanthropy'. They have, indeed, continued to form a dominant feature of the American scene ever since.[14]

Why does a Maussian perspective nevertheless still apply?

The problem with the above presentation is not that it is wrong, but that it is only a very partial rendering both of the actual workings of modern philanthropy and of the applicability of Mauss's conception of the gift process. If this is easier for us to realise now than some thirty years ago, it is perhaps simply because we have since arrived (from the point of view of a late-twentieth-century sociological perspective) at a very different understanding of the nature of so-called 'modern' society itself, and of the workings of bureaucratic organisations in it. I shall briefly refer here to at least two major aspects of Mauss's approach that are still immensely useful and insightful: first, the gift's intrinsic and paradoxical combination of interestedness and disinterestedness; and second, the deep interconnection between the gift and of the donor's personal identity. Significantly, both features continue to obtain even as the three-fold sequence of obligations, and especially the obligation to return, seems to have otherwise largely collapsed.

That philanthropic giving is not a totally disinterested 'pure' gift, has of course been a leading axiom of the many virulent critiques of philanthropy (often in the Marxist mode) that view it as an instrument of big business interests, or even American capitalist imperialism: such critiques argue that it lends legitimacy to huge amounts of wealth accumulated in often illegitimate ways at the expense of the working classes, or that in other ways it contributes to an even better imposition of capitalist power and control over social structures that are increasingly dependent upon philanthropic funding and so-called 'expert' one-sided criteria of performance.[15] Similarly, more moderate attacks have also viewed philanthropy as a convenient, self-serving, and self-righteous way for the social elite to avoid state taxation, display its financial superiority, and last but not least, finance its very own exclusive range of educational, cultural, and leisure institutions in a way that could not be allowed through centralised and standardised state policy and funding. Only a very small part of the financial contributions made by the wealthy, it is argued, has redistributive value extending beyond their own class, or can be channelled to causes and institutions of use to the lower strata — something that in any case wealthy philanthropists often claim should rather be the responsibility of religious charities or the state.[16]

While such criticisms may very well be to the point, they still do not explain why the promotion of class interests should take the form of giving, rather than of simple and blunt purchase and control of whatever goods and institutions are fancied by the wealthy. Underlying the critical assessments is often a strictly narrow approach, refusing to accept as a 'gift' any form of prestation that does not conform to the idea or ideal of the 'pure', totally disinterested, nearly self-sacrificial gift; or on the contrary, the denial of the very existence of such gifts and the reduction of all gifts to some form of interest best understood in terms of some variant of exchange or rational-choice theory.

By contrast, from a Maussian point of view, one may grant that much of philanthropic giving is ultimately self-serving and may even be facilitated by a whole range of internal and external rewards (such as self-esteem or pleasure; social prestige among both peers and inferiors or even upward social mobility; business connections; public relations improvement, etc.); and yet one may still consider it as a gift because it nevertheless also entails, simultaneously, an element of uncertainty and disinterestedness. Not only are such rewards as may occur not an automatic and expected entitlement but, as recognised in what I have called above the Tittmus line of thinking, they do not usually come from the recipient, nor even from a third or *n*th party to whom the recipient passes on a roughly equivalent gift, as happens, for example, in what Lévi-Strauss called processes of generalised exchange. What matters is not whether the philanthropic gift is utterly disinterested or interested (since most often it is unavoidably both); more important is rather from where or whom rewards may be expected to come, if at all, and whether there is or is not any law of rough equivalence between the philanthropic gift and its eventual rewards.

It is significant, in this regard, that American philanthropists themselves do not display any tendency, by and large, to define their giving as disinterested or self-sacrificial, but often prefer to emphasise the rewarding effects of giving, such as the power to shape their environment as they see fit, or a whole set of subjective, psychological 'good feelings', such as pleasure, self-fulfilment, self-esteem, etc.[17] While this is true of individual donors, it is even more explicitly true of corporate donors who have been careful to promote their philanthropic giving not as disinterested 'good citizenship', but rather as 'enlightened self-interest,' or at least as a mix of both.[18]

Thus the point is not to posit a total disinterestedness in a sort of hypothetical social vacuum where one would receive or expect no rewards whatever (internal or external) for one's giving, but that such rewards are not expected from the recipient, are not the main impulse for giving, and are in any case intrinsically underdetermined and incommensurable in kind to the donor's philanthropic contribution. Philanthropic giving, moreover, does not seem to be rooted in the donors' hope or trust that they would be able to rely on the good will of other donors were they themselves ever in need of help — the kind of trust Tittmus thought operated in the modern context, and should be encouraged. Such trust in the existence of some form of a diffuse, generalised store of good will, in any case, cannot be taken to imply that the gift is consciously made in order to obtain such a return, or that the act of donation is motivated by such a hope.

Although hardly utterly 'disinterested', philanthropic giving seems thus hard to account for in terms of extant ideas of either direct or indirect reciprocity and exchange.[19] In other words, notions of reciprocity and exchange are not very useful here in accounting for philanthropic giving's specific blend of interestedness and disinterestedness — a vital and paradoxical feature, in the Maussian conception, of the gift more generally. Much more evident and explicit, in my mind, is the impact of the donor's personal structure of preferences (including a particular conception of the 'good' society) and his or her personal and collective sources of identity — confirming the second major aspect of the Maussian perspective singled out here, namely the insistence on a deep connection between the gift and the donor's identity, and complementing Tittmus's accurate but partial rendering of the gift in highly differentiated and bureaucratised societies.

Beyond and despite the otherwise undeniably and increasingly impersonal, anonymous, and bureaucratised nature of modern giving, philanthrophy actually maintains very significant aspects of personalisation, and even a lasting interpenetration of gifts and personal identities. Some of this is simply due to the realities of fund raising, often operating through informal if very effective networks of personal relationships: one wealthy individual gives in answer to the personal petition of a close professional peer, business partner, or even friend. Providing further evidence against the idea of fully impersonal and anonymous giving, much giving is done within very localised, communal frameworks where donors and recipients know each other quite well, or can easily, if they want to, get to know each other and meet face to face. In fact, trends show a decrease in trans-local giving and increased giving to local, communal goals and institutions, which in turn increases the probability and weight of such informal and personalised networks of interaction.[20]

But perhaps even more important for our purposes, the amount of philanthropic giving and the choice of a recipient are very much matters of personal commitment, taste and identification. This has, of course, far-reaching implications, since between 86 and 90 percent of all giving in the United States is made by individuals, and only around 5 percent each by foundations and corporations. Personal involvement was already a trait of the *mécène*, or patron of the arts, in premodern times.[21] But it was also explicitly recognised and even commended as such by Andrew Carnegie — one of the founding figures of American 'scientific' philanthropy — who after defining in his famous *Gospel of wealth* of 1900 what seemed to him to be the best fields for philanthropy, added: 'It is not expected, neither is it desirable, that there should be general concurrence as to the best possible use of surplus wealth... What commends itself mostly highly to the judgment of the administrator is the best use for him, for his heart should be in the work. It is as important in administering wealth as it is in any other branch of a man's work that he should be enthusiastically devoted to it and feel that in the field selected his work lies.' Although the early great philanthropic founders entrusted their boards with the authority to change the foundation's goals in response to changing conceptions of public needs and priorities, foundations' programmes were and still are often cast in the image of their creators' personal concerns.[22] For instance, basing their choice of cause on personal taste or ideological bent, a younger generation of wealthy Jews are now displaying a greater interest in progressive, environmental, and non-Jewish causes than their parents did.[23]

While modern giving is characterised by a much stronger element of individual choice, and by a much greater range of options as to what to give and to whom, than could possibly be contained by Mauss's law of triple obligations, this also means that a much heightened importance is given to personal taste, commitment, and involvement with the choice and management of one's giving. Far from becoming detached from the gift, the identity of the donor does seem thus to leave its imprint and remain attached to the gift, which in fact often becomes a vehicle for that identity and a mechanism for its self-definition and expression.[24]

Even if the gift is made in the medium of money (as is of course most usually the case in the context of modern philanthropic giving), this does not entail an automatic process of depersonalisation. This is evident when wealthy donors opt to give through setting up their own private foundation, largely out of preference for a vehicle of giving that allows them maximal personal choice of and control of the goals and process of giving.[25] But the lasting tendency to connect between the gift and the donor's person also shows in the refusal, by certain organisations, to accept tainted money from a donor considered ethically dubious or threatening. More subtly and only recently investigated, it also transpires in some donors' tendency to give money a place of personal significance in their own life-stories (relating to its acquisition as well as giving away), and of course, as is much better known, in frequent attempts by donors to specify the use to be made of their money by the recipient in light of their own preferences and intentions.

In fact, a major feature of current philanthropy is precisely the contempt for anonymous, impersonal giving, and the search of many actual or potential philanthropists for enhanced personal involvement or, as it is often called, 'partnership' with the cause and the organisation sponsored. Unlike the previous and accepted tendency to give 'with no strings attached', new formulas are now trying to allow for ongoing communication and greater symmetry between donors and recipients, while also avoiding total donor control over the recipient organisation's goals and activities. As powerfully argued, for example, in Francine Ostrower's study of New York patterns of elite philanthropy, 'elite philanthropy involves far more than monetary contributions' and 'is part of an overall involvement with nonprofit organisations.'[26] The point about modern giving is thus perhaps that we have developed not only the capacity and willingness to give to strangers (as stressed by Tittmus), but also the capacity, no less paradoxically, and *contra* our dominant mythology of modern bureaucracy, to develop a deep and lasting personal involvement with so-called bureaucratised organisations.

True, Mauss mostly dealt with gift exchange between groups, that is, situations where the personal identity of the donor was in fact to a large extent merged with that of the group to which the person belonged and in the name of which he or she gave or received gifts. Such an emphasis on group, collective identity has even been invoked as one more reason making Mauss's approach inapplicable to modern, 'private' individual giving especially in the primary sphere of family and friends.[27] With regard to philanthropic giving, however, there is evidence that individual giving is not only shaped by totally idiosyncratic tastes and preferences, but also by the religious, ethnic, or even economic and professional group to which the individual belongs or (the distinction is important) with which they choose to identify. Moreover, and much less noticed, even the recipient, as a rule, is selected as representative of a certain social group or category, carefully assessed in terms of whatever criteria (socioeconomic, ethnic, intellectual, religious, artistic, and so forth)[28] are deemed important by the donor individual and organisation. Last, but not least, one has to recall that all the early great American foundations were family foundations, bearing the name and otherwise perpetuating a certain family tradition and identity. Far from disappearing, family foundations (of all sizes) have since thrived and multiplied. Even when not through the vehicle of such family foundations, innumerable donations are made 'in memory' of a (usually deceased) close relative, and with the double intent of not only contributing to a specific cause or organisation, but also somehow perpetuating his or her memory. In all such ways, we are very far from the Titmuss-like picture of a wholly impersonal and anonymous modern philanthropic giving. In fact, philanthropic giving may even be one of the most significant vehicles for the expression of both individual and collective 'personal' identity in contemporary American society.

I hope by now to have sufficiently conveyed the lasting relevance of much of Mauss's analysis. I could in fact pursue it much further, and argue, for example, that modern philanthropic giving is no less a total phenomenon than archaic gift exchange, that it has remained a blend of economic, legal, aesthetic, moral, and even religious dimensions, and that it is still often accompanied, as in the archaic settings studied by Mauss, by festive, celebratory, ritual activities, such as dedication ceremonies, dinners, galas, reunions, and concerts, where artists and other celebrities contribute to what Durkheim called an intensified sense of social effervescence;[29] that it is still able, again as in more archaic contexts, to define, confirm, or modify prestige and status distinctions, or to nurture, as it did with Mauss's primitive clans and tribes, some form of relationship between otherwise disconnected social groups (such as, for example, businessmen and artists); that while much attention has been paid to donors, one also needs to explore more fully what it means to be on the receiving or accepting end of philanthropic giving, and so forth.[30] In a sense, research on philanthropy has only started to scratch the surface of what a Maussian perspective could help bring to light and conceptualise. In the little space that remains, however, I shall try to suggest some of the ways in which we may be able to go beyond Mauss, if always with him, to reach for a fuller understanding of modern philanthropy.

Beyond Mauss?

First, and most simply, one would have to add an important step to Mauss's three-fold sequence of obligations, a kind of 'fourth' phase nowadays rather conceived as a 'right', albeit one at times bordering on a 'duty': an important feature of modern philanthropy, beyond the act of giving, receiving, and returning, is the act of asking or soliciting philanthropic giving. This act has now acquired an unprecedented level of legitimacy and explicitness, and in fact possesses its very own structures of organisation and professionalisation — powerful ones. Studying transformations in what counts as legitimate and efficient techniques of fund raising would no doubt help understand much about the nature and place of giving in contemporary settings.

On a more general conceptual level, breaking away both from Mauss and a long tradition of gift analysis, I would suggest trying to bracket out the notions of reciprocity and exchange — conscious or unconscious, restricted, generalised, or even in the latest version, 'serial' (see note 19). These notions cannot fail to evoke the underlying assumptions of economistic thinking and the root metaphor of a constant circulation and redistribution of material and symbolic goods — a strand present indeed in Mauss[31] but perhaps overemphasised as a result of Lévi-Strauss's specific reinterpretation. Converging with the work both of Annette Weiner and Maurice Godelier, and pursuing a line of thinking I have already developed with regard to donations to monasteries in the medieval West, I would rather opt for an analysis of philanthropic giving in terms of *symbolic constitution and communication of personal and collective identities;* and propose to understand this very distinctive symbolic operation of the gift as furthered not only by the flow or circulation of wealth, but also by its partial immobilisation and withdrawal from circulation. In the context of modern philanthropic giving, it is precisely such partial immobilisation of donated wealth (mainly in foundations, universities, and museums,[32] or the accumulated philanthropic endowments of any other institutions) that underpins the capacity of philanthropic giving to serve also, as suggested above, in the perpetuation of the memory of specific individuals or families, in the provision of concrete, visible expression, perhaps even consolidation, for otherwise invisible and volatile identities, and in the ongoing constitution of a highly dispersed and localised sphere of 'public' goods and institutions.

Although Mauss's main emphasis was on the underlying similarity and continuity of the gift phenomenon across periods and civilisations, the thrust of his essay also contributed to the historicisation and contextualisation of the ideas of self-interest and market exchange, and of the related dichotomic distinction between interest and disinterestedness, which both he and a number of more recent scholars (such as Albert Hirschmann, Pierre Bourdieu, Jonathan Parry, Alain Caillé, Jacques Godbout, and James Carrier), each on different grounds, have recognised to be a specific and relatively recent historical development.[33] In the same line, one of the most challenging tasks is to try to understand philanthropy in the context of historical developments and transformations in the cultural construction not only of gift giving, but also of interest and market, and in fact of the relation between them.

In such terms, and confronting an issue that Tittmus had totally overlooked, the fact that philanthropic giving developed the most strongly precisely in the cultural context where market and self-interest have received the greatest valorisation, is not without significance. Far from being mutually undermining, market capitalism and philanthropy in the American context seem to have developed a relation not only of coexistence, but even of mutual, if dialectic, support — further encouraged, it would seem, by the traditional relative weakness of the state in that very same context. In any case the topic merits much more investigation and conceptual elaboration.[34]

On the other hand, such an overall macro-institutional constellation may very well prove to be a rather brittle and temporary one. A most significant development, in this regard, is the increasing interpenetration of the three sectors (market, state, third or nonprofit) through the multiplication of institutions and endeavours sponsored by a mix of these three main sources of funding and of their respective modes of management and criteria of legitimacy and accountability.[35] In the context of such an increasing intermingling of the three sectors, one may wonder what will be the power of resilience, if at all, of the patterns of philanthropic giving that I have just described and that seemed to be an integral part of American culture of capitalism; and what will be the future resilience of dichotomic conceptions of the relation between gift and market, or interest and disinterestedness that, as we saw earlier, had anyway been identified as a historically recent and distinctively 'modern' cultural development.

Such a historicising and contextualising approach, if truly pursued, seems inevitably to lead us away from any possible ontological statements with regard to gift giving. Further undermining the possibility of an 'ontological' stance, moreover, is the astonishing variety and multiplicity of forms and functions of gift giving, often coexisting even within a single society. The dilemma we face now is therefore the following: shall we keep searching, like Mauss, for an essential, ideal-typical kernel of what the gift is about? Or should we perhaps give up the idea of a unified gift theory and start rather 'deconstructing' the very idea of the gift in the same way that many are now engaged in the 'deconstruction' of the idea of the market? The task, to my mind, is to search for the conceptual tools which may help us tackle the problem in a comparative historical way and thus perhaps find a middle way between these two extremes.

NOTES

1. M. Mauss, *The gift: the form and reason for exchange in archaic societies* [1923-4], trans. W.D. Halls, London, 1990.
2. I have in mind above all the group of scholars associated with the *Revue du MAUSS* published in France, although not all scholars of modern giftgiving are necessarily related to, or have published in that journal. See D. Cheal, *The gift economy*, London, 1989; J.T. Godbout with A. Caillé, *L'esprit du don*, Paris, 1992; A.E. Komter, ed., *The gift: an interdisciplinary perspective*, Amsterdam, 1996; A. Petitat, 'Les circuits du don: "kula", charité et assurances,' *Cahiers internationaux de sociologie* 90, 1991, pp. 49-65; G. Schmied, *Schenken: über eine Form sozialen Handelns*, Opladen, 1996. In the United States, see especially T. Caplow, 'Rule enforcement without visible means: Christmas gift-giving in Middletown', *American journal of sociology* 89, 1984, pp. 1306-23; J. Carrier, *Gifts and commodities: exchange and Western capitalism since 1700*, London, 1995.
3. Even in that sphere, though, the applicability of Mauss's approach has not yet been fully and explicitly assessed. For some reservations, focusing on Mauss's emphasis on gift-interaction between groups rather than individualised 'persons' and feelings, for example, see Cheal, *The gift economy*.
4. R. Tittmus, *The gift relationship: from human blood to social policy*, New York, 1971, pp. 71-5.
5. See especially Godbout with Caillé, *L'esprit du don*, p. 29ff.
6. For example, Mauss sees in the modern liberal professions an emphasis on honour, disinterestedness, and corporate solidarity as integral rather than contrary to the necessities of the job. See Mauss, *The gift*, p. 76.
7. Mauss, *The gift*, pp. 75-7. Mauss seems to allude here to the kind of giving that would be later explored by Paul Veyne in his monumental study of Graeco-Roman 'euergetism' (P. Veyne, *Le pain et le cirque:sociologie historique d'un pluralisme politique*, Paris, 1976). Veyne's contribution and precise positioning *vis-à-vis* Mauss's work would deserve fuller attention. See I.F. Silber, 'Le champ du don: pour une perspective historique comparée', paper presented at the conference on *L'Héritage de Marcel Mauss*, Collège de France et Maison des Sciences de l'Homme (Paris, 22-24 Mai, 1997).
8. Mauss, *The gift*, pp. 68-9. Mauss, however, would also refuse the idea of a society based solely on giving, which he saw as harmful both for individuals and society at large: men have to work, be self-reliant, and defend their personal or collective interests, and excessive generosity is no less harmful than excessive egoism (ibid., p. 75).
9. Mauss, *The gift*, pp. 3-4).
10. See J. Parry, '*The gift*, the Indian gift and the 'Indian gift'', *Man* n.s., 21, 1986, pp. 453-73.
11. Parry's remarks assume that contract and gift are very different phenomena, as they are indeed in many ways — if only because one is sanctioned in formalised law, while the other remains an informal process, with informally defined sanctions; on

the other hand, the contract itself may be said to entail a component of gift (for example, if one agrees to moderate one's self-interest for the sake of a fair, normative, or lasting relationship, etc.).

12. We may perhaps assume that he would have simply followed Durkheim's stance on this last issue.

13. Tittmus's study was explicitly meant to have practical implications for social and welfare policy making. Many of Tittmus's supposedly 'empirical' or ambitious 'comparative' statements, however, were advanced with no supporting evidence.

14. Not entirely different reasons have already led some scholars to find Mauss's insights of limited application even in the framework of traditional societies. This applies especially with regard to patterns of religious giving which entail a break in reciprocity and are encouraged by other-worldly orientations, patterns which are exemplified by charity and by certain types of donation to religious specialists and institutions (Parry, '*The gift*'). For other possible differences between archaic and religious giving in the 'greater' traditions, see I.F. Silber, 'Gift-giving in the great traditions: the case of donations to monasteries in the medieval West,' *European journal of sociology* 36, 1995, pp. 209-43.

15. See, for example, R.F. Arnove, *Philanthropy and cutural imperialism: the foundations at home and abroad*, Boston, 1980; D. Fischer, 'The role of philanthropic foundations in the reproduction and production of hegemony,' *Sociology* 17, 1983, pp. 206-33.

16. See, for example, T. Odendahl, *Charity begins at home: generosity and self-interest among the philanthropic elite*, New York, 1990; F. Ostrower, *Why the wealthy give: the culture of elite philanthropy*, Princeton, 1995, pp. 113-31.

17. See, for example, P. Schervish, 'Introduction: the wealthy and the world of wealth,' in *Gospels of wealth: how the rich portray their lives*, eds P. Schervish, P.E. Coutsoukis and E. Lewis, Westport, 1994, pp. 1-19.

18. Incidentally, even Titmuss retains this most essential aspect of Mauss's conception: even the free gift of blood, he emphasises, cannot and should not be expected to be utterly disinterested: 'No donor can of course be said to be characterized by complete, disinterested, spontaneous altruism. There must be some sense of obligation, approval and interest; some awareness of need and of the purposes of the blood gift; perhaps some organized group rivalry in generosity; some knowledge that fellow-members of the community who are young or old or sick cannot donate, and some expectation and assurance that a return gift may be needed and received at some future time — as with many examples of gift-exchange in other societies. Nevertheless, in terms of the free gift of blood to unnamed strangers there is no formal contract, no legal bond, no situation of power, domination, constraint or compulsion, no sense of shame or guilt, no gratitude imperative, no need for penitence, no money and no explicit guarantee of or wish for a reward or a return gift' (Tittmus, *The gift relationship*, p. 89).

19. Such ideas, moreover, hardly ever appear in the many reports (all U.S. based) of wealthy donors' motivations for giving. I would not reject, however, the applicability of some form of 'serial reciprocity', i.e., repaying the benefits one has received by providing benefits to a third party other than the original benefactor (see M.P. Moody, 'Serial reciprocity: a preliminary statement', Working Paper II-93, Department of Sociology, Princeton University, 1993). This concept, however, entails a number of problems which I cannot treat here, and in any case cannot be assumed automatically to apply to all forms of philanthropic giving.

20. See J. Galaskiewicz, *Social organizations of an urban grants economy*, Orlando, 1985; Odendahl, *Charity begins at home*; R.A. Prince and K.M. File, 'Philanthropic cultures of mind,' in C.H. Hamilton and W.F. Ilchman, eds, *Cultures of giving II: How heritage, gender, wealth and values influence philanthropy*, San Francisco, 1995, p. 130.

21. See, for example, R. Mousnier and J. Mesnard, *L'Age d'or du mécénat (1598-1661)*, Paris, 1985. There is no Maecenas-type patronage in the absence of 'taste, pleasure, joy, blossoming, happiness given by beauty, the search for the beautiful, aesthetic

quality, truth in relations with the creator' (ibid., pp. 437-40).

22. See A. Carnegie, *The gospel of wealth and other timely essays*, New York, 1900, p. 41. This was perhaps less felt in the first, progressivist phase where priority was often given to scientific research with potential social implications, but became increasingly evident later. For the personal concerns of donors (or initiators, often lawyers or administrators advising the donor or the wider family) and their impact on programmes in the humanities emerging in the mid-1920s, see K.D. McCarthy, 'Twentieth century cultural patronage,' Working Paper, Center for the Study of Philanthropy, City University of New York, 1996. Ultimately, however, and despite the legal enforcement of perpetuity, a donor's wishes are not immune to modifications by later generations. See F. Ostrower, 'Donor control and perpetual trusts: does anything last for ever?', in R. Magat, ed., *Philanthropic giving: studies in venture and variety*, Oxford, 1989.

23. See Barry A. Kosmin and P. Ritterband, *Contemporary Jewish philanthropy in America*, Savage, 1991.

24. However, money does allow recipients much greater freedom in adapting the gift to their own, rather than the donor's, personal needs, including the freedom to pass the money on to someone else. See V. Zelizer, *The social meaning of money*, New York, 1994.

25. Odendahl, *Charity begins at home.*

26. Ostrower, *Why the wealthy give*, pp. 9, 29, 135-6.

27. Cheal, *The gift economy*, p.173. To my mind, however, Mauss's concluding chapters clearly show that he was aware of the individual basis of giving — as well as, if only because of his close relation to Durkheim, of that of individualism more generally.

28. Somewhat ironically, such criteria may even include the bureaucratic grading of 'individual originality.'

29. An interesting difference here is that while in a primitive setting, giving is part of and accompanies ritual occasions, it now becomes the occasion of ritual.

30. While the interest has usually focused on issues of autonomy of the recipient from the donor's eventual interference and control, there are many other important issues, such as the ways of expressing gratitude, maintaining contact, or engaging in 'serial reciprocity' (when reciprocating the initial donor's gift is impossible).

31. According to Mauss, the gift is the vector of a dynamic flow, incessant motion, or circulation of goods, which can 'throb more (or less) intensely and speedily' (Mauss, *The gift*, p. 40) — largely in response to the propelling motor force of the triple obligation to give, receive, return.

32. An interesting phenomenon is the giving by wealthy philanthropists of the works of art they have collected over a lifetime, to museums of their choice; in contrast to money gifts, these are very personalised and precious gifts, in some cases also reflecting a commitment to specific aesthetic choices and orientations.

33. See for example: 'One can almost date — since Mandeville's *The fable of the bees* — the triumph of the notion of individual interest' (Mauss, *The gift*, p. 76).

34. There is thus much to commend in Parry's conception, building on Mauss, that 'the ideology of a disinterested gift emerges in parallel with an ideology of a purely interested exchange' (Parry, '*The gift*,' p. 458). On the other hand, as suggested above, philanthropic giving is often closer to Mauss's perception of the gift, and seldom couched in an unambiguous discourse of 'disinterestedness.'

35. See D. Billis, 'Sector blurring and nonprofit centers: the case of the United Kingdom', *Nonprofit and voluntary quarterly* 22, 1993, pp. 241-57; L. Salomon, 'Partners in public service: the scope and theory of government-nonprofit relations', in *The nonprofit sector: a research handbook*, ed. W.W. Powell, New Haven, 1987, pp. 99-117, and 'The marketization of welfare: changing nonprofit and for-profit roles in the American welfare state', *Social service review* 67, 1993, pp. 15-39.

This interpenetration, as well as a tendency to assess the performance of philanthropic organisations in terms of economic rationality and efficiency, are in fact experienced by partisans and practitioners of philanthropy as entailing a potential threat to the future of philanthropy. 'Any of the three sectors (voluntary, not for profit, private, public-interest/government and business) can be compromised by borrowing too many of the core values of the other. Some overlap is necessary as well as desirable; too much leads to an essential compromise of purpose and method' (R.L. Payton, 'Philanthropic values,' in *Philanthropic giving: studies in venture and variety*, ed. R. Magat, Oxford, 1989, p.40).

Chapter 10

MAUSS, DUMONT, AND THE DISTINCTION BETWEEN STATUS AND POWER

Jonathan P. Parry

For the student of Indian society Mauss's legacy is both more profound and, I would like to think, more enduring than is generally realised today. The main legatee was Dumont; and in the first part of this paper I want to try to locate the latter's theory of the relationship between status and power in 'traditional' India in the context of a wider comparative project inspired by Mauss — a context without which, I believe, it is barely comprehensible and of which we lose sight at our peril. While Dumont's understanding of this relationship has been so widely berated that my defence of it may seem merely pig-headed, in the latter part of the paper (which briefly summarises an argument spelled out in more detail elsewhere[1]) I compound the perversity by proposing that his related — though this time generally accepted — stress on the symbiotic complementarity of the high and the low is actually quite problematic. The conclusion attempts to bring these two arguments together, suggesting that the development of a soteriology, and of the values of renunciation which accompany it, may provide an ideological impetus for both some kind of separation between status and power, and for a one-sided repudiation of interdependence between superior and inferior.

Dumont's debt to Mauss

Dumont's debt to Mauss — 'the source of all my efforts'[2] — is generously acknowledged, though largely unnoticed by anglophone Indianist commentators on his work. And there is perhaps something as much 'temperamental' as intellectual in his identification with his teacher, for Mauss himself personified a conception of sociology as a cooperative and collaborative endeavour with which he could deeply sympathise.[3] The intended (though disappointed) model for *Contributions to Indian sociology* had been the *Année sociologique*.[4]

It was with Mauss, Dumont claims,[5] that sociology in France 'reached its experimental stage', and it is surely no accident that he chose to describe *Homo hierarchicus* as an 'experiment'.[6] Though Dumont would later follow Durkheim in discovering that the values of modern individualism have their roots in religion,[7] *Homo hierarchicus* follows Mauss's essay on the person in offering an oblique critique of *The Division of Labour*:[8] the Individual is not an epiphenomenon of social morphology but rather the product of a specific cultural development.

It also clearly represents an exemplary instance of Mauss's strategy of studying in detail particular cases (like the potlatch or the seasonal variations of the Eskimo[9]) where certain *general* social facts are highlighted in a particularly prominent form, these cases representing 'the *maxima*, excesses, which can better show the facts than those societies where, although no less essential, they are still tiny and involuted' (quoted by Lévi-Strauss in his introduction to Mauss's work[10]). Like the potlatch, caste is a 'total social fact' in which the whole society is — as it were — present in a condensed form. Though Dumont is preoccupied with difference, he nevertheless sees ideologies as being built up out of a finite number of universal elements, and difference as lying in their combination. In any society one aspect of social life tends to be given primacy, and this aspect can then be put under the microscope by examining it in that context. Caste society is the Maussian 'maximum' of hierarchy; and Mary Douglas is chided for attempting to 'evolve a general theory of pure and impure based on that which a Congolese tribe possesses of it in an infinitely weaker and less articulated form ... (for) each sort of representation must be grasped where it is fully accepted and elaborated'.[11] The case was chosen 'precisely because the relations to which we wish to call attention are exaggerated and amplified among them; because they stand out we can clearly understand their nature and significance. As a result, it is easier to recognise them even in other societies where they are less immediately apparent or where the configuration of other facts conceals them from the observer.' Though these words actually belong to the introduction to Mauss's essay on the Eskimo,[12] they might equally well have appeared on the first page of Dumont's essay on caste.

Mauss too, Dumont claims, had stressed difference; in particular that between 'modern' and 'traditional' society. One crucial aspect of this 'great principle which arises from Mauss's teaching and which has directed all my efforts' is that it is only modern societies which have partitioned ethics, politics, and economics off into separate domains.[13] Here we come to what is, for my purposes, the most significant legacy of Mauss's teaching, the progressive fragmentation of an originally unified conceptual order. Just as Mauss's essay on *The gift*[14] was concerned with the way in which purely economic exchanges have evolved out of the 'total prestations' of primitive and archaic societies[15] — prestations in which the religious, political, and economic aspects were inseparable — so a great deal of Dumont's intellectual effort has been devoted to charting the process by which religion, politics, and economics come to be conceptualised as autonomous domains in Western ideology. 'The modern era has witnessed the emergence of a new mode of consideration of human phenomena and the carving out of a separate domain, which are currently evoked for us by the words *economics, the economy*. How', he asks at the beginning of the first instalment of his study of *homo aequalis*, 'has this new category appeared .... ?'[16] And his answer, of course, gives considerable prominence to Mandeville's *Fable of the bees* which Mauss's essay on the gift had already identified as marking 'the triumph of the notion of self-interest'.[17] There is even in Dumont, I claim, a kind of implicit and residual evolutionism taken over from Mauss which finds in the Indian formulation of the relationship between the priest and the king a kind of halfway house along a path of development which leads from an undifferentiated 'traditional' world in which religion, politics, and economics are inseparable, to the modern world in which they constitute conceptually autonomous spheres.[18]

The Guénon red herring

In emphasising his debt to Mauss and other members of the Durkheimian school I am consciously accepting at face value Dumont's own version of his principal intellectual debts, rather than the representation of them offered in two recent, and rather less sympathetic, accounts. These unexpectedly come from closer to home than we are used to, the still-smoking gun suggesting a possible case of attempted parricide.

According to Lardinois, the Dumontian corpus — *Homo hierarchicus* is singled out for special attention — reveals an unresolved tension 'between two epistemically contradictory intellectual and social spaces which structured the field of Indian studies in the 1930s'.[19] One of these is the 'positivist and rationalistic type of scholarship' of Durkheimian sociology (as preeminently represented by Mauss), and of classical Indology (as preeminently represented by

Sylvain Lévi, one of Mauss's most influential teachers). The other is that of the 'esoteric essayist', René Guénon, whose work represents an 'apology for tradition' and 'a criticism of the modern world and the development of Western individualism',[20] and whose social attitudes were those of 'a conservative Catholic and nationalist culture ... (which) denigrated reason while strongly supporting the concepts of social order and hierarchy'.[21] Dumont's text represents a 'structure of compromise' between these two contradictory positions, and Lardinois warns that it can be reduced to neither[22] — a warning he promptly proceeds to ignore by directing all his attention to the putative influence of Guénon.

For this there are esssentially two kinds of evidence. The first consists of a small number of references Dumont makes to Guénon's work. Of these the most significant is his answer to the question 'Why have I chosen India?', to which he is on record as saying that he had read Guénon 'very early'.[23] But if this seems hardly compelling testimony to a major intellectual influence, that is only because Dumont has exercised 'self-censorship' to 'repress' the traces of such a disreputable intellectual pedigree, 'his earlier intellectual and social links (being) abandoned in a process of selective oblivion that characterises his memory'.[24] So it is that in *Homo hierarchicus* Tocqueville comes to be invoked merely as 'camouflage' to disguise the true provenance of ideas that were really derived from 'that man (who was said to have) introduced the tone of *Gringoire* into metaphysics'.[25] In the 1930s *Gringoire*, we learn, was a newspaper of the extreme right, famous for the violence of its anti-Semitic and anti-Marxist views. Of this outrageous innuendo — that Dumont is tarred by association with the same brush — the best that can be said is that it provides the anglophone author with a salutary warning of the possible dangers of acknowledging any childhood acquaintance with the works of Enid Blyton. In fact, as Lardinois concedes in a footnote,[26] Guénon was widely read in the 1930s by people with very different political views. If, in any event, the value of an idea were to be judged only by the social and political attitudes of its originator, the life expectancy of many of us today would be a good deal lower than it is. Not a few might feel compelled to ignore the laws of gravity.

The second piece of evidence seems, at first sight, more substantial. It consists supposedly of a close convergence of views on the nature of Indian society, and — what is of particular interest to me here — on the relationship between spiritual authority and temporal power in 'traditional' Hindu India, the implication being that Dumont's theory of encompassment is directly derived from Guénon's earlier discussions.[27] In a subsequent paper in the same collaborative publication, Assayag elaborates. Like Dumont, Guénon was concerned to understand the genesis of (modern) individualism, and is held to have 'anticipated the Dumontian theory of the secularisation of Indian kingship',[28] as well as the Dumontian notion of hierarchy. What Lardinois and Assayag fail to note, however, is that an equally good case might be made for tracing the provenance of most of these ideas back to Célestin Bouglé, in whose *Essays on the caste system* we find a clear statement of the separation of the temporal power of the king from the spiritual authority of the Brahman; of the ideological subordination of the first to the second; of the argument that in the past the two functions were not so 'strictly specialised', and of the argument that in Hinduism it is the religion of caste rather than the religion of the gods that is truly fundamental.[29] Moreover, Bouglé too had used India as a kind of counterpoint, or mirror, for a central preoccupation with an investigation of the egalitarian values of the West; while, as I have already suggested, the central problem of Dumont's comparative work had already been laid down by Mauss's discussion of the fracturing of a 'primordial' unity in which religion, politics, and economics remained ideologically undifferentiated.

Given that either Bouglé or Guénon might have provided Dumont with crucial hints towards his own formulation, and given the clear inspiration of Mauss's investigation, it is surely quite unnecessary to accuse Dumont of deliberately covering his tracks by suppressing his real debts. To both Bouglé and Mauss he has acknowledged them copiously, and it seems entirely gratuitous to doubt his own account of where his influences came from. Guénon is simply a red herring — or perhaps just a red rag to be waved in the faces of the Parisian Indianist establishment.

But there is a more general point to be made about the Bouglé/Guénon convergence. Bouglé was, of course, a leading — if not always entirely orthodox — member of the *Année sociologique* school, and was politically one of its most engaged and 'progressive' adherents. An active supporter of the Radical and Radical-Socialist Party, one of the earliest members of the Ligue des Droits de l'Homme formed during the Dreyfus affair and for some time its Vice-President, he also devoted more of his energy to demolishing the theories of 'scientific' racism than almost any other member of the group.[30] The moral is plain. As Trautmann has recently cautioned in the context of his lucid and compelling history of the Indo-European concept, people who hold very different social and political attitudes may sometimes subscribe to the same idea; and it may be unwise to dismiss an idea without pausing to consider its content.[31] While 'orientalism' may currently serve as a convenient term of abuse, its meaning is often quite vague. If, in the Indian case, it means knowledge which Orientalist scholars (like Sir William Jones) produced about India, then we must acknowledge that some of it has proved of lasting value; and that their representations of

Indian society and culture were a great deal more sympathetic to it than were those of their critics (like James Mill).

What, then, was the *content* of Dumont's idea about the relationship between status and power in 'traditional' India? It is, I fear, necessary to re-tread some old ground — and to do so, if that is still possible, without succumbing to Pavlovian reflexes triggered by the 'orientalist' expletive, which is about to recur.

Dumont's theory of the relationship between status and power

Hierarchy is glossed as 'rule or dominion over holy things' in the *Shorter Oxford English Dictionary*. As Dumont emphasises, 'the original sense of the term concerned religious ranking';[32] and — though the idea has a long pedigree — it is Dumont who has most systematically elaborated the view that 'traditional' India provides social science with its most privileged instance of the hierarchical ordering of society.

Recently, however, this picture of the Indian social order has received a severe battering from the latest 'new wind' — the title used of an earlier storm — to blow out of Chicago.[33] Dumont's theory of caste is now revealed as a modern mutation of an old-fashioned, self-serving 'orientalism'.[34] Writing twenty years after its first publication, Appadurai observes that although *Homo hierarchicus* had then seemed to offer a fresh way of approaching our data, it now appears to have been 'the swan-song for an older one'. By placing hierarchy at the centre of the sociology of India, Dumont had merely 'composed an elegy and a deeply Western trope for a whole way of thinking about India ...'[35] Consistent with the 'appropriately restricted role' it should now be assigned, a number of recent writers have advocated a return to Hocart's view of caste society as centred round the king rather than the Brahman, the significance of whose values and place in the system has seemingly been exaggerated.[36]

We cannot quite speak of consensus, however. In the same year as this Appadurai piece, Richard Davis — himself writing from 'the windy city' — concluded his review of T.N. Madan's Festschrift collection, *Way of life*, by likening hierarchy to a 'current that seems to flow through Indian social thought as continually as the Ganges'; and by judging this concept to be Dumont's 'most significant and long-lasting contribution to the study of India'.[37]

For Dumont, hierarchy is inseparable from holism, the valorisation of the social whole rather than the human individual. Hierarchy is said to be 'the *principle by which the elements of a whole are ranked in relation to the whole*, it being understood that in the majority of societies it is religion which provides the view of the whole, and that ranking will thus be religious in nature'.[38] In the modern West, by contrast, 'religion, as an *all-embracing* principle, has been replaced by individualism'.[39] In any holistic society there is assumed to be some overarching value in terms of which the whole is ordered, and everything else is as far as possible expressed. Those who are held to most fully incarnate this value are accorded the highest status, represent the whole, and thus 'encompass' the rest of the social order. As an illustration of this relationship of hierarchical encompassment, we are invited to think of God's creation of Eve out of Adam's spare rib. From an undifferentiated being, the prototype of 'mankind', Adam becomes male as opposed to female. 'There could not be', says Dumont, 'a more pictorial symbolism of the normative subordination of women to men', nor a better illustration of a hierarchical relationship.[40] Man encompasses woman who derives from *a part* of him, and represents the species in relation to God and the animals. The hierarchical superior thus encompasses what is in a sense both complementary and contrary to himself.

As this example suggests, hierarchy is also represented as inseparable from complementarity. In 'traditional' India, the encompassing principle is held to be the opposition between purity and pollution. Both conceptually and practically, the pure can only exist in relation to the impure. '.. society is a totality made up of two unequal but complementary parts'.[41] And just as there can be no pure castes without impure ones, so it is with the deities and the cults devoted to them.[42] In Hinduism the concept of the divine, like the concept of caste, is a relational one, and

> ... belief in the gods is ... subject to an overriding belief in the necessary coexistence of opposites, in the complementary relationship of the pure and impure. The religion of the gods is secondary; the religion of caste is fundamental.... The interdependence of high and low is not only observable in behaviour; it is also interiorized as the fundamental belief.[43]

The relationship between (religious) status and temporal power, and between those who represent these principles, is again one of hierarchical complementarity. The two functions are clearly distinguished; and the temporal power of the king (or the locally dominant caste) is ideologically subordinated to the spiritual authority of the Brahman. While each is preeminent in his own sphere, the Brahman is superior on the superior level — in terms of the values which order the whole. But each is dependent on the other, the one materially and the other spiritually. '*Comparatively speaking*, the king has lost his religious prerogatives: he does not sacrifice, he has sacrifices performed....'.[44]

I underscore 'comparatively speaking' for two reasons. The first is that the hierarchical disjunction between status and power is precisely what permits Dumont to argue that India provides sociology with its paradigmatic case of 'the pure type of hierarchy, completely separated from that with which hierarchy is usually mixed, namely power'.[45] The second reason is that he is centrally concerned to contrast the Indian pattern with the configuration of values elsewhere: at one extreme with the many societies — ancient Egypt or Sumeria, the Chinese empire and various Polynesian chiefdoms are cited as examples — in which the king is also the chief priest of the nation.[46] Dumont believes that in the remote past this was also true of India; but that at an early date the two functions were split apart. At the other extreme is the modern West, where the whole is held to be made up of 'autonomous, equal realms resembling the juxtaposition of individuals in society',[47] and where the political domain is therefore absolutely autonomous from religion — by contrast with its *'relative'* autonomy in the Indian situation.[48] Dumont is presumably thinking here of France or the United States rather than Britain.

So on one side the contrast is with, say, Polynesia where status and power are often combined. Here the realm of the sacred includes both the holy and the unclean, and is — by contrast with the Indian opposition between purity and pollution — therefore said to remain undifferentiated in relation to the profane. Such a system is held to be a 'logical and genetical' precursor to the Indian configuration.[49] Now with regard to status and power, Europe too has passed through, *and beyond*, such a transformation. In 'Hellenistic times and later' it also knew the sacral kingship of the priest-cum-ruler; but this gave way in the early Christian West to a separation of the two functions, and by the beginning of the sixth century Pope Gelasius had elaborated a theory of the relationship between the priest's *auctoritas* and the king's *potestas* precisely comparable to the Indian pattern. This formulation did not take deep roots, however, and the Church in Italy was soon claiming superiority to the temporal power *'on the temporal level itself'*.[50] In India, by contrast, 'the supremacy of the spiritual was never expressed politically'.[51] The historical trajectory, then, has been a development from a priest-king at the apex of a hierarchy which is simultaneously religious, political, and economic, to a configuration — like that of traditional India — in which a separate politico-economic domain is subordinated to the transcendent realm of religion, to the more absolute differentiation in modern ideology of religion from the politico-economic, a domain which has now itself been bifurcated.

Much the same point might be made with regard to the individual: the modern West has come from where India is (or at least was until rather recently). There the individual exists only in the person of the world-renouncer. Much like the Hindu ascetic, the early Christians were individuals outside the world — individuals, that is, in relation to God — while in the profane world they continued to be governed by a collective conception of man. In the West the historical development was to lead this outwordly individual into the world, while in India he remained outside it.

In short, the Indian social order is seen as growing out of something very like that of Polynesia (or rather Dumont's version of it, for in fact some kind of split between status and power is by no means unknown in the region[52]); while the conceptual order of the modern West is seen as growing out of something very like that of India. As in Mauss's essay on the gift, India would therefore seem to represent a kind of arrested development of the evolutionary history of western Europe.[53] Phrased in this way, the charge of 'orientalism' seems to stick (though the charge that Dumont's 'relativism' precludes comparison is plainly way off the mark[54]). Given a more charitable gloss, however, the theory is surely not unreasonable. The implicit *assumption* — which seems to me plausible and which is perhaps reminiscent of Durkheim[55] — is that in the course of human history the tendency is for more differentiated forms to evolve out of less differentiated ones as societies increase in scale and economic complexity. The *empirical proposition* — which seems to me right — is that the sacral polities of *certain* Polynesian societies, 'traditional' India, and the modern West represent three distinctively different, and increasingly differentiated, configurations of the relationship between religion, politics, and economics. India is *not* a variant on Firth's Tikopia, nor even on Hocart's Fiji.[56]

The neo-Hocartian revisionism: an exemplary instance

The most radical, best documented — and thus for my purposes exemplary — statement of the neo-Hocartian position that it is such a variant is Dirks's 'ethnohistorical' study of the 'little kingdom' of Pudukkottai in present-day Tamilnadu. The central thesis of his book is that in precolonial India it was the king and not the Brahman who played the central organising role in the social organisation of caste, and that there was no fundamental separation between politics and religion. 'Kings were not inferior to Brahmans; the political domain was not encompassed by the religious domain ... ritual and political forms were fundamentally the same'.[57] But Dumont was deluded for a reason. Building on, but greatly extending, the earlier arguments of Cohn and Fuller, Dirks claims that 'colonialism ... created much of what is now accepted as Indian 'tradition', including an autonomous caste structure with the Brahman clearly at its head'.[58] By removing the king, the British in effect decapitated the social system, allowing the Brahmans to assume a position of unrivalled supremacy, and creating Dumont's — supposedly ancient — hierarchical disjunction between status and power.

In the precolonial state worship was the root metaphor for political relations. The subject serves the king as the devotee serves the deity, and receives back gifts which are the analogue of the transubstantiated offerings which the deity returns to the worshipper. The king in his court is the counterpart of the god in his temple; and it was his royal gifts — rather than relative purity — which defined hierarchy 'through a logic of variable proximity to the king', and which constituted the polity. By the mid-nineteenth century, around 70 percent of all Pudukkottai's land had been granted to subordinate lords, themselves at the centre of miniature replicas of the 'little kingdom'; to village officers, artisans, and servants; and to temples, monasteries, and Brahman communities. But these gifts are not to be seen as a symptom of royal weakness; they were the very basis of statecraft. What the king gave out in the form of land grants, titles, emblems, honours, and privileges of service, was some part of his own sovereign substance by which he conferred on the recipients a subordinate share in his sovereignty and bound them to him. Giving away land was a means of incorporating 'new people into the moral-political economy in which the king was at the centre'.[59] Dumont is therefore in error to speak of the 'secularisation' of Indian kingship, and with his separation between religion and politics he has imposed on India 'a fundamentally Western ideology'.[60]

Since one of Dumont's central preoccupations had been to *distinguish* between Indian and Western ideologies, the second of these charges seems somewhat misplaced; while the first — which is routinely rehearsed by the critics — seems to be based on a misreading of Dumont's work and a misunderstanding of his comparative enterprise. It is 'speaking comparatively' — remember the priest-cum-ruler — that the Indian king can be said to have 'lost his religious prerogatives'; and his 'secularisation' is a question of level. It is in relation to the world of the orthodox Brahman (deeply influenced as he is by the values of renunciation) that kingship is a profane concern; while it is acknowledged that from another perspective 'the king has kept the magico-religious character inherent in his person and function'.[61] It is simply wrong to assert that Dumont believes that the magico-religious function has become the 'unique preserve' of the Brahman.[62] That kingship must in some measure be a religious phenomenon is, of course, precisely what the theory of encompassment requires. Dirks's demonstration that political relations are expressed in the language of religion is therefore entirely consistent with the theory he criticises.

Not all of the facts are, however, quite consistent with his own thesis in which status and power go together. The territorial division of the royal subcaste to which the king belonged was ranked only second in order; and *within* this division the king's lineage was again only second in rank.[63] Similarly, at the royal assembly in the contiguous state of Ramnad, the Maravar king would rise to offer a seat to the Kontaiyankottai and Vanniya chiefs in token of their superior subcaste status.[64] Far from being a mere 'peculiarity', as Dirks describes the Pudukkottai case, this pattern is a positive embarrassment in that it is uncomfortably reminiscent of reports from other parts of Tamilnadu where secular leadership and ritual office are vested in different descent groups within the subcaste, and where it is ritual office which claims precedence — in short, where there is a hierarchical distinction between status and power.[65]

As for the bold proposition that it was only with the demise of kingship that the Brahman gained supremacy, a radical qualification is later conceded: 'while the Brahman was superior to the king as Kallar (that is, by caste), he was inferior to the Kallar as king'.[66] The context, in other words, is crucial,[67] leaving open the likelihood that the king is superior to the Brahman only on an ideologically inferior plane. This situational logic is, however, hard to unravel from Dirks's account, in which the Brahman's role in the system is difficult to fathom. The sovereignty of subordinate lords, we are told, was dependent on the sovereignty of greater ones.[68] But if the Brahmans were quite so irrelevant to this process of royal legitimation as Dirks's silence about them implies, it is surely surprising that of the 70 percent of the total area of the state which had been granted away by the king, 22 percent had been given directly to Brahmans, and a further 51 percent to various kinds of religious endowment of which the Brahmans must have been the chief beneficiaries,[69] and that a high proportion of this land was at the kingdom's most valuable core. Similarly, of the 2,167 villages in the state of Ramnad, around 865 had by the end of the eighteenth century been given away for the support of religious institutions (431 of them as charitable grants — *dharmasanam* — to specific Brahman families); while in the four years of her rule (1803-7), Rani Mangaleswari Nachiar built or restored four *chattirams* (pilgrim hostels), four temples, and one monastery, and returned eighty-six villages to their Brahman grantees.[70]

The munificence of these royal subventions to the Brahmans would surely suggest that their superiority did not only exist in their own minds and that the king was forced to recognise in them some quality which guaranteed his rule. That the neighbouring Ramnad rulers denied the unqualified religious preeminence of their *kulagurus* (the spiritual preceptors of their lineage) — who were none less than the Jagatgurus of Sringeri, the direct spiritual descendants of the Shankaracharya himself — is hard to credit. It was the Jagatguru's priests who performed the raja's installation ceremonies; and it was to his authority that the raja appealed when he wanted to change the form in which his tutelary goddess was worshipped within the temple inside his own palace.[71] And at the Ramnad Navaratri — the royal ritual *par excellence* at which the ruler's divine status is most fully manifest — it was everybody *but* the Brahmans who prostrated before him.[72]

Certainly, Peabody's work on the 'little kingdom' of Kota provides a different picture of the relationship between kings and Brahmans.[73] The latter controlled the movements between kingdoms of miniature images which were held to embody the deities themselves. In theory, a deity would only remain with a deserving and virtuous king; and the Brahmans' decision to remove an image was seen as a withdrawal of divine support and legitimacy. What Peabody convincingly demonstrates is that the wanderings of the deities were not merely an index of the current distribution of power; they actually affected it.

What his evidence also suggests is that when the *Pax Britannica* finally succeeded in fixing the boundaries of the kingdom, the Brahmans lost much of their ability to play one ruler off against the other, and control of their temples increasingly fell into royal hands.[74] In other words, rather than subordinating the king to the priest (as Dirks argues), colonial rule seems to have shifted the balance of advantage in the favour of the king. Elsewhere, and much closer to base for the Pudukkottai king, colonial rule in the former kingdoms of Ramnad and Sivagangai (which had been reduced to *zamindari* territories by the Permanent Settlement of 1801-3) had the effect of breeding a new competition between erstwhile rulers on the one hand, and the priests and administrators of the major temples in their kingdoms on the other, as the former continually sought to involve the latter in the reproduction of their increasingly shaky authority, and as the latter sought to break free of royal control. The effect was to radically subvert the old complementarity between the priest and the king; in the long term to undermine the authority and legitimacy *of both*, and to lay the ground for *zamindari* support for the nascent anti-Brahman Dravidian Movement which was to dominate Tamilnadu politics throughout much of the twentieth century.[75] In Tamilnadu of all places, it can hardly be said that the emasculation of the king left the Brahmans in a position of unquestioned supremacy. Though their armies were now disbanded, and their royal prerogatives radically reduced, the former rulers — now *zamindars* — continued to exercise a critical influence on the social and political ordering of their domains. There *was* no sudden and absolute decapitation of the caste system, and it would rather soon prove that there had been no marked increment in the popular standing of the Brahman priest. As Galey has put it for a different corner of the country, 'kingship has survived the eviction of the king and the disappearance of the dynasty', for its values have remained intact.[76] Kingship, in other words, is more than the king, whose removal (which — as in the case of Ramnad — was anyway rarely complete) does not at a stroke destroy the principle of dominance for which he (amongst others) stands.

Nor, to return to Kota, is the historical data entirely consistent with Dirks's picture of the well-oiled way in which the gifts of the king unproblematically integrated the kingdom. The precolonial state was beset by 'perennial rebellions, cut-throat politics, and shifting political alliances that destabilised the polity throughout much of its existence'.[77] Authority was perpetually contested: subordinate lords trying to assert their independence or claim that their land was held from a superior sovereign; the king trying to resume land granted them in times of weakness and to reduce his dependence on the military levies they owed him. Gifts were as much a symptom of royal enfeeblement as a symbol and method of hegemony and incorporation.

Given all this, it seems rather more plausible to argue that it is Dirks — not Dumont — whose model is an artefact of colonialism. In the British period, Pudukkottai was the one remaining princely state in Tamilnadu, and — as Peabody points out[78] — this encourages Dirks to treat it in isolation rather than as part of a series of overlapping polities making rival claims, and to ignore the fact that the state was continually subject to subversion from within and without. Again, Price's account of precolonial Ramnad and Sivagangai stresses the way in which the king's legitimacy was constantly contested; and Price plausibly argues that the effect of colonial rule was to enhance the importance of royal munificence as an instrument of statecraft 'as other strategies of royal status were cut off'.[79] In short, both the king's apparent inviolability and the inflation of his largesse may well have been historical products of the *Pax Britannica*. Given Dirks's reliance on oral history, one might even wonder how the more recent past — specifically, an ideological climate profoundly affected by the militantly anti-Brahman Dravidian movement — might have influenced an analysis that so radically downplays the sanctioning authority of the Brahman. And given the prominent part that a number of ex-rulers played in the formation of that movement, it seems quite likely that they themselves had become prone to do so, suggesting the possibility that what we are being offered to replace an allegedly 'Brahmanical' view of caste is that of the enfeebled late nineteenth-century *zamindar*-king.

There is, at any rate, a peculiar irony about the current tendency to conjure up Hocart's ghost in order to taunt the 'idealist' Dumont with the crime of perpetuating the old 'orientalist' fantasy of India as a land in which religious ideology is preeminent. It was, after all, Hocart for whom, as one recent commentator has put it, 'in the beginning everything originated in and evolved from ritual; corporate social life is nothing, at least originally, but another form of ritual organisation'.[80] Centred on the king and oriented towards the maintenance of life through the sacrifices which he sponsors, the Indian caste system is just such an organisation.

If Dumont is to be accused of taking the ritual out of kingship, it seems to me that Dirks can be said to have taken the religion out of worship and the politics out of power. Worship, as Fuller complains, is treated 'as if its primary function is to constitute rank and authority among powerful men';[81] while it is ritual — not *realpolitik* — that is represented as the key to the reproduction of power. I have tried to suggest that this is not only a somewhat implausible picture of the precolonial polity, but that — given the scale on which he was prepared to fund them — there is every reason to suppose that the Kallar king looked to Brahmans to legitimise his rule. But what did they have, which he lacked? The answer must surely be some kind of transcendent authority. The Indian king was not after all a sacral king of the type from which Dumont had sought to distinguish him.

Hierarchical complementarity?

But if Dumont's characterisation of the relationship between status and power has rather more to recommend it than his numerous critics allow, it seems to me that the seemingly self-evident way in which he brackets the notions of hierarchy and complementarity is rather more problematic than is generally recognised. I have argued this case in detail elsewhere,[82] and for present purposes a brief re-statement will suffice.

Much of the problem derives from his over-stark opposition between the householder and the renouncer. As Dumont sees it, both the king and the Brahman are comfortably ensconced within a world 'of strict interdependence, in which the individual is ignored', while the renouncer 'puts an end to interdependence and inaugurates the individual'.[83] Consistent with the 'yawning gap'[84] which separates these persons goes an equally sharp break between their goals. Salvation is seen as opposed to the *trivarga* — the three *worldly* goals of human existence: the moral order of *dharma*, the politico-economic domain of *artha*, and the sensual pleasures of *kama* — and is said to be 'fatal' to them.[85] But if salvation is superior to the *trivarga*, it is hard to see why it should not be said to encompass them — as the *dharmic* realm of the Brahman is said to encompass the politico-economic realm of the king. And in fact, of course, there is a great deal of evidence that renunciation does provide a pervasive language in terms of which these other domains are ordered.[86] If, to put it more pointedly, the renouncer represents the autonomous individual, and if — as Dumont also argues[87] — his teachings have been the principal source of ideological innovation in the world he has left behind him, it is surely to be expected that these teachings will have a potentially subversive impact on the cultural recognition of complementarity.

That such misgivings are not without substance is clear from Fuller's important discussion of the Hindu pantheon in South India which shows how the cult of the village deities constructs their solidarity with, and dependence on, the higher Sanskritic deities, while the rituals and representations surrounding the latter deny their dependence on the former.[88] I myself found a similar pattern in the relationship between priesthood and possession in the Banaras region.[89] The interdependence between higher and lower becomes an intransitive relationship which exists only from the inferior's point of view. The efficacy of the exorcist's endeavours rests ultimately on the powers of the Brahman and of the rituals over which he presides; but the efficacy of the latter in no way depends on the former. The message is also repeated in the rules laid down in the Dharmashastra texts with regard to the periods of ritual incapacity incurred on the death of a connection. Pollution is held to seep, as it were, through the body particles shared with the deceased — the closer the relationship, the greater the pollution and the longer the duration of mourning. The consistent principle, I argue, is that where there is a difference in status between them, the lower is held to be more polluted by the death of a superior than the latter is by his death, implying that the inferior is more closely related to the superior than the latter is to him.[90] Or take the theory of gender encoded in many Brahmanical texts: while a woman's social and ritual existence is dependent on her husband, a man can stand alone — not only can, but indeed must do so, if he is follow the path of the renouncer. On a popular level, something of this pattern emerges in the way in which the expression of grief is structured by gender. As against the calm resignation expected of men, the weeping and wailing of women reveals that they are more bound to the world of social and bodily relationships than men, and are therefore inferior to them.[91] The lower are more mired in materiality and must recognise their connection to — and dependence on — the higher, who for their part pretend to an autonomy from their inferiors. So while Dumont is routinely charged with purveying a Brahmanical view of Hindu ideology, it ironically seems that his stress on complementarity is essentially a view *from the bottom up* — a point which he himself gets half way to recognising in his essay on world renunciation, when he speaks of 'the complementarities of common religious practice becoming blurred and indistinct when we move to the level of Brahmanic practice' and tending 'to disappear altogether at the level of Brahmanic theory'.[92]

This kind of asymmetry is also already implicit in the definition of hierarchy as a relationship of 'encompassment' in which the higher subsumes or contains the lower within itself. Since the superior encompasses the capacities of the inferior, it would seem to have no absolute need of others to represent them. *Shastrik* theory, for example, associates each *varna* with a specific form of power, the superior encompassing the inferior.[93] Thus the all-embracing mystic power of the Brahmans endows them with the ability to control the cosmos through their knowledge of the Vedic texts and the science of sacrifice. Subsumed within this power is both dominion over the earth and human beings (the function of the Kshatriya), and dominion over cattle and production (the function of the Vaishya). But the converse does not, of course, apply: the Kshatriya cannot pretend to the cosmic power of the Brahman, and the Vaishya cannot pretend to the capacities of either. So while the texts allow the Brahman to assume the temporal power of the Kshatriya in times of distress (or to perform the duties of the Vaishya), there are no circumstances in which the lower can legitimately arrogate to themselves the functions of the higher. Again, the six conventionally enumerated duties of the Brahman are to study and teach the Veda, to sacrifice and to preside over the sacrifices of others, and to give and receive gifts. By contrast, the duties of the Kshatriya are to study, offer sacrifice, and make gifts. In both these examples, then, the higher is more complete and therefore less reliant on others, than the lower. Relative superiority implies relative autonomy. The apogee is clearly the renouncer.

Now I am not, of course, claiming that interdependence is simply a matter of inescapable social reality, and that it remains unrecognised at the ideological level. As the much-quoted saying has it, 'Shiv(a) without Shakti (his consort) is a corpse (*shav*).' My point is simply that there is another strand in the ideology which denies this social imperative; that if hierarchy is a matter of encompassment then a repudiation of complementarity is an open possibility, and that it is the prestige and influence of the renouncer's message which gives this possibility real ideological salience.

One side of this ambivalence — the denial of relatedness — is perhaps nowhere more clearly illustrated than in Brahmanical ideas about gifts. The religious gift — the gift of *dan* — is said to be a surrogate for asceticism appropriate to the debased epoch in which we now live; its orientation is not to this world but the next, and the donor must on no account receive any kind of wordly reciprocation for it. The theory, in short, denies the world of social interdependence by denying the moral norm of reciprocity on which that world must be based. The gift is geared to salvation, and salvation turns its back on society and disregards its basic axioms.[94]

A concluding hypothesis on soteriology

In different degrees, this deeply uneasy relationship between the ultimate goals of religious striving and the social order seems to be common to all of the major world religions. As a first approximation, it seems possible to draw a distinction between those systems of thought in which there is a radical distinction between this world and the other world, and those in which they are represented as being broadly homologous. Take Evans-Pritchard's account of Nuer conceptions of the afterlife — such as they are, for the Nuer are notably vague on the topic. 'General opinion', however, is that the dead 'live a life like that they lived when they were on earth amid their cattle and dung fires in villages and camps'.[95] In salvation religions, by contrast, there is a complete antithesis between the world of human existence and a transcendent world which is entirely free from suffering, misery, and death. Life in this world is plainly devalued, and movements of ascetic withdrawal from it are clearly a logical development.

So much is obvious. But what is perhaps less obvious — or what has at any rate received less notice — is that some form of hierarchical distinction between status and power also seems to be inherent in such a conceptual order.[96] Those who embody the values of the transcendent world cannot be fully committed to this world, and represent a superior order of being to those who preside over it. If, to put it differently, the two kinds of world are radically opposed, then we would also expect those who represent these worlds to be opposed. Now I am not, of course, claiming that a notion of salvation is a *necessary* condition for the development of a clear separation between status and power; but I am suggesting that a radical opposition between this world and the other world is likely to encourage its development, and to make the temporal rulers dependent for the legitimation of their power on those with transcendent authority.[97]

As we saw above, in the early sixth century Pope Gelasius formulated a theory of the relationship between priesthood and power that was strictly analogous to the Indian one. One of Gelasius's central arguments was that *before* Christ it had been possible to have kings — like Melchisedech — who were also priests, but that after him this blending of the two functions is a work of the devil.[98] What seems to me striking is that on this theory it was only after *salvation* had been brought into the world that the function of priest-cum-ruler had to be split in two. By the same token, it is surely no accident that the earliest texts to which Dumont can trace his picture of 'secularised' kingship in India are the products of heterodox *renouncers* .[99] In both cases it is, in other words, a soteriological perspective that seems to demand a separation between status and power.

The millenarian exception seems to prove (or at least support) the rule. The chasm between this world and the other is about to be bridged; salvation will shortly come down to earth when sacred status will no longer be incompatible with the exercise of power. In Whitehouse's recent and remarkable account of the Pomio Kivung, for example, the 'Period of Government' is held to be imminent and will bring an end to suffering, death, reproduction, labour, and conflict.[100] But how imminent is not, of course, clear. At a stage when millenarian expectations were high, status and power were combined in the person of the founding prophet. But with the routinisation of the cult under the aegis of his sucessors, and under the pressure of delay, sacred and secular leadership has been split apart. The splinter movement with which much of Whitehouse's ethnography is concerned initially reproduced this split, but as millennial enthusiasm waxed and the return of the ancestors became an immediate expectation, the two kinds of role were recombined.

It is with these soteriological considerations that the two strands in my argument come together. Having begun by claiming that Dumont's characterisation of the relationship between the priest and the king is rather more compelling than his critics allow, I went on to suggest that the relationship between hierarchy and complementarity is rather more uneasy than he recognises. What I am now trying to suggest is that both propositions are already implicit in the radical opposition between the transcendent and the mundane that is set up by a soteriology. In a world in which ultimate value is located in the transcendent realm, status is likely to be distinguished from power, and complementarity is liable to be called into question by the values of ascetic autonomy.

With the first of these propositions at least I hope to signal my faith in the importance of continuing Mauss's much broader enquiry into the way in which religion, politics, and economics come to be understood as separate domains. To this enquiry, Dumont has I believe made a lasting — though today sometimes undervalued — contribution which has kept alive the breadth of his teacher's comparative vision in a way that the rather more parochial concerns of his Indianist critics have tended to obscure.

NOTES

1. J. Parry, *Death in Banaras*, Cambridge, 1994.
2. L. Dumont, *Essays on individualism: modern ideology in an anthropological perpective*, Chicago, 1986, p. 1.
3. M. Mauss [1930], 'An intellectual self-portrait', included in the present volume.
4. J.-C. Galey, 'A conversation with Louis Dumont: Paris, 12 December 1979', in T.N. Madan, ed., *Way of life: king, householder and renouncer*, New Delhi, 1982, pp. 13-22.
5. Dumont, *Essays on individualism*, p. 184.
6. L. Dumont, Preface to the complete edition of *Homo hierarchicus: the caste system and its implications*, Chicago, 1980, p. xvi.
7. Dumont, *Essays on individualism*, chap. 1. E. Durkheim, 'Individualism and the intellectuals' [1898], in W.S.F. Pickering, ed., *Durkheim on religion*, London, 1975.
8. M. Mauss [1938], 'A category of the human mind: the notion of person, the notion of 'self', in *Sociology and psychology: essays by Marcel Mauss*, London, 1979, pp. 57-94. E. Durkheim [1893], *The division of labour in society*, trans. G. Simpson, New York, 1964.
9. M. Mauss in collaboration with H. Beuchat, *Seasonal variations of the Eskimo: a study in social morphology* [1906], trans. J.J. Fox, London, 1979.
10. C. Lévi-Strauss [1950], *Introduction to the work of Marcel Mauss*, trans. F. Baker, London, 1987, p. 51.
11. Dumont, *Homo hierarchicus*, p. xxxix. Cf. M. Douglas, *Purity and danger: an analysis of concepts of pollution and taboo*, London, 1966.
12. Mauss, *Seasonal variations of the Eskimo*, p. 19.
13. Dumont, *Essays on individualism*, p. 4.
14. M. Mauss, *The gift: the form and reason for exchange in archaic societies* [1925], trans. W.D. Halls, London, 1990.
15. Cf. J. Parry, 'The gift, the Indian gift and the "Indian gift"', *Man* 21, 1986, pp. 453-73.
16. Louis Dumont, *From Mandeville to Marx: the genesis and triumph of economic ideology*, Chicago, 1977, p. 33.
17. Mauss, *The gift*, p. 76.
18. On the evolutionary preoccupations of Mauss's study of the gift, see Parry, 'The gift, the Indian gift and the "Indian gift"'.
19. R. Lardinois, 'Genesis of Louis Dumont's anthropology: the 1930s in France revisited', in J. Assayag, R. Lardinois and D. Vidal, eds, *Orientalism and anthropology*, Pondy Papers in Social Sciences, 24, Pondicherry, 1997, pp. 25-54, at p. 34.
20. Ibid., p. 27.
21. Ibid., p. 33.
22. Ibid., p. 34.
23. Ibid., p. 26.
24. Ibid., p. 44.
25. Ibid., quoted by Lardinois on p. 47.
26. Ibid., p. 44.
27. Ibid., p. 28.
28. J. Assayag, 'Indianism and the comparative theory of Louis Dumont: the construction of the 'object' in anthropology', in J. Assayag et al., eds, *Orientalism*, pp. 55-81, at p. 70.
29. C. Bouglé, *Essays on the caste system* [1908], Cambridge, 1971. See especially chapter 3, at pp. 53, 66.
30. W.P. Vogt, 'Durkheimian sociology versus philosophical rationalism: the case of Célestin Bouglé', in P. Besnard, ed., *The sociological tradition: the Durkheimians and the*

founding of French sociology, Cambridge and Paris, 1983, pp. 231-247, at pp. 232, 242.

31. T.R. Trautmann, *Aryans and British India*, Berkeley, 1997.

32. Dumont, *Homo hierarchicus*, p. 65.

33. K. David, *The new wind: changing indentities in south Asia*, The Hague and Paris, 1977.

34. R. Inden, *Imagining India*, Oxford, 1990.

35. A. Appadurai, 'Is homo hierarchicus?', *American ethnologist*, 13, 1986, pp. 745-61, at p. 745.

36. For example, see N. Dirks, *The hollow crown: ethnohistory of an Indian kingdom*, Cambridge, 1987; D. Quigley, *The interpretation of caste*, Oxford, 1993; G.G. Raheja, *The poison in the gift: ritual, prestation, and the dominant caste in a north Indian village*, Chicago, 1988; Inden, *Imagining India*. Cf. A.M. Hocart, *Caste: a comparative study*, London, 1950.

37. R.H. Davis, review of *Way of life: king, renouncer, householder*, ed. T.N. Madan, *Contributions to Indian sociology*, n.s., 20, 1986, pp. 135-48, at p. 147.

38. Dumont, *Homo hierarchicus*, p. 66; original emphasis.

39. L. Dumont, 'Religion, politics, and society in the individualistic universe' (The Henry Myers Lecture), *Proceedings of the Royal Anthropological Institute*, 1970, pp. 31-41, at p. 33. Original emphasis.

40. L. Dumont, 'On putative hierarchy and some allergies to it', in 'On the nature of caste in India: a review symposium on Louis Dumont's *Homo hierarchicus*', ed. T.N. Madan, *Contributions to Indian sociology*, n.s., 5, 1971, pp. 58-78, at p. 69.

41. Dumont, *Homo hierarchicus*, p. 55.

42. L. Dumont, *Religion/politics and history in India*, The Hague, 1970, chap. 2.

43. L. Dumont, 'Pure and impure', *Contributions to Indian sociology*, 3, 1959, pp. 9-39, at pp. 34-5.

44. Dumont, *Homo hierarchicus*, p. 71. My emphasis.

45. Ibid., p. 213.

46. Dumont, *Religion/politics*, pp. 67-8; 'Pure and impure'.

47. Dumont, 'Religion, politics and society', p. 33.

48. Dumont, *Religion/politics*, p. 87; cf. P.M. Kolenda, 'Seven types of hierarchy in *Homo hierarchicus*', *Journal of Asian Studies*, 35, 1976, pp. 581-96, at p. 586.

49. Dumont, 'Pure and impure', p. 29.

50. Dumont, *Essays on individualism*, chap. 1.

51. Dumont, *Homo hierarchicus*, p. 72.

52. This version seems to have been based primarily on the example of Fiji. See in particular Dumont, *Homo hierarchicus*, pp. 364-5. For a sceptical discussion of the debate as to whether the Fijian material is more appropriately seen as Polynesian or Melanesian, see N. Thomas, 'The force of ethnology: origin and significance of the Melanesia/Polynesia division', *Current Anthropology*, 30, 1, 1989, pp. 27-41. On the relationship between status and power, see, for example, A. Gell, *Wrapping in images: tatooing in Polynesia*, Oxford, 1993, at pp. 48-9.

53. Parry, '*The gift*, the Indian gift and the "Indian gift"'.

54. Quigley, *The interpretation of caste*, p. 44.

55. Durkheim, *The division of labour*.

56. R. Firth, *Rank and religion in Tikopia: a study in Polynesian paganism and conversion to Christianity*, London, 1970. A.M. Hocart, *Kings and councillors* [1936], Chicago, 1970.

57. Dirks, *The hollow crown*, pp. 4-5.

58. See B.S. Cohn, 'Is there a new Indian history? Society and social change under the raj' [1970], in B.S. Cohn, ed., *An anthropologist among historians and other essays*, Delhi, 1987, pp 172-99, at pp. 195-6; C.J. Fuller, 'British India or traditional India?

An anthropological problem', *Ethnos*, 3-4, 1977, pp. 95-121. Dirks, *The hollow crown*, p. 8.

59. Ibid., p. 137.
60. N. Dirks, 'The original caste: power, history and hierarchy in South Asia', *Contributions to Indian sociology*, n.s. 23, 1989, pp. 59-77, at p. 60.
61. Dumont, *Religion/politics*, pp. 68, 73.
62. Quigley, *The interpretation of caste*, p. 29.
63. Dirks, *The hollow crown*, pp. 222-8.
64. P.G. Price, *Kingship and political practice in colonial India*, Cambridge, 1996, p. 27.
65. B.E.F. Beck, *Peasant society in Konku: a study of right and left subcastes in south India*, Vancouver, 1972, pp. 93-5; and 'The right-left division of south Indian society', in R. Needham, ed., *Right and left: essays on dual symbolic classification*, Chicago, 1973, pp. 391-426, at p. 397.
66. Dirks, *The hollow crown*, p. 291.
67. Cf. G.G. Rajeha, 'India: caste, kingship, and dominance reconsidered', *Annual review of anthropology*, 17, 1988, pp. 497-522, at pp. 516-7.
68. Dirks, *The hollow crown*, pp. 47-8.
69. Ibid., p. 117.
70. Price, *Kingship and political practice*, pp. 109-11.
71. Ibid., pp. 153-5.
72. Ibid., p. 157.
73. N. Peabody, 'In whose turban does the Lord reside?: the objectification of charisma and the fetishism of objects in the Hindu kingdom of Kota', *Comparative studies in society and history*, 33, 1991, pp. 726-54.
74. N. Peabody, 'Logic of the fish: Hindu kingship and polity in Kota', doctoral dissertation, University of Harvard, 1992, p. 262ff.
75. Price, *Kingship and political practice*.
76. J.-C. Galey, 'Reconsidering kingship in India: an ethnographic perspective', *History and anthropology*, 4, 1989, pp. 123-87, at p. 130.
77. N. Peabody, 'Kota *Mahajagat*, or the Great Universe of Kota: territory and sovereignty in eighteenth century Rajasthan', *Contributions to Indian sociology*, n.s., 25, 1991, pp. 29-56, at p. 34.
78. Ibid.
79. Price, *Kingship and political practice*, pp. 17, 77, 100.
80. B. Schnepel, 'Durga and the king: ethnohistorical aspects of the politico-ritual life in a south Orissa jungle kingdom', *Journal of the Royal Anthropological Institute*, 1, 1995, pp. 145-66, at p. 161.
81. C.J. Fuller, *The camphor flame: popular Hinduism and society in India*. Princeton, 1992, p. 81. Cf. Schnepel, 'Durga and the king', p. 160.
82. J.P. Parry, *Death in Banaras*, Cambridge, 1994, p. 264ff.
83. Dumont, *Homo hierarchicus*, pp. 185-6.
84. Dumont, *Essays on individualism*, p. 26.
85. Dumont, *Religion/politics*, p. 44.
86. For example, see V. Das, 'Kama in the scheme of purusharthas: the story of Rama', in Madan, *Way of life*, pp. 183-203; K.J. Shah, 'Of artha and the Arthasastras', in Madan, *Way of life*, pp. 55-73; Davis, review of Madan, *Way of life*.
87. Dumont, *Religion/politics*, chap. 2.
88. C. J. Fuller, 'The Hindu pantheon and the legitimation of hierarchy', *Man*, n.s., 23, 1988, pp. 19-34.
89. Parry, *Death in Banaras*, chap. 7.
90. Ibid., p. 218ff.
91. Ibid., p. 152ff.
92. Dumont, *Religion/politics*, p. 40, and cf. p. 63.

93. F.A. Marglin, 'Power, purity and pollution: aspects of the caste system reconsidered', *Contributions to Indian sociology*, n.s., 11, 1977, pp. 245-70.
94. Parry, *Death in Banaras*, chap. 4.
95. E.E. Evans-Pritchard, *Nuer religion*, Oxford, 1956, p. 159.
96. S.N. Eisenstadt, 'Transcendental visions — other-worldliness — and its transformations: some more comments on L. Dumont', *Religion* 13, 1983, pp. 1-17, at p. 6.
97. Cf. R.N. Bellah, 'Religious evolution', *American sociological review*, 29, 1964, pp. 358-74.
98. Dumont, *Essays on individualism*, p. 47.
99. Dumont, *Religion/politics*, p. 75.
100. H. Whitehouse, *Inside the cult: religious innovation and transmission in Papua New Guinea*, Oxford, 1995.

Materiality, body, history

Chapter 11

THE CATEGORY OF SUBSTANCE:

A MAUSSIAN THEME REVISITED

N. J. Allen

> *pāṅktaṃ vā idaṃ sarvam*
> 'Fivefold verily is this world as a whole'
> Taittirīya Upanishad 1.7.1.

Mauss several times refers to his interest in the category of substance. In 1924, in a well-known passage discussing categories Aristotelian and non-Aristotelian, he refers to one of the former: 'Let us take for example that of substance, to which I have given some highly technical attention. What a lot of vicissitudes it has undergone! For example it has had among its prototypes another notion, especially in India and Greece: the notion of food'.[1] Similarly, in 1938, at the start of *The person*, referring again to the Aristotelian categories, he says: 'For many long years I have been preparing some work on the notion of substance, but from it I have only published an extract which is pretty abstruse and, in its present form, scarcely worth reading.' In 1930 he was envisaging publishing this work as the second in a series of two or three volumes, the first of which was to have been based on unpublished writings left by Hubert.[2]

Three questions arise. To what extent can one recover Mauss's views on this theme? How do they relate to his (and our) view of the discipline to which he was trying to contribute? And, most important, given the orientation of this volume, can one carry his line of thought

beyond the point which he himself reached? In other words, can one
do for his work on substance something analogous to what I attempted
for his 1931 essay on social cohesion?[3]

Mauss on substance

Mauss wrote on substance in two main places. The 'abstruse extract'
appeared in a Festschrift for his Sanskrit teacher, Sylvain Lévi, whom
he loved and honoured as his 'second uncle';[4] the book was published
in 1911 to celebrate Lévi's completion of twenty-five years at the Ecole
Pratique des Hautes Etudes. The article was originally intended to form
an appendix to a longer paper on the notion of food in Vedic literature,
but Mauss failed to finish the latter in time for the deadline. The seven-
page article is called 'Anna-Virāj'.[5] The Sanskrit word *anna* means
grain or food, while Virāj (literally Wide-shining or Wide-ruling) has a
number of applications, of which three need to be noted here. Virāj is
a Vedic poetic metre which (to simplify slightly) consists of four groups
of ten syllables; it is the name of a cosmogonic being, originally female,
later also presented as male; and it (or she) is also the primal substance
of the universe.

Mauss has no difficulty in assembling citations from the
Brāhmaṇas, the ritual texts of the early first millennium B.C., to the
effect that the metres in general and Virāj in particular 'are' food.
Primarily they are food for the gods, and above all for the Creator
Prajāpati, but to feed the gods is to feed oneself, via the abundance the
gods can provide. The idea clearly relates to the fact that the metres are
used for the invocations that accompany animal and vegetable
offerings to the gods, and are thus drawn into the all-pervasive
sacrificial discourse. However, there is more to it, since Virāj is more
strongly associated with food than are the other metres, and this
association operates via the number ten. Ritual elements often come in
tens, and the ritualists' explanations link number, metre, and food.
Thus, in building the fire-altar, one lays down ten sets of ten bricks,
and part of the explanation given in the Śatapatha Brāhmaṇa[6] is that
Virāj consists of ten syllables, and Virāj is all food; one is thus offering
all food to the Fire God.

Mauss makes some brief comments on the history of Virāj in
cosmogonic myth, but his main interest is in her link with the number
ten. The ritual specialists themselves speculate on the explanation, but
unconvincingly, mentioning ten fingers, ten breaths, and the like.
Without being fully explicit, Mauss takes it as 'axiomatic' (n. 28) that
the reason has to do with royal power, and with the mystic relations
between royal power and abundant harvests.[7] In any case, in offering

his own explanation, he calls attention to a passage, not from the ritualistic Brāhmaṇas, but from the somewhat later and more speculative Upanishads.[8] One reads here that 5+5=10 is the highest throw in dice, that ten is Virāj, and that ten is food. In early Indian dicing the possible throws were often associated with the numbers 4, 3, 2, 1, and since another passage in the same text says essentially that winner takes all, Mauss proposes that in some scoring methods Virāj represented the totality, i.e., the sum $4+3+2+1 = 10$.

It is difficult to know how much weight to give to this hypothesis — there might be other reasons for the significance attached to ten (for instance, if one uses two six-sided dice ten faces are exposed at each throw). When he says that the article is scarcely worth reading (*bien inutile à lire*), Mauss himself seems to display a certain lack of confidence in his idea, and a recent learned study of this complex field mentions Mauss's paper only in passing and without comment.[9] However, its importance for my purposes lies not in its explanation of the number ten but in its recognition of a complex of ideas connecting substance, number, femaleness, and food.

Mauss took up several of these themes again at a workshop on the notion of matter held in 1939.[10] In his seven-page contribution he talks as usual about categories, which are abstractions from the mode of thinking and feeling current in a particular society, and not, *pace* some philosophers, entities transcending social history. In early seventeenth-century Europe, as in the Melanesia of his own times, matter was not the inanimate stuff that we think of today. The very word 'matter' derives from Latin *mater* 'mother', and the notion has a complex history involving feminine-gender Latin and Greek words for wood (*hulê, silva*), which is or has been alive. Apart from female versus male, the idea relates to a number of other dyads: ethnographically, to the dangerous forest outside the settlement versus the cosmos within it, philosophically to matter versus form and, at least since Spinoza, to extension (or substance) versus spirit. The complete despiritualisation of matter was an important step in the history of the category.

Mauss now turns back from modern thought to more traditional materials, claiming that food is one of the most important notions underlying that of matter — the idea of subsistence connects with that of substance. Thus numerous tribal peoples (he instances the Australian aboriginals studied by Spencer and Gillen) practise initiation rites at which the males are for the first time introduced to the eating of their totemic species, thereby gaining the power of the eater over the eaten. After alluding to the contrasting diet of the Eskimos in summer and winter, he pursues the theme of eating into the theology of the Maori, envisaging their cosmology as a hierarchical system of classification and offering the useful image of a mythological corpus as a spider's web that only makes sense when studied as a whole. He briefly notes the contrast within Indo-European languages between female and neuter words for water (thereby perhaps incidentally implying that for his purposes food includes drink). Emphasising again the male-female opposition, he concludes by repeating that for many cultures matter is an animate principle, or even a living body.[11]

The 1939 text is typical of late Mauss — dense and allusive, extremely demanding on the reader, stuffed with facts, ideas, and references whose connections are difficult to grasp and sometimes elude me altogether. It contains no bibliographic references, and a full commentary would necessitate considerable work on the various authors he refers to — for instance Spinoza, a philosopher whom he had particularly studied in his youth.[12] Comparing this paper with the earlier 'Anna-Virāj', one might note that, while it deals not at all with numbers, it shares the earlier concern with the complex of ideas embracing substance, food, and femaleness; and that it puts more explicit emphasis on the hierarchical relation between eater and eaten. It is also, of course, far broader, referring to India only in passing, and drawing on a range of societies — tribal, archaic literate and modern.

The map of learning

In reflecting on Mauss's ideas on substance, and on how they might be developed, it seems helpful to use three frames of reference: Mauss the Indologist, Mauss the anthropologist, and Mauss the Indo-Europeanist. For other purposes there would be other Mausses, for instance Mauss the collaborator of Durkheim, or Mauss the citizen and political activist.

Since he started studying Sanskrit with Lévi in 1895, at the age of twenty-three, early Indian culture was among the very first to which he was exposed in any depth, and although Sanskritic material occupies only a small percentage of his *oeuvre*, one can be pretty certain that it nourished his thinking throughout his life.[13] Apart from book reviews, none of his texts is so exclusively Sanskritic as 'Anna-Virāj', but India is central to the essay on sacrifice (1899), and in most of the wide-ranging essays it helps to form a sort of bridge between tribal societies and Europe (as it does in *Primitive classification* 1903, *The gift* 1925 and *The person* 1938). Had either study been finished, Sanskritic material would have contributed major sections both to his thesis on prayer and to the projected work on substance.[14] But often the references to India are quite discreet. Thus the last paragraph of *Techniques of the body* (1935) mentions his reading of Sanskrit texts on yoga, and the essay on matter states in five words that the conceptual evolution from subsistence to substance in India is analogous to that among the Romans. The more alert one is to such references, the more one understands why, as Denise Paulme recalled in 1967, Mauss regarded Sanskrit as 'indispensable'.[15]

Since Mauss liked facts, and was usually reluctant to theorise, his global conception of his own field of study is notoriously difficult to pin down. It was certainly the study of 'social facts',[16] but what else can one say? Two of his fundamental orientations are worth noting here, namely towards history and towards philosophy. As regards the former, he clearly and consistently thought in world-historical terms, welcoming improvements in the writing of 'l'histoire de l'esprit humain'.[17] This is an orientation which, despite abuses by some sorts of evolutionist and the dangers of Eurocentric 'Grand Narratives', seems to me in principle an entirely respectable academic interest and one which anthropology ignores at its peril. As regards philosophy, Mauss thought primarily in terms of the categories of Aristotle and Renouvier, as I have discussed elsewhere.[18] If one interprets *The gift* and *Sacrifice* as preliminary studies of the category of relation, one can view much of his *oeuvre* as oriented towards categories and hence towards philosophy. Since his interest in the categories was precisely in the different forms they had taken throughout world history, the two orientations are interwoven.

Between the level of the individual culture, such as India from Vedic times onwards, and the level of world history, there lies an intermediate level of study which Mauss did not undervalue. He gave considerable emphasis to intersocietal relations (emphasising refusal to borrow no less than 'diffusion'), and already in 1931 was criticising ethnographers for presenting societies as if they were isolates.[19] From an early stage he believed in an ancient civilisation, regionally subdivided but embracing 'all the shores and islands of the Pacific'.[20] But the intermediate unit that most concerns India is that of the Indo-European speakers.

This unit of analysis was of course first recognised by comparative philology, and continues to be used predominantly by linguists. However, at the start of this century it was also much used in work on culture, partly no doubt because nearly all Western students of India were then at home in Latin and Greek. Numerous relevant comments by Mauss are therefore to be found in his reviews of authors who construed particular cultural elements as of Indo-European origin — Meyer and Nutt on the afterlife (1899), Usener on deluge myths and Caland on ritual circumambulation (both 1900), Dieterich on reincarnation (1906), and so on. Although he quite often criticises lack of rigour in the arguments of cultural comparativists, his attitude was not simply dismissive. As he says when reviewing von Schroeder in 1910, 'one must not forget the definite kinship not only of the Vedic language but also of Vedic religion with primitive forms of the religions of early Europe, both Graeco-Roman and other'.[21] Similarly, reviewing Dumézil's first book in 1925, he was severe but not discouraging: after its eclipse (due to the unacceptable speculations of Max Müller and his contemporaries), Indo-European comparative mythology was due for a revival.[22]

His most enthusiastic endorsement of Indo-European comparison is probably to be found in his references to Meillet, with whom he had once studied Avestan[23] and who collaborated in the *Année sociologique*. Meillet, Dumézil's supervisor, combined his pure linguistics with a sociological attitude of mind, and his genealogical comparativism was a necessary method for *sociologie* — a precision tool for studying the evolution of social phenomena.[24] Moreover, it was a method Mauss himself sometimes used, for instance in his arguments for the existence of potlatch among the Indo-Europeans.[25]

Perhaps Mauss's views on substance would have been developed within the same framework. He certainly saw the Greece-India comparison as essential to his undertaking: the provisional title of his book was *Forme archaïque de la notion de nourriture: Grèce et Inde védique comparées*. But rather than deriving them from a common origin, he might perhaps have explained similarities by east-west contacts, as he did when discussing the oriental 'feel' of Plotinus and of Plato's account of the soul.[26] In general too, he emphasised the role of the non-Aryan substrate in India, ascribing to it (debatably, and in disagreement with Lévi) much of what distinguishes the Upanishads from earlier Vedic texts.[27]

All in all, although Mauss the Indo-Europeanist certainly existed, this is not a particularly salient component of the whole scholarly persona. Nevertheless, as I have argued elsewhere,[28] Mauss's contribution to the successful use of the language-family framework by others was fundamental, though it operated indirectly. The 1903 essay on *Primitive classification* has been severely criticised (not always justly), but whatever its defects, it was this paper that particularly inspired Mauss's friend, the Sinologist Granet, at the time when Dumézil was studying with him, and it was to the influence of Granet at this very time that Dumézil himself attributed his 'breakthrough' in Indo-European comparativism. Before 1938 he was groping in the dark; thereafter, with the discovery of the three functions, he had the basis for real progress. Though he himself did not put it in quite this way, what he had found was that the Indo-European ideology was a form of primitive classification.

Mauss might almost have predicted such a discovery. Already in the 1903 essay he had compared the Greek system of divination with the

Chinese form of primitive classification. As he saw it, every mythology is fundamentally a classification, and if in some cultures it is clans that divide up the universe between them, in others it is the pantheon. Thus 'India distributes things, and simultaneously their gods, between the three worlds of heaven, atmosphere and earth.'[29] These mythic classifications merge into the philosophical ones of Greece and India. In a sense, all that Dumézil did was set these insights firmly in the Indo-European framework, give them greater precision, and document their ramifications.

Thus, if one hopes to carry further Mauss's work on substance, one way of proceeding is to start from Dumézil. I cannot here take up the Greek limb of Mauss's proposed comparison, though Virāj's link with the number ten might recall the fact that the same number, construed as 1+2+3+4, constituted the *tetraktys*, the sacred symbol of the Pythagoreans. I confine myself to India, and the purpose of the next section is to look at one particular classical Hindu ontological doctrine in the light of Dumézilian formulations and attempts to elaborate them.

Sāṃkhya

To introduce Sāṃkhya we can start from Virāj. As Mauss notes, Virāj appears first in the best-known Rig Vedic creation hymn, the Puruṣasūkta,[30] which contains the first list of the four varṇas or social estates recognised by Hindu doctrine, and tells of their origin from the body parts of the dismembered Puruṣa, the Primal Man. The birth of society occupies only two of the sixteen stanzas, leaving space for many other aspects of creation, and in stanza 5 we read: 'From Puruṣa was born Virāj, and from Virāj Puruṣa.' Sometimes called 'reversible parenthood', the same mytheme applies to some other male-female cosmogonic pairs, and its interpretation is not obvious. It is clear at least that Virāj, 'the female Creation-Principle',[31] is in some sense paired with the male Puruṣa, and that this cosmogonic pairing appears in many forms. In particular, as O'Flaherty says, 'the active female creative principle Virāj is later replaced by Prakṛti or material nature, the mate of Puruṣa in Sāṃkhya philosophy.'[32] Prakṛti, and its three components, will be our main concern in the rest of the paper, but a few words are needed to introduce the philosophical doctrine as a whole.

Sāṃkhya is paired with yoga as one in the traditional list of six Hindu schools of philosophy.[33] It was of extraordinary influence and pervasiveness, and has been described as lying 'at the fountainhead of systematic Indian reflection', and as influencing Hindu medicine, law, statecraft, mythology, cosmology, theology and devotional literature, as well as Jain and Buddhist philosophy.[34] Although it barely survives as a living school of philosophy, it lives on vigorously in other forms, as we shall see. It is classically expressed in a text called the *Sāṃkhyakārikā* (henceforth *SK*), which consists of seventy-two stanzas and dates from the fourth/fifth century A.D. However, as has already been implied, the roots of the doctrine go back to the Vedas, and there has been much technical discussion about its development. Like all Indian philosophies it is primarily soteriological, and its aim is to offer salvation through knowledge. This knowledge certainly concerns the composition of the cosmos and how it evolved, but one of the difficulties in understanding it is that it does not sharply distinguish macro- and microcosm. One can think of it as combining the mythological and macrocosmic with the psychological and microcosmic.

In its standard form Sāṃkhya sees the world as consisting of twenty-five *tattvas* or principles, of which Prakṛti or primal nature is one. Prakṛti itself (or herself) is made up of three gunas, literally 'strands', as in a rope.[35] The gunas are regularly given in a standard order and, as in most such lists, the highest-valued entity comes first. Thus nature is composed of *sattva*, *rajas* and *tamas*, which have the following associations:

sattva	being, goodness, luminosity, purity, tranquillity
rajas	energy, passion, dynamism
tamas	inertia, heaviness, darkness

The gunas are also often linked with the colours white, red, and black respectively. They are not themselves enumerated in the list of principles, but are an important feature of the doctrine.[36]

From Prakṛti emanates *buddhi* (Intellect) and from that *ahaṃkāra*, literally the I-maker, i.e., the Ego or Ego-principle. From Ego in turn come mind and the five sense-capacities, the five action-capacities, and the five subtle elements; and from the latter come the five gross elements. Since the focus here will be on the start of the series, I do not list the individual *tattvas* making up the various pentads. The whole system is diagrammed by Larson,[37] in a form resembling a genealogy.

If Prakṛti and her evolutes make up the twenty-four principles so far mentioned, the twenty-fifth is *puruṣa*. In classical Sāṃkhya, this word refers to something like individual consciousness. Although usually spoken of in the singular, it is here sometimes explicitly plural,[38] but this plurality seems to have arisen relatively late in the psychologisation of the macrocosmic Puruṣa presented in the Puruṣasūkta. On the one hand *puruṣa* is contentless, inactive, detached, and isolated, a mere witness and enjoyer of nature and the world; yet on the other hand it or he is absolutely fundamental. His passive presence somehow motivates the evolution of *prakṛti*, and salvation lies in achieving perfect discrimination between *prakṛti* and *puruṣa*. This may seem paradoxical, since *prakṛti* contains and evolves into entities such as Intelligence and Mind, which seem to us to fall under consciousness. Luckily we need not here wrestle with such essentially philosophical problems, nor with the many other complexities in the doctrine.[39]

At this point, I would emphasise that, although Sāṃkhya may seem an esoteric aspect of elite culture, such as many anthropologists would prefer to leave to textual specialists, it or elements of it have in fact often come to the attention of fieldworkers. The gunas in particular are extremely widely known: the Sanskrit words and their derivatives can be found in ordinary Hindi dictionaries, and the triadic schema is applied in a wide variety of contexts. Here are a few unsystematically assembled examples. In contemporary Banaras a *śrāddha* ritual performed after a bad death involves the offering of three balls of rice or wheat, which are correlated one for one with the gunas, as well as with colours, metals, and deities (Brahmā, Vishnu, and Śiva, i.e. the Trimūrti).[40] Here, as in Bali,[41] the gunas are also used to classify human personality types or dispositions, and they are sometimes applied to food.[42] In Maharashtra they are used to contrast humans with animals and plants.[43]

Moreover, some anthropologists have given them an important theoretical role. Kondos, who worked in the Central Valley of Nepal, not only relates the gunas to (*inter alia*) the Trimūrti, three forms of the Goddess, and the larger categories of the caste system, but also proposes that the guna scheme is 'far more extensive than hitherto envisaged', and that 'the recurrent guna scheme is involved not just in classification and evaluation but contains the core idea of a world view which is processual in nature'.[44] A good deal of what her informants told her is in fact potted Sāṃkhya. In a comparable manner, when attempting to found a new approach to the sociology of India, Marriott starts by recalling some of the lists so characteristic of Hindu abstract thought; the gunas are the first of his lists and are one of the four around which he builds his argument.[45] The theory he proposes is entirely ahistorical and contains too many arbitrary and subjective linkages to be acceptable, but I think he is looking in the right direction: the gunas do indeed have something to tell us about the structure of Hinduism as an ideology.

Mauss was, of course, well aware of such a major component of Hindu tradition as Sāṃkhya, and in *The person* his half-page treatment of India is largely devoted to it.[46] He would certainly have seen its relevance to the complex of ideas he had discussed in 'Anna-Virāj', which we summarised above as bringing together notions of substance, number, femaleness, and food. As regards substance, Prakṛti has as its final evolutes the gross elements (ether or space, wind, fire, water, earth) that form the matter of the world. As regards number, the very word *sāṃkhya* seems to mean 'enumeration', and although the number ten is not salient, its most obvious factor, five, certainly is.[47] As for the femaleness of Prakṛti, it is not in doubt. Admittedly, the feminine-gender word is quite often replaced by neuter forms (*pradhāna, avyakta* plus *vyakta*), and absolutely no reference is made to sexual relations between her and Puruṣa. However, this lack of emphasis on Prakṛti's sex, which surely reflects the on-going shift from myth to philosophy, is not complete: for instance, *SK* stanza 59 compares her to a female dancer (*nartakī*) performing before Puruṣa. There are also a number of stanzas which present Puruṣa as 'enjoying' Prakṛti, and the verb in question (*bhuj*, noun form *bhoga*) connotes both food and sex, a linkage familiar enough to anthropologists. A more explicit reference to food comes in stanza 57, where Prakṛti's assistance to Puruṣa is compared to a cow feeding its calf. Similarly, in a text which is cited by Mauss (Atharva Veda 8.10), Virāj herself is compared to a cow who is milked.

Two questions now arise. Do the gunas reflect the three functions which Dumézil sees as characteristic of Indo-European ideology? And do they relate to the hypothesis that I have been exploring for some years, namely that, *pace* Dumézil, the ideology was in fact pentadic and included a bifurcated fourth function, whose two halves 'bracket' the classical triad of functions? The rest of the section addresses these two questions.

Dumézil naturally asked himself whether the three gunas reflected or manifested the three functions, but while noting that they were often correlated with representatives of the three functions, he carefully avoided claiming that they were intrinsically or by origin trifunctional. As he said:

> India related the three varṇas [social estates], with their principles, to numerous triads of notions either pre-existing or created ad hoc. These harmonies or correlations, important for the sympathetic [magical NA] action to which the cult tends, are sometimes profoundly meaningful, sometimes artificial and puerile. For example, if the three functions are attached one-for-one to the three gunas...or to the three levels of the cosmos [i.e. meaningfully NA], one also finds them attached with equal forcefulness [but artificially NA] to various Vedic metres and melodies, to various sorts of livestock....[48]

Dumézil later repeated the point when rebutting some misconceived criticism by Gonda, and leaves us in no doubt that for him the gunas are only secondarily linked to the three functions.[49] They do not derive from them.

But here he may be wrong. The two triads resemble each other formally, i.e., in their ordering and valuation, as well as in their colour associations — white, red, and black in that order, except that the third-function colour may also be green or blue.[50] Of course, to show that a triad manifests the three functions one has to show that each element conforms to the definition of the appropriate function, and here there is at least room for argument. In maintaining that the guna-to-function linkage was secondary, Dumézil presumably felt that the fit was too loose. On the other hand, the three gunas have been labelled respectively intelligence stuff, energy stuff, mass stuff,[51] and it is worth lining up these definitions with Dumézil's fullest definitions of the functions.[52] The first function relates to the sacred..., to sovereign power..., and finally more generally, to knowledge and understanding (*la science et l'intelligence*), which at that time were inseparable from the meditation and manipulation of sacred objects: cf. intelligence stuff. The second relates to physical brute force and the uses of force, principally but not solely in warfare: cf. energy stuff. The third includes the important idea of large number, applied not only to goods (*abondance*) but also to the men who compose the body of society (*masse*): cf. mass stuff. The fit is not bad, and I conclude that those who first propounded the gunas were, whether consciously or not, directly expressing or adapting the functional ideology.

The problem can be approached directly by exploring the earliest passages relating to gunas, as was done briefly by Naudou.[53] Drawing on the Upanishads,[54] Naudou saw the gunas not only as reflecting the three functions but also as linked with a considerable number of other triads occurring in the same texts. I doubt some of his arguments,[55] but he needs to be mentioned as the first scholar to interpret the gunas trifunctionally. Moreover, in answering my second question, I hope to show that his interpretation was right, albeit incomplete.

Again and again, as I have argued elsewhere, Dumézilian triads are substructures within pentadic wholes. I give just two examples. Dumézil's theory of the three functions arose in 1938 from his comparison between the three Roman *flamines maiores* (ritual specialists) and the three twice-born social estates. But the flamens are the central members of the *ordo sacerdotum*, which consists of *five* specialists. Again, the myth of origin of the estates in the Puruṣasūkta exhibits a fivefold narrative structure: the three twice-born estates, originating from the mouth, arms, and thighs of Puruṣa, are complemented, not only by the Śūdra or Servants originating from the feet, but also by the notion of totality implicit in the whole body of Puruṣa before his dismemberment. These two additional elements belong respectively, I think, to the negatively and positively valued halves of the fourth function, which is defined as pertaining to what is other, outside or beyond, relative to the classical functions.

The question now becomes: are the three gunas a substructure within a pentadic framework? Given the general salience of pentads in

Sāṃkhya and the total number of principles ($25 = 5 \times 5$), it would not be surprising. But first we should eliminate a dead end. Since twenty of the principles fall neatly into four pentads, and there are five left over (Puruṣa, Prakṛti, Intelligence, Ego, and Mind), one might wonder if this residue is what we are looking for. Certainly not: the five do not form a coherent whole within the philosophy, and cannot be construed four-functionally. The question is rather whether the three gunas that constitute Prakṛti can be seen as bracketed by two other principles.

As regards the positive pole, there is no problem. Outside and beyond the gunas,[56] and superior to them, stands Puruṣa, unique and absolute. As for the negative pole, I have long hesitated. The most obvious candidate is perhaps *buddhi*, Intelligence, since it is enumerated immediately after the principles that sum up the gunas. It stands outside the triad, and is lower valued than they are in the sense that it is a departure from the totality or quasi-totality represented by Prakṛti, and a departure that leads towards the gross elements, Prakṛti's final evolutes. On the other hand, Intelligence is not convincing as the end-point of a pentad, and the devaluation is implicit and slight. On both counts the Ego-principle provides a much better candidate. Firstly, it constitutes a sort of threshold in the evolutive process, since whereas Prakṛti gives rise directly only to Intelligence, and Intelligence only to Ego, Ego gives rise directly both to the group of eleven principles and to the five subtle elements.[57] Secondly, it is definitely devalued, being equated with *abhimāna* 'self-conceit, haughtiness'.[58] If Dumézil-style analysis is to avoid the charge of being arbitrary, it must deal with totalities that are indisputably present as such in the material to be analysed. Convenient though it would be to do so, one cannot simply ignore the fact that the pentadic sequence Puruṣa — three gunas — Ego is interrupted by Intelligence. The difficulty must be faced head on, but it is not insuperable. All authorities now agree that classical Sāṃkhya has a complex history behind it.[59] Like myself, but for different reasons, Hulin seems puzzled by the relative order of Intelligence and Ego in the classical scheme,[60] and suggests in effect that a precursor of the learned concept of *ahaṃkāra*, namely the *mahān ātmā* of *Kaṭha Upanishad* 3.10, formerly came after Prakṛti and before *buddhi* in the sequence. This is the simplest way of dealing with the difficulty, though there may be others.

In other words, the proposal is that not only the gunas as constituents of Prakṛti, but also the larger structure that forms their setting in Sāṃkhya philosophy derive from an application of the Indo-European functional ideology. Exactly what historical processes embedded this five-fold structure within the twenty-five-fold ontology propounded by the *SK* is another matter, and far outside the scope of this essay.

One objection might be that the influence of the Indo-European ideology should be greatest in the earliest period of Indian history, and should lessen later. One would expect it to be clearest in the Vedas, above all in the earlier books of the *Rig Veda*, and less clear in classical Hinduism. But Virāj belongs to the Vedic period, the triune Prakṛti to the later one, and it is on the latter that the analysis has concentrated. However, this objection overrates the importance of the relative dating of texts that originate from the orally transmitted traditions of a nonliterate culture, and underrates the importance of Dumézil's discovery (building on Wikander) of the greater salience of the Indo-European heritage in the epics of classical Hinduism than in the mythology of the Vedas.[61] Much of the heritage simply bypassed the Vedas.

Moreover, even if the more copious later sources provide better opportunities for recognising the Indo-European heritage, once it is clear what to look for the earlier and more cryptic sources may offer more than at first appears. Any account of the origins of Sāṃkhya will cite the above-mentioned *Śvetāśvatara Upanishad* 4.5:

> With the one unborn female, red, white and black,
> Who produces many creatures like herself,
> There lies the one unborn male taking his delight.
> Another unborn male leaves her with whom he has had his delight.[62]

Hume glosses the tri-coloured female as Prakṛti, the first male as Puruṣa, the second as the individual soul, and although not all commentators would agree, at least the five-fold structure is patent.

In the final analysis, the plausibility of the four-functional argument cannot be assessed without taking account of the wider Indo-European picture. A convenient way of summarising such arguments is to draw up a matrix diagram (as below), with one column for each function or half-function and one row for each pentadic context. We referred above to two such contexts, namely the Roman *ordo sacerdotum* (row 1) and the mythic origin of Hindu society (row 2), and we have just added an important part of Sāṃkhya philosophy (row 3).

F4+	F1	F2	F3	F4-
1. rex sacr.	fl. dialis	fl. mart.	fl. quir.	pontifex
2. Puruṣa	his mouth	arms	thighs	feet
3. Puruṣa	*sattva*	*rajas*	*tamas*	Ego

The same format has been used in some previous papers,[63] to explore about twenty contexts, and this mass of material adds weight to the present argument.

An innovation here has been the proposal that in this particular philosophical context, the relation between the bifid fourth function and the classical triad is as male principle to female. It would be premature to generalise, but the question of how the functional ideology relates to gender is obviously important, and there are again resonances to be explored with the ethnography of the Hindu world. For instance, after a death, the expression of grief by males contrasts with its expression by females. The men (superior) are expected to show a calm and aloof autonomy, while the women (inferior, 'mired in materiality') should weep and wail loudly.[64] Compare the contrast between the detached Puruṣa and the material Prakṛti.

Concluding remarks

How would Mauss have reacted to this attempt to develop his ideas? He might have had a niggle of regret that its tendency is to agree with Lévi, and to disagree with himself, on the relative unimportance of the non-Aryan substrate in the Upanishads. In any case, with his prodigious range of knowledge, he would have seen at once that the paper only scratches the surface, that it hardly begins to organise the vast quantities of relevant facts, and in particular, that it does not even attempt the comparison he planned to make with ancient Greece.[65] As regards India, he might have missed a fuller discussion of goddesses. In the Atharva Veda text which presents her as a cow, Virāj is also addressed as Tapodhā 'Concealment',[66] which recalls the later goddess Māyā 'Illusion' — Prakṛti, Māyā, and Śakti are three major forms of the classical Devī, 'The Goddess' par excellence.

Mauss was well aware of deities, many of them female like Prakṛti, who are in some sense triple or triune (three in one, *dreieinig*); his review in 1904 shows that he had enjoyed the discussion of the subject by Usener.[67] I like to think that he would also have enjoyed this attempt to apply his concept of forms of classification to Sanskritic notions of substance, and that he would have seen it as a contribution towards the *sociologie* to which he aspired, a science of social facts combining ethnography with philology and history. Perhaps he would even have revised his judgement that 'Anna-Virāj' was not worth reading.

NOTES

1. M. Mauss, *Sociologie et anthropologie*, Paris, 1966, p. 309. Dictionary definitions of substance include 'the permanent substratum of things, that which underlies phenomena, the material of which a body is formed'.
2. M. Mauss, 'An intellectual self-portrait', this volume. Hubert had died in 1927.
3. N.J. Allen, 'The division of labour and the notion of primitive society: a Maussian approach', *Social anthropology*, vol. 3, 1995, pp. 49-59.

4. M. Mauss, *Oeuvres*, vol. 3, p. 535 [1935].
5. Mauss, *Oeuvres*, vol. 3, pp. 593-600; the reprint often mangles the original, especially, but not only, by omitting diacritics from Sanskrit vocabulary.
6. ŚB 8.1.2.11, trans. J. Eggeling, *The Śatapatha Brāhmaṇa*, part IV, Oxford, 1897, p. 12.
7. What was axiomatic may have been that ideological phenomena need to be related to sociopolitical ones. Perhaps he also has in mind the connection on the one hand between Creation or Cosmogony and totality (God creates the whole Universe), and on the other between royalty and totality (the King represents society as a whole).
8. *Chāndogya Upanishad* 4.3.8 (the 4.1.8 in the text is a slip).
9. H. Falk, *Bruderschaft und Würfelspiel*, Freiburg, 1986, p. 119.
10. The papers were not published until 1945. See *Oeuvres*, vol. 2, p. 161ff.
11. Mauss does not discuss the distinction present in Aristotle between matter (*hulē*) and substance (*ousia* — from the verb 'to be'). In the discussion following his paper he anticipated much that was characteristic of structuralist writing in and around the 1960s: 'The duality of the principles of male and female, high and low, right and left, descent (matrilineal or not), and so on, constitutes the essential character of all cosmogonies.' The North American comparisons he referred to would have included the Omaha — cf. *Oeuvres*, vol. 2, p. 101 [1913].
12. Mauss, 'An intellectual self-portrait', this volume. Cf. M. Fournier, *Marcel Mauss*, Paris, 1994, p. 128.
13. For instance his whole attitude towards religion, and in particular his unease over Durkheim's doctrine of the sacred, may derive from India: 'The distinction of the magical and the religious has never really been made by the Hindus', *Oeuvres*, vol. 1, p. 337 [1898]. Cf. S. Martelli, 'Mana ou sacré: la contribution de Marcel Mauss à la fondation de la sociologie religieuse', *Revue européenne des sciences sociales* 34, 1996, pp. 51-66.
14. Mauss, 'An intellectual self-portrait', this volume. Of Mauss's references to India no doubt the ones that have received most attention come in *The gift* — see most recently A. Michaels, 'Gift and return gift, greeting and return greeting in India: on a consequential footnote by Marcel Mauss', *Numen* 44, 1997, pp. 242-69.
15. D. Paulme, 'Avertissement à la deuxième édition', in Mauss, *Manuel d'ethnographie*, Paris, 1967. If a personal note is permitted, this epithet, combined with the influence of Hocart and Dumont, has helped me considerably in developing my own conception of the field called 'Social anthropology of South Asia'.
16. As he said when criticising Radcliffe-Brown for separating the study of tribal and non-tribal societies, 'there is only one science of social facts', *Oeuvres*, vol. 3, p. 267 [1925].
17. *Oeuvres*, vol. 3, p. 262 [1925]; N.J. Allen, 'The category of the person: a reading of Mauss's last essay', in M. Carrithers, S. Collins and S. Lukes, eds, *Anthropology, philosophy, history*, Cambridge, 1985, p. 27.
18. N.J. Allen, 'Mauss and the categories', to appear in *Durkheimian studies*, 1998. While critical of aspects of Mauss's undertaking, one writer who cites the paper on matter recognises him as a founder figure for those working on the borderline between *ethnologie* and philosophy — F. Zimmermann, *Le discours des remèdes au pays des épices: enquête sur la médecine hindoue*, Paris, 1989, p. 142.
19. *Oeuvres*, vol. 3, p. 367 [1931].
20. *Oeuvres*, vol. 2, p. 463 [1929]; vol. 3, p. 469 [1923].
21. *Oeuvres*, vol. 2, p. 259. One might recall here the well-recognised influence exercised on Durkheim by the historian Fustel de Coulanges, who in studying Graeco-Roman religion in 1864 had drawn on material from the Hindu world because of the Indo-European common heritage — cf. R.A. Jones, 'Durkheim and *La cité antique*', in S.P. Turner, ed., *Emile Durkheim: sociologist and moralist*, London, 1993, pp. 25-51.

22. *Oeuvres*, vol. 2, p. 315 [1925]; vol.3, p. 440 [1933].

23. *Oeuvres*, vol.3, p.548ff. [1937].

24. *Oeuvres*, vol.3, p. 444 [1933]; cf. B. Karsenti, *L'homme total*, Paris, 1997, p. 158ff.

25. Mauss, 'Wette, wedding', *Revue historique de droit français et étranger*, vol. 7, 1928, pp. 331-33.

26. *Oeuvres*, vol. 2, p. 558 [1928]; vol. 3, p. 618 [1920].

27. *Oeuvres*, vol. 2, p. 557 [1928]; vol. 2, p. 159 [1937].

28. N.J. Allen, 'Primitive classification: the argument and its validity', in W.S.F. Pickering and H. Martins, eds, *Debating Durkheim*, London, 1994, pp. 40-65.

29. Trans. R. Needham, *Primitive classification*, London, 1963, p. 78.

30. *RV* 10.90; trans. W.D. O'Flaherty, *The Rig Veda: an anthology*, Harmondsworth, 1981, pp. 29-32.

31. 'Das weibliche Schöpfungsprinzip', K.F. Geldner, *Der Rig-Veda aus dem Sanskrit ins Deutsche übersetzt*, vol. 3, Boston, 1951, p. 287. We can probably distinguish the primeval Puruṣa from his namesake, born from Virāj.

32. O'Flaherty, *Rig Veda*, p. 31. This statement disagrees with Geldner, who regarded the Puruṣa of the *Rig Veda* as unrelated to that of Sāṃkhya.

33. See G.J. Larson, *Classical Sāṃkhya: an interpretation of its history and meaning*, 2nd edn, Delhi, 1979; M. Hulin, *Sāṃkhya literature*, Wiesbaden, 1978.

34. R.S. Bhattacharya and G.J. Larson, *Sāṃkhya: a dualist tradition in Indian philosophy*, Delhi, 1987, p. 43.

35. The image would have appealed to Mauss's sense of the historical workings of *bricolage*, cf. Allen, 'Category of the person', 1985, p. 37. I shall anglicise the frequently occurring and essentially untranslatable *guṇa*, but doubt if I shall achieve consistency in the transcription of entities like *prakṛti*, which are sometimes individualised as persons, sometimes not, and are sometimes indeterminate (cf. the problem of *agni* 'fire' and Agni the Fire God — the Sanskrit script lacks the upper case/lower case distinction).

36. *SK* stanzas 11-20.

37. Larson, *Classical Sāṃkhya*, p. 236.

38. *SK* stanza 18.

39. E.g., its account of causation and transmigration. I also confine attention to the gunas as they relate to *prakṛti*, ignoring their relevance to *buddhi* and *ahaṃkāra*. *SK* stanza 54 gives them macrocosmic correlates, linking them respectively with the upper, middle and lower worlds.

40. J. Parry, *Death in Banaras*, Cambridge, 1994, p. 242 and note.

41. M. Hobart, 'Is God evil?', in D. Parkin, ed., *The anthropology of evil*, Oxford, 1985, p. 187.

42. R.S. Khare, *Cultural reality: essays on the Hindu system of managing foods*, Simla, 1976, pp. 34, 78-85.

43. A.T. Carter, 'Hierarchy and the concept of the person in Western India', in A. Östör, L. Fruzzetti, and S. Barnett, eds, *Concepts of the person: kinship, caste and marriage in India*, Delhi, 1992, p. 122.

44. V. Kondos, 'The triple goddess and the processual approach to the world: the Parbatya case', in M. Allen and S.N. Mukherjee, eds, *Women in India and Nepal*, Canberra, 1982, p. 274.

45. M. Marriott, in *Contributions to Indian sociology*, vol. 23, 1989, pp. 1-39.

46. His plausible comment that the Sāṃkhya term for the Ego-principle is a learned coinage is endorsed by M. Hulin, *Le principe de l'ego dans la pensée indienne classique: la notion d'ahaṃkāra*, Paris, 1978, p. 3.

47. For the arithmetical sophistication apparently implicit in a late Sāṃkhya text, cf. G.J. Larson, 'The format of technical philosophical writing in ancient India: inadequacies of conventional translations', *Philosophy east and west*, vol.34, 1980,

pp. 375-80, who notes that there are twenty-five prime numbers between 1 and 100 and suggests a link between Puruṣa and zero.

48. G. Dumézil, *L'idéologie tripartie des Indo-européens*, Brussels, 1958, p. 19.
49. G. Dumézil, *Les dieux souverains des Indo-européens*, Paris, 1977, p. 253.
50. Dumézil, *Idéologie tripartie*, p. 25, and *La courtisane et les seigneurs colorés*, Paris, 1983, p. 17.
51. S. Dasgupta, *A History of Indian Philosophy*, vol. I, Cambridge, 1922, p. 244.
52. Dumézil, *Idéologie tripartie*, p. 19.
53. J. Naudou, 'L'analyse ternaire de la nature dans la pensée indienne', *Revue de l'histoire des religions* 197, 1980, pp. 7-26.
54. *Chānd. Up.* 6.4.3ff., *Śvet. Up.* 4.5.
55. The same applies to a recent work which focuses on triads in the Vedas — B.K. Smith, *Classifying the universe: the ancient Indian varṇa system and the origins of caste*, New York, 1994.
56. *SK* stanza 17.
57. *SK* stanza 22.
58. *SK* stanza 24.
59. E.H. Johnson, *Early Sāṃkhya*, London, 1937.
60. Hulin, *Le principe de l'ego*, 1978, p. 83.
61. N.J. Allen, 'Hinduism as Indo-European: cultural comparativism and political sensitivities', to appear in J. Bronkhorst and M.M. Deshpande, eds, *Aryan and non-Aryan in South Asia: evidence, interpretation and ideology*, Michigan.
62. Trans. R.E. Hume, *The thirteen principal Upanishads*, 2nd edn, London, 1931. The word *aja* 'unborn' also means 'goat', which is preferred by some translators.
63. Notably in 'Hinduism, structuralism and Dumézil', to appear in E. Polomé, ed., *Varia Indo-Europea*. Using arguments independent of the functions, I have also tried to show the Indo-European roots of yoga, a branch of Hindu philosophy to which Sāṃkhya is closely allied — see 'The Indo-European prehistory of yoga', to appear in *International journal of Hindu studies*, 1998.
64. Parry, drawing on his fieldwork in Banaras — this volume, his note 91.
65. The comparison between Sāṃkhya and Greek philosophy, especially that of Pythagoras and Plato, goes back to the first substantial paper on the Hindu doctrine, and there are brief references even earlier. See chap. 8 in H.T. Colebrooke, *Essays on history, literature and religions of ancient India*, Delhi, 1977 [1823].
66. *AV* 8.10.28, trans. W.D. Whitney, ed. C.R. Lanman, *The Atharva Veda Saṃhitā*, Cambridge, Mass. 1905, vol. 2, p. 515.
67. In his review Mauss cites in Latin: *Hermes omnia solus et ter unus*, 'Hermes — all things in one and thrice unique.' This is the last line of Martial *Ep.* 5.24 (see H. Usener, *Dreiheit: ein Versuch mythologischer Zahlenlehre*, Hildesheim, 1966, p. 36). The epigram is addressed not to the god but to a gladiator who bore the god's name, and it parodies a hymn — see H.S. Versnel, 'A parody on hymns in Martial V 24 and some trinitarian problems', *Mnemosyne*, no. 27, 1974, pp. 365-405. Usener argues that the line implies a customary view of divine being as comprehended in three gods.

Chapter 12

THE STUDY OF TECHNIQUES AS AN IDEOLOGICAL CHALLENGE:

TECHNOLOGY, NATION, AND HUMANITY IN THE WORK OF MARCEL MAUSS

Nathan Schlanger

It is frequently said of Marcel Mauss, by critics and admirers alike, that he was something of an inconsistent genius, all too prone to let his 'fulgurating insights' dissipate and fade away through lack of discipline and concentration. While this portrayal is generally accurate, we must acknowledge that there was one topic of research in which Mauss consistently invested the best of his conceptual and didactic efforts. Starting around 1920 and up to 1941 — that is, from the time when he became a somewhat reluctant standard-bearer of the Durkheimian school until the very end of his active career — hardly a year passed in which Mauss did not write or lecture on the topic of technology: the study of techniques, practices, and products from anthropological and sociological perspectives. Together with two full-length articles and numerous comments, notes, and digressions throughout his major writings, Mauss dedicated to the topic a year-long lecture series, at both the Institut d'ethnologie and the Collège de France.[1]

To better appreciate the importance of this work, a few words must be said on the meanings of the terms 'techniques' and 'technology'. In their common Anglo-Saxon usage, both these terms have substantive connotations related to tools, artefacts, material culture, the transformation of matter, etc. However, 'techniques' is usually applied in 'low-tech' ethnographic or artisanal situations, while 'technology' is invariably reserved to the rationalised and science-based forms of production characteristic of modern postindustrial societies. This widespread distinction is not the one followed here. Like virtually all French-speaking scholars of his times, Mauss used 'technology' (*technologie*) in its grammatical sense, as a composite term designating a 'logos' or discourse about techniques. While 'techniques' refers for Mauss to the whole range of material practices, objects, and skills devised and used by human beings in their interactions with their surroundings and with each other, 'technology' is the systematic body of scientific theory and practice by which these phenomena are identified, described, analysed, and interpreted. Technology is thus to techniques what musicology is to music, what criminology is to crime, indeed what sociology or anthropology are to society and to humanity: the study, in relation to its subject.[2]

Following this terminological distinction has two important implications. First, by using technique as a single substantive term, it becomes possible to assess for its worth the ethnocentric divide which supposedly separates primitive 'techniques' and modern 'technology', and eventually show that, for example, there may be as much systematic knowledge in basketry manufacture as there is skilled *bricolage* in experimental physics. Next, by restricting the term technology to the study of techniques, it becomes easier to acknowledge that technology is itself a full-fledged scientific discipline. Besides having its own history, methods of enquiry, and explanatory ambitions, this field also raises distinct intellectual and ideological challenges which effectively place it at the very heart of the social sciences.

These salutary implications can readily be perceived in Mauss's contribution. To begin with, and most obviously, the body of writing he produced over the years goes a long way to confirm that Mauss is important for technology, for the scientific study of techniques from anthropological and sociological perspectives. The evocative potency of such concepts as 'body techniques' (*techniques du corps*) or 'traditional effective actions' (*actes traditionnels efficaces*) has long been recognised and exploited by Mauss's students and readers, ranging from Haudricourt and Leroi-Gourhan through to Cresswell and Lemonnier.[3] In marked contrast, Anglo-Saxon scholars have remained almost completely oblivious to this aspect of Mauss's work. This is so partly because his main theoretical and methodological statements have not yet been translated (except for the 'Techniques of the body'), but also, more importantly, because studies of techniques and material culture were themselves long considered to be marginal, if not discreditable, to the goals and practices of mainstream anthropology.[4] With this impoverishing restriction in the process of being lifted, it is high time to acquaint a wider readership with the tenets and achievements of Mauss's work in the field of 'technology'. An understanding of Mauss's contribution is not simply indispensable for making contact with the 'anthropology of techniques' and the 'cultural technology' developed on the other side of the Channel. As we will amply appreciate in the coming pages, the insights and interrogations contained in his technology are well able to inform and to stimulate further research in these directions.

Together with that, there is another possibly even more fundamental lesson to be learned from Mauss's contribution. It is, quite simply, that technology was important for Mauss. Inconsistent genius as he may have otherwise been, shifting with allegedly detrimental haste from 'the gift' to 'the notion of the person' to 'the obligatory expression of sentiments', technology was one topic to which he repeatedly returned. Not only did he consistently urge that we give to technical phenomena 'the formidable place they deserve' as 'a special and very eminent part of sociology', not only did he caution against the neglect of the subject, he was also ready and willing to invest in its elaboration and to pursue its implications.[5] As a confirmation, we need only record that Mauss's interest in techniques and their study was in itself a radical thematic departure, which cannot be readily aligned with his prior professional concerns with classification, ritual or religion, or for that matter with his participation in the mapping of the sociological domain at large. On the contrary, discussions of techniques and technology were by and large ignored or dispensed with in mainstream Durkheimian sociology, and all the more so once Durkheim had begun to shift his research interests towards the collective representations and effervescent rituals of primitive societies. This idealist orientation in no way compels the automatic neglect of technological considerations, but it so happens that such considerations are missing, and at times glaringly so, from both the essay on 'Primitive classification' and the dualist masterpiece that is *The elementary forms of religious life*.[6] Whatever the reasons for this state of affairs, it can be advanced that techniques and their study had little role to play, at either practical or theoretical levels, in the sociological framework under which Mauss operated and which he undertook to develop.

If so, if Mauss's interest in the topic did not grow out of the research tradition of which he formed part, how and why did he come to 'discover' the anthropological importance, indeed centrality, of techniques and their study? The fact that we cannot invoke here a preexisting pattern of 'internal' disciplinary logic is actually helpful in focusing this question, since it invites us to try and situate this breakthrough within the specific historical, intellectual, and cultural circumstances which informed and motivated it. In this light, the argument I develop in this article is the following. Mauss's newly developed interest in techniques and their study emerged, in chronological, conceptual, and existential terms, from his involvement in what may be conveniently called *the fieldwork of modernity* — that is, the life-shattering experiences of the Great War and the intense 'intellectual organisation of political passions' that ensued (to use Julien Benda's phrase).[7] To substantiate this broad-ranging proposal, I will distinguish and discuss here two such 'intellectually passionate' themes: they are the postwar crisis of humanity, and the associated problem of nationality. In both cases, my main concern will be to show how, in its underlying aims as well as its practical implications, the technology elaborated by Mauss throughout the 1920s and 1930s enabled him to confront and engage in some of the key ideological challenges of his turbulent times.

Techniques and the crisis of humanity — between *homo faber* and *l'homme total*

On both patriotic and personal grounds, Mauss did not hesitate to leave his pacifism behind and volunteer for the front as soon as the First World War was declared. As he pointed out, the unprecedented combination of mechanised brutality and routinised anxiety he endured during the following years left their permanent intellectual and existential marks on him. Since Mauss was obviously not alone in this, an initial appreciation of the ways by which other members of his generation came to terms with this experience will help us understand his subsequent 'discovery' and valorisation of techniques.[8]

Together with the demographic, political, and economic perturbations that followed it, the Great War generated a veritable flood of emotional, artistic, and intellectual responses. Among these can be singled out a substantial body of eschatological writings, explicitly concerned with the causes and consequences of this catastrophic trauma. *The decline of the West* or *The end of the Renaissance* are some of the better known titles of this literature, whose stylistic and topical diversity is underscored by the pervasive leitmotif of doubt, despondency, and disintegration.[9] Within the dimensions of this genre, the themes of techniques and the machine were subjected to particularly probing apocalyptic discussions: now that their efficiency as agents of death and destruction was made so evident, their inescapable presence throughout the reaches of life could be seen as a tangible objectification of the moral crisis, and even as one of its original causes. With the examples of over-industrialised America and Bolshevik Russia looming large, it was felt by many in Europe that humanity, for all its impressive material achievements (if not because of them) had dismally failed to improve its present condition and future prospects. Not only did civilised human beings insist on behaving like an uncontrollable swarm of insects irresistibly attracted to the flames (as Valéry put it), they also appeared bent on accelerating the process of their consummation through their self-devised machinations.[10]

A particularly eloquent discussion of techniques can be found in the essay to which I will give particular attention here; Henri Bergson's *The two sources of morality and religion*.[11] When he finally completed his book in 1932, the ailing Collège de France philosopher was long past the peak of his extraordinary prewar popularity, but the influence he exerted over French intellectual, scientific, artistic, and political life was still considerable and multifaceted. Bergson's authoritative standing ensured that his reflections would continue to be read and discussed by admiring disciples as well as virulent detractors.[12] So far as techniques were concerned, Bergson argued in *The two sources* that it was instrumental ingenuity and inventiveness that enabled human beings to become what we are. These same abilities now threaten to run out of control, to wreak havoc and to spread emptiness. Industrialisation and mechanisation have encouraged artificiality and luxury, widened the gap between town and country, transformed the relations between labour and capital, and, in general, fostered a growing disparity between 'the human dimension' and the enormity of its technical creations: 'In this bloated body, the soul remains as it was, too small now to fill it, too weak to direct it'. Indeed, clamoured Bergson, we desperately need a 'deeper soul' (*supplément d'âme*), we need a *mystique* to oversee, control, and moralise the *mécanique* if the world is ever to fulfil its universal vocation and become, as he asserted at the conclusion of his essay, 'a machine for the making of gods'.[13]

As this famously ambiguous phrase intimates, Bergson's argument was not limited to the theme of techniques as an uncontrollable monster or 'golem'. As a complement to this classic critique, he also promoted a markedly different conception of techniques, around a reinterpretation of the notion of *Homo faber*. When it first appeared in the 1907 *Evolution créatrice*, *Homo faber* could well be understood in a relatively weak sense, as a diagnostic classificatory feature distinguishing humanity from animality.[14] In the 1932 *Two sources*, however, it became clear that Bergson conceived of *Homo faber* in a far stronger ontological sense, as an essential and constitutional attribute of humanity itself. As he argued, civilisation is but a superficial, acquired veneer: scratch it, and you will reveal behind it natural humanity — a natural being who is inherently moral because morality comes from nature, from biology and not from reason, from lived intuition and not from detached intellect. This natural morality has as its purpose the continuation of the original form of life, when human beings lived in 'closed societies' — self-centred and belligerent societies where the 'aberration' of democracy was unknown, and where cohesion was related to the need to exclude others: 'Humanity might have civilised itself, society might have been transformed [but] the organic tendencies of social life have remained what they were at the origin ... It is for the simple and closed society that the original and fundamental moral structure of man is made'.[15]

For Bergson, the leading members of these original closed societies are privileged and superior individuals: the margin of instinct that remains in their subconscious shelters them from the egoistic and destructive excess of intelligence, and it is this intuition that guides their creative activities, their vital thrust, their wilful fabrication of matter — far from being mere *Homo sapiens*, they are, in the strong sense of the word, *Homo faber*. Thus, Bergson proceeded in *The two sources* to divide techniques along an ethical fault-line. He attached negative, destructive, and amoral properties to the techniques associated with intelligence, rationality, civilisation and modernity, and he attributed positive, revitalising, and moral qualities to techniques associated with individual organic tendencies, vital forces, mystique, and volition.[16]

Mauss reacted to this thesis in two distinct ways. At a formal and immediate level, he pursued the long-standing confrontation initiated between Durkheim and Bergson over the epistemological merits of intuitionism and objectivism.[17] In his 1933 panoramic overview of French sociology, Mauss singled out Bergson and his latest book as being one of the multiplying forces opposing Durkheimian sociology: 'Bergson ... relegates the facts studied by sociologists to the domain of the "closed", of the frozen (*figé*): he reserves to psychology, to philosophy, and even to the philosophy of mysticism, all that is 'open', vital, really psychic and creative in the realm of moral and religious life.'[18] But Mauss was not simply responding to the challenge as a defender of Durkheimian orthodoxy. For lack of competence or more probably inclination, he did not pursue his criticism in the abstract philosophical terms Durkheim would have preferred. Likewise, he did not himself seek to explore the roots of Bergson's views in the *Lebensphilosophie* of Schopenhauer or Nietzsche, and he left it to such scathing critics as Julien Benda to expose the political and moral implications of Bergson's pragmatic anti-intellectualism.[19] Over and above these overt and punctual reactions, Mauss responded to the whole of Bergson's *oeuvre* also at a deeper, substantive level — a level that, crucially, bore upon his deeply felt experiences of the Great War. It was with his technology, with the study of traditionally efficacious actions (*actes traditionnels efficaces*) which he now advocated, that

Mauss sought to overturn Bergson's individualist and mystical *Homo faber* with a rationalist and humanist conception of the whole human being, *l'homme total*.

To begin with, Mauss was in no doubt about the inherently social, rather than individual, nature of techniques. Granted, the term *Homo faber* had the merit of claiming a place of honour for techniques in the history of humankind. Nevertheless, this formula could be used only on the crucial condition that 'it does not denote a creative quality (*vertue créatrice*) which strongly resembles the soporific property of opium, but rather a characteristic trait of life *in common*, and not of *the individual and profound life of the spirit*'.[20] Mauss was even more clear-cut in another essay, where he argued that 'the Bergsonian idea of creation is actually the precise opposite of the technical (*technicité*)', that is creation from matter which human beings have not themselves created, but which they adapt and transform, guided by collective effort.[21] Indeed, 'the invention of the movement and of the tool, the tradition of its usage, usage itself, and the practical arts are essentially social'. What needs to be explained — he goes on to argue — is 'the extent to which all social life depends on techniques'.[22]

To flesh out this fundamental interdependence by which techniques create and mediate social relations, and thereby to combat Bergson's vitalist tendencies, Mauss invoked the notion of tradition. Instead of being some sort of organic tendency, a form of species memory to be revealed beneath the superficial veneer of civilisation, techniques are for Mauss traditional because they are learned, acquired, transmitted. Learning and carrying out techniques takes place in a collective context, a context which forms and informs the social constitution of its practitioners. 'Each traditional practice which has a form, and which is transmitted by this form, is to a certain degree symbolic. When a generation transmits to the next the science of its gestures and of its manual acts, there is as much authority and social tradition in this transmission as there is in linguistic transmission.'[23]

To further argue that gestural and manual actions are significant because they are both symbolically and physically efficacious, Mauss went literally to the heart of the matter: the body itself. Our 'most natural' daily actions — walking, sleeping, eating — are acts that are mounted by the collective, that form part of the social make-up of the individual, that are open to approval, recognition, and evaluation. In advancing this argument, Mauss was in no way oblivious to the biological foundation of the human being. However, what attracted his attention about the organic body was not the vitalist and teleological thrust that Bergson sought to identify in it, but rather, more prosaically, its physiology; the coordination of articulated motions by which it functions and by which it embodies and conveys meaning. Indeed, in so far as they vary with individuals and societies, with education, fashion, and prestige, these efficacious bodily acts confirm the social nature of the *habitus*.[24]

Just as Mauss undertook to socialise the organic endowment of the living body, so he attempted to restore the reasonable nature of its thinking activities. In view of Bergson's ostensibly anti-intellectual conception of *Homo faber* — engaged in purely instinctive creative action — we can better appreciate the links forged by Mauss between techniques and reason. It was now fashionable, he wrote in 1927, to interrogate sociology on 'the origins of reason' — a fashion actually launched some twenty-five years earlier with the famous essay on 'Primitive classification' coauthored with Durkheim. But now, contrary to 1903, Mauss argues that the origin of the categories was not only institutional or religious, but also — as in the case of *number* or *space* — technical. Thus, much more needs to be known about the role of weaving, basketry, or the potter's wheel in the origins of geometry, arithmetic, and mechanical sciences.[25] In a complementary way, Mauss stressed here and in his other writings those aspects of knowledge and of consciousness deployed and acquired by technical actions. To weave, to navigate a canoe, to construct a spear, to set a trap — all are activities which suppose and at the same time generate knowledge, knowledge which is practical rather than discursive in its nature, without being for that any less social.[26]

As can be seen, then, Mauss did not put in opposition to each other the rational and the irrational in human life. In technical matters as well as in others, 'The human being makes reasonable things out of unreasonable principles, and uses sensible principles to accomplish absurdities ... these are however the beginnings of great social institutions.'[27] Or, put even more forcefully, in the language of the time, 'Man creates and at the same time he creates himself; he creates at once a means of livelihood, purely human things, and his thoughts inscribed in these things. Here is elaborated true practical reason.'[28] There is in this statement an echo of Marx's conception of *praxis* (with which Mauss grappled on several occasions), but it also contains an evident reply to Bergson's irrationalism. For Mauss, techniques are not the expression of an individual will to power, nor an instrument to achieve mastery over nature. If they are 'a tactic for living', to use Spengler's phrase, they are a tactic for living, thinking, and striving in common; they are above all means and mediums for the production and reproduction of social life. Likewise the practitioner of techniques, in the course of being social, is as much *Homo sapiens* as *Homo faber*; far from being some Nietzschean *Übermensch*, this practitioner is above all *l'homme total*.

Alongside its epistemological and ontological dimensions, the Maussian concept of *l'homme total* possesses also an 'existential' facet that needs to be recognised. In effect, Mauss's 'discovery' of the totality of the human condition as a physical, psychological, and social nexus seems to have occurred alongside his recognition of the significance of techniques, and following similar formative experiences. Given his attitude, it makes perfect sense for Mauss to recognise just how difficult it is to distinguish the traditional efficacious acts of technique, magic, or religion — they are all performed by *l'homme total*.[29] At a methodological level, this provides another reason why all technical activities should be observed in their entirety — who does what, when, with whom, how are tools used, in what sequence, how is the tie worn, how does the wearing of shoes affect walking, how is the gait that ensues subject to evaluation and approbation, indeed how techniques, objects, and activities work together in a manner that is both efficacious and meaningful. To say that 'the tool is nothing when it is not handled', is to stress that nothing can be understood if it is not in relation to the whole, and recognised to be changing and dynamic.[30] Thus, to follow the trajectory of transformations involved in all technical acts is to gain entry into a process of ongoing construction, mediation, and re-combination involving material, social, and symbolic elements.

Under the premises of this totality, the object itself becomes a document that informs at many levels, that can be itself 'the proof of the social fact'.[31] This particular conception of the object is all the more interesting in that it links the anthropology of Mauss — and more specifically his technology — with various surrealist activities of the 1920s and 1930s. By drawing attention to the intricate interpenetration of the technical, the symbolic, the materially effective, indeed the reasonable and the arbitrary, Mauss rejected prevailing fixations with the aesthetic, the representational, and the extraordinary. By giving prominence to the functional, the representative, the ordinary, Mauss sought, however implicitly, to transcend the prevailing dichotomy between Low and High culture. Indeed, Mauss could well be said to have promoted (if not actually inspired) a version of what Bataille has called, in the well-known avant-garde review *Documents*, a *bas matérialisme*. It must, however, be stressed that beyond the commonalities of themes and of authors juxtaposed in *Documents*, there remain important differences between the author of 'Les techniques du corps' and that of 'Le gros orteil'. Much as he willingly paid extraordinary attention to the ordinary and magnified the mundane, much as he recognised the inseparability of the symbolic and the practically efficacious, Mauss did not for that set out to be unconventional, let alone to subvert or to destabilise established orders and patterns of meaning.[32]

In fact, we have already gathered that his primary intention was redemptive, almost therapeutic. While so-called 'primitives' had previously been valorised by the Durkheimians for their primeval status, they are now studied because 'They defamiliarise us and teach us to think otherwise than as *Homo Sorbonnais* or *Oxonois*'.[33] Likewise their activities, their techniques, the range of objects which they produce and use — and which they know so well to give, to receive, and to return — serve a new purpose. They help us 'civilised' occidentals to expose and repel the ill-founded sentiments of alienation, decadence, and loss of bearing enforced on us by the enormity of historical events, indeed they help us transcend the chimera of disintegration with an ideal of wholeness and of plenitude.[34] In contrast to many apocalyptic responses to the Great War, the message articulated and expressed by Mauss through his technology is resolutely upbeat, as if techniques were a means of recovery, indeed of re-enchantment. Far from being overrun by our uncontrollable techniques, far from crying out for a mystical 'deeper soul' to alleviate our existential angst, far from glorifying in our instinctive precivilised will to create power, it is in our traditional efficacious actions that we will be able to find practical help and moral solace:

> The history of human techniques [*industries*] is effectively the history of civilisation, and vice versa. The spread and discovery of techniques [*arts industriels*] ... it is this that, via the development of societies, has enabled the development of reason and sensibility, as well as of volition ... It is this that renders human beings equal to each other and worries the gods; it is this that, without any doubt, will save humanity from the moral and material crisis in which it struggles.[35]

Techniques and the problem of nationality — purity and synthesis

It may appear somewhat naive to place such faith in the salutary potential of techniques, but Mauss's pronouncements cannot for that be dismissed as the inconsequential daydreams of an unreformed worshipper of Progress. To do so would not only keep us from appreciating that Mauss promoted the humanity of techniques as a redeeming feature of the postwar 'total human being'. It would also blind us to the fact that his technology was thoroughly implicated in yet another 'intellectually passionate' debate, it too exacerbated by the Great War and its geo-political aftermath. In effect, the study of techniques as advocated by Mauss also bore upon the increasingly urgent problem of the nation, its making and its identity. In this respect, technology was important for Mauss precisely because it enabled him to convey in theoretical and empirical terms his preferred conception of the nation, as a synthesis of common values and shared civic duties.

During the interwar years, this republican model of the nation was coming under sustained criticism from various political, intellectual, and indeed anthropological quarters. Whereas the idea of the nation had strong liberal connotations throughout the nineteenth century, designed to instil sentiments of liberty, equality, and allegiance among the postrevolution citizens of the state, the successive political and economic upheavals of the early Third Republic — chief among them the Boulanger crisis and the Dreyfus affair — brought about a gradual redefinition of nationalism in right wing and reactionary terms, as an emotive concept explicitly designed to counter enlightenment universalism with an overpowering sense of group identity and territorial affiliation.[36] As Charles Maurras, a leading intellectual of the right, defined it: 'The nation is not the sum total or the majority of the adult individuals who happen to be at a certain time in the country. The nation is the people, organised in families, in corporations, in communes, in provinces, united in accordance with traditional customs and in solidarity with past and future generations'.[37]

The staunchly republican and pro-Dreyfusard Durkheimians of the Nouvelle Sorbonne found this conception of the nation, with the opportunities for exclusion and discrimination it entailed, thoroughly objectionable. Nonetheless, the conception gathered increasing support among other intellectuals and scientists, and notably those associated with the prestigious Société d'anthropologie de Paris. The Society, created in the mid nineteenth century by Paul Broca to promote the positive 'natural history' of man, initially had strong materialist and antimonarchist leanings. By the first decades of the century, however, many of its members had veered towards a more conservative and even reactionary stance. Under the leadership of Louis Marin, himself a right-wing parliamentarian as well as a career anthropologist, the ethnographic and folkloristic study of the 'traditional customs' of various '*ethnies*' and '*civilisations*' took on many of the nationalist and essentialist connotations valorised by Maurras and like-minded thinkers. It is indeed no coincidence that Marin published his *Questionnaire d'ethnographie* in 1925, the very year when Mauss, Lévy-Bruhl, and Rivet established the Institut d'ethnologie. The professional rivalry between these institutions corresponded to deep-rooted ideological and political divergences over the concept of the nation and its foundations: civic and participatory, or on the contrary territorial, genealogical, or indeed racial.[38]

These divergences were notably played out in the field of technology. In this respect, the work of one of Marin's most active protégés, the Swiss-born and medically trained Georges Montandon, deserves special mention. Montandon acquired his ill fame during the Vichy regime, when he eagerly put his expertise in physical anthropology at the service of the infamous *Commissariat aux affaires juives* and of Nazi racist policies in general. But Montandon's increasingly virulent anti-Semitism should not detract attention from his anthropological contributions, which were actually well known and influential during the early 1930s. Indeed, his 1934 ethnographic manual was at that time unique, and therefore frequently used, *faute de mieux*, even by Mauss and his students.[39]

In the first part of this manual, bearing on *ethnographie cyclo-culturelle*, Montandon provided an articulate (if not always accurate) review of current anthropological theories, including a rejection of Durkheiman sociology and an endorsement, with some idiosyncratic modifications, of the claims and achievements of the German *Kulturkreise* school. The second part, entitled *Traité d'ergologie systématique*, contained the most comprehensive survey of ethnographic techniques available in French. Organised along the general lines of Marin's *Questionnaire*, this five hundred-page text was mostly descriptive, but it also raised a number of theoretical points. For our present purposes, the most telling claim is undoubtedly this:

> It will be an error, in the technological domain as much as in any other, to believe that the customs of primitives and savages are a threshold which we have occupied and then moved on. Their ways are often different and divergent from those followed by the occidental civilisation. The indigenous procedures of fabrication, construction ... etc., are *sui generis*. When the lineage of the constructors who had the secret [of these techniques] becomes extinct, the procedures they used are definitively lost.[40]

Needless to say, Montandon was not perturbed by the disappearance of 'primitive' crafts and peoples, a state of affairs he saw as biologically inevitable and even welcome. There were however two clear implications in his work. First, and precisely because of their alleged *sui generis* nature, technical practices and products could serve as apparently faithful markers of the extension and limits of different ethnic groups.[41] Next, it follows that the late coming 'occidentaloid civilisation' was not only absolutely superior in technical, social, and moral terms, it also owed nothing whatsoever to those 'primitives' and 'savages' who preceded it or who still survive in the colonies. Montandon's eccentricities and extremism notwithstanding, his work appears to have expressed a prevailing world-view among conservative anthropologists of the time. For them, the processes of evolution, of civilisation, and of nation-formation were primarily processes of distillation, concentration, and purification — in the realm of technical activities and objects, in the realm of customs and institutions, and indeed in the realm of biology and race.

Returning at this point to Mauss, we can understand that the message he sought to promote with his own technology would be of an altogether different sort. Before we examine the unfolding of Mauss's arguments, however, it must be noted that they were actually set within the same diffusionist anthropological paradigm as that followed by Montandon. Since this paradigm is usually considered to be ideologically and ethically antithetical to the kind of message Mauss aimed to promote, his somewhat paradoxical relationship to it requires explanation. Mauss actually undertook most of his anthropological work in a Durkheimian evolutionist frame of mind,[42] and this no doubt rendered him sceptical of many diffusionist claims and results, notably as advanced by members of the *Kulturkreise* school. To summarise, Mauss's main objections were that these scholars failed to combine the study of elements with the study of forms, that their views on the topic of imitation were far too naive and reminiscent of those promoted by G. Tarde, Durkheim's erstwhile antagonist, that they overlooked the problem of refusals of innovations, and more generally that they failed to appreciate the systemic and holistic character of civilisations. In addition, he considered that these scholars enforced an unwarranted distinction between primitive and modern, and that they deprived ethnology of any sociological content by reducing it to the study of areas and layers.[43]

And yet, despite and alongside these apparently damning criticisms, it remains the case that Mauss did not reject diffusionism as such. Besides his careful monitoring of the writings of its advocates, he also dedicated considerable constructive attention to diffusionism in several of his own essays, as well as in his well-attended lecture series. While expressing his misgivings, Mauss also retained many of the outlooks, expressions, and methods used by the diffusionists, and he notably endorsed the collection of series of objects and the drawing of distribution maps. What is more, Mauss also actively encouraged his students and colleagues (among them Haudricourt, Leroi-Gourhan, Métraux, and Rivet) to engage in diffusionist studies.[44]

This endorsement may have to do with the perceptible decline of the evolutionist paradigm, but it can also be understood in the light of the importance of diffusionist studies in conservative anthropology, in France and abroad. Quite simply, Mauss recognised that it was there — in the study of traits, layers, and spatial distribution — that the scientific claims of nationalist ideologies were being played out. In order to assess and contest in their own terms the various claims advanced, Mauss accepted the diffusionist framework as the ideological battle-ground for the promotion and justification of national conceptions.[45] Both the thrust of his position and the role played by technology in its elaboration are encapsulated in the following passage, extracted from the posthumously published essay on 'La Nation' written shortly after the 1918 Treaty of Versailles.

'Some are so certain that this thing they call civilisation is a national fact that they make of it the basis of their territorial claims. It is almost comic to see poorly known and badly studied facts of folklore being presented before the Peace Conference as a proof that such and such nation should extend here or there because one still finds in it such and such form of dwelling or this or that bizarre usage.'[46]

Mauss's awareness of the political stakes surrounding anthropological studies of civilisation could not be clearer, but his characterisation of these facts of folklore as 'poorly known and badly studied' should not mislead us as to his intentions. His argument was that once these various forms and usages *are* well known and well studied by adequate ethnographic and technological means, they can serve to *defuse* rather than strengthen would-be territorial claims — they can confirm that 'this thing called civilisation' is by its nature an *international* phenomenon, and indeed that nations are not the purified products of organic development or immemorial traditions, but rather the creators of these distinctive traditions, through continuing contacts and admixtures.

Modern nations, as Mauss deplored in this key essay, tend to have an exaggerated and indeed illusory belief in *their* civilisation, always considered to be the first and the best. They have a veritable 'fetishism' of their literature, their arts, their language, and their institutions, and they portray their techniques as if they had themselves invented them single-handedly. In fact, it is simply erroneous to consider these elements as 'the products of national genius by virtue of some sort of sociological vitalism'. However distinctive, all these traits and customs emerge from the milieu of other societies, since all societies are to some degree immersed in a shared pool of civilisation (*bain de civilisation*). Pursuing his arguments in terms highly reminiscent of Durkheim's 1893 'organic solidarity' thesis, Mauss asserted that with the passage of time all nations became increasingly open, in moral and material terms, to each other, continuously augmenting the quality, quantity, and intensity of their interactions. Indeed, 'contrary to the absurd reticences of the *littérateurs* and the nationalists, one cannot stress enough the importance of technical borrowings, and the human advantages that ensue'.[47]

Mauss seems to have anticipated some of Montandon's *sui generis* claims when he noted a few years later that techniques, like all social phenomena, are arbitrary and particular to the society which engenders them. That granted, he crucially added: 'But at the same time, more than any other social phenomenon, [techniques] are able to transcend the limits of societies, they are eminently borrowable ... From earliest times they have been open to trade and imitation ... they are the expansive social thing *par excellence*. By their nature, techniques tend to generalise and multiply themselves among people.

They are the most important factor among the causes, the means and the ends of what are called civilisations, and also of progress, not only social but also human'.[48]

In his contribution to the 1929 colloquium on *La civilisation, le mot et l'idée* organised by Febvre, Mauss brought home the implications of this conception. Well aware that Marin and his colleagues had attempted to make of *'civilisations'* the specific objects of their nationalist studies, Mauss argued that facts and phenomena of civilisations are international rather than national, and indeed that civilisations themselves are a sort of 'hyper-social system of societies'. Working against a 'simplistic history [that was] naively political and unconsciously abstract and nationalist', Mauss aimed to demonstrate in concrete ways that nations and civilisations are the ever-developing products of transfers and interactions. A clear example of this stance is embodied in Mauss's admiring exclamation, *à propos* the diversity of styles at the temples of Angkor: 'Already a miscegenation (*métissage*), as magnificent as it is unique.' Both the transfer of the term *métissage* from its racial discourse, and its evident valorisation, could not be more significant. They confirm that Mauss envisioned a free flowing and generative admixture of an increasingly voluminous and important stock of traits and forms, a common stock which is now resolutely cross-cultural and all-embracing, creating the possibility of new forms of civilisation in which once marginal populations now have the scope to contribute, to give as well as to receive. Fully attentive to the cultural movements of his times, Mauss wrote: 'The success of primitive arts, music included, demonstrates that the history of all this will take many unknown roads'.[49]

The routes of this cultural, artistic and indeed artefactual *métissage* may be difficult to predict, but the traffic is essential, and must be maintained. What was anathema to the conservative anthropologists, who sought through their diffusionist studies of traits and techniques to establish their version of 'True France' as the inalterable essence of the land (*terroir*), the destiny, and the blood, was for Mauss a constituent condition of the moral and material progress of the republic, in which there should be as much room for the famous black American cabaret dancer Josephine Baker as there was for the archetypal patriotic martyr Jeanne d'Arc. There is no doubt that the internationalist conception which Mauss promoted throughout his writings of the interwar years did recognise the importance of the material and ideal attachment to the *patrie* and its symbols. Gone was the socialist cosmopolitanism of the prewar years, when class membership was supposed to brush aside national allegiances with uncompromising pacifism. But then, sober and accommodating as it may have become, Mauss's understanding of the nation still remained miles away from the 'closed' and exclusive society portrayed by Bergson and endorsed by conservative circles. For Mauss, the nation was rather an avenue towards an 'open', inclusive society, one that invites opportunities for dialogue and cross-fertilisation, one that values possibilities of contacts and of borrowing.

Techniques, and their anthropological and archaeological study, were in this respect both a model and a confirmation of this ideal. In contradistinction to the conception promoted by Montandon and other conservative anthropologists, technical products and practices are not the markers of innate identity or essence, but rather the embodiment of convergences and interactions. Seen in this light, diffusionist studies should not be limited to revealing the territorial march of national genius from their original core areas — they can rather show that material and moral changes in societies across time and space are best understood in relation to the interactive milieu of other societies, in contact with each other and with their respective physical environments. Diffusionist studies can show that societies, like techniques and like their user *l'homme total,* are made out of synthesis rather than distillation; that their lack of 'purity' is their source of strength, that hybridisation or creolisation is not their worst nightmare but their salvation. Diffusionist studies can show, as Mauss's closest student André-Georges Haudricourt did, that the origins of the plough and the harness are to be found in Central Asia — contrary to the Aryan claims of the *Kulturkreise* school.[50] They can show, as Mauss's colleague Paul Rivet attempted to do, that the American Indian civilisation is a unique synthesis emerging out of several cumulative inputs from the Bering Straits, from Japan, from Malaysia, from Oceania.[51] The case of Rivet — the arch-diffusionist who founded the *Comité de vigilance des intellectuels antifascistes,* and who then fostered the first resistance network in German-occupied France — can serve as an appropriate conclusion, since it amply confirms that the study of techniques is fraught with ideological challenges and opportunities to which we would be well advised to pay heed today. The congruence between Mauss's technological message, and the cultural politics of the Front Populaire was nowhere made as evident as in the corridors of Rivet's Musée de l'Homme, where the display of humanity's technical achievements served as a concrete and intelligible moral lesson for the republican masses to absorb and hopefully to live by.

NOTES

1. For Mauss's articles on techniques and technology, see 'The notion of body techniques', in *Sociology and psychology: essays by Marcel Mauss,* [1935] trans. B. Brewster, London, 1979, p. 95ff.; 'Les techniques et la technologie' [1941], in

Oeuvres, vol. 3, pp. 250-6. For Mauss's lectures, see his *Manuel d'ethnographie* [1947], 3rd edn, Paris, 1989. Mauss's other comments on technology can be found in his 'La nation' [1920], in *Oeuvres*, vol. 3, p. 573ff., at 613ff.; 'Real and practical relations between psychology and sociology' [1924], in *Sociology and psychology*, p. 1ff.; 'Divisions et proportions des divisions de la sociologie' [1927], in *Oeuvres*, vol. 3, p. 178ff. at 194ff.; 'La civilisation: éléments et formes' [1929], in ibid., p. 456ff., *passim*; 'Fragment d'un plan de sociologie générale descriptive', ibid., p. 302ff. at 328ff.; 'Conceptions qui ont précédé la notion de matière' [1939], in *Oeuvres*, vol. 2, pp. 161-68.

2. The terms 'techniques' and 'technology' have received a wide range of meanings and definitions since their first uses in classical Greece. Most of these meanings, as well as current engineering and social sciences uses in English, are discussed in C. Mitcham, *Thinking through technology: the path between engineering and philosophy*, Chicago, 1994; see particularly pp. 143-54. In anthropology, a distinction between techniques as a body of practices or skills and technology as a corpus of knowledge has been proposed by T. Ingold, mostly recently in his 'Tool-use, sociality and intelligence', in K.R. Gibson and T. Ingold, eds, *Tools, language and cognition in human evolution*, Cambridge, 1993, pp. 429-45. A strong argument for maintaining the distinction between techniques (the subject) and technology (its study) is advanced on both historical and conceptual grounds by F. Sigaut; see for example his 'Preface. Haudricourt et la technologie', in A.G. Haudricourt, *La technologie, science humaine: recherches d'histoire et d'ethnologie des techniques*, Paris, 1987, pp. 9-34, esp. 9-10; 'More (and enough) on technology', *History and technology* 2, 1985, pp. 115-32; 'Technology', in T. Ingold, ed., *Companion encyclopedia to anthropology*, London, 1994, pp. 420-59, esp. 422; and see also J.-P. Séris, *La technique*, Paris, 1994.

3. A.G. Haudricourt, 'Relations entre gestes habituels, formes des vêtements et manière de porter les charges', *Revue de géographie humaine et d'ethnologie* 3, 1948, pp. 58-67; 'La technologie, science humaine', *La pensée* no. 115, 1964, pp. 28-35; 'La technologie culturelle: essai de méthodologie', in J. Poirier, ed., *Ethnologie générale*, Paris, 1968, pp. 731-822; see Haudricourt, *La technologie*; A. Leroi-Gourhan, *L'Homme et la matière*, Paris, 1943; *Le geste et la parole*, Paris, 1964. R. Cresswell, 'Les trois sources d'une technologie nouvelle', in J. Thomas and L. Bernot, eds, *Langues et techniques, nature et société. II, Approche ethnologique, approche naturaliste*, Paris, 1977, pp. 21-7; idem, *Prométhée ou Pandore? Propos de technologie culturelle*, Paris, 1996; P. Lemonnier, *Les salines de l'ouest: logique technique, logique sociale*, Lille, 1980; idem, 'The study of material culture today — towards an anthropology of technical systems', *Journal of anthropological archaeology* 5, 1986, pp. 147-86; idem, *Elements for an anthropology of technology*, Ann Arbor, Anthropological papers no. 88, Museum of Anthropology, Michigan, 1992. For a detailed discussion of Mauss's technology, see N. Schlanger, 'Le fait technique total: la raison pratique et les raisons de la pratique dans l'oeuvre de Marcel Mauss', *Terrain* 16, 1991, pp. 114-30.

4. On the neglect and 'rediscovery' of technology and material culture studies in British and North American anthropology, see among others B. Pfaffenberger, 'Social anthropology of technology', *Annual review of anthropology* 21, 1992, pp. 491-516; D. Tayler, 'A Temple of the muses or a forum for debate? Oxford's anthropological collection', *Anales del Museo Nacional de Antropología* 1, 1994, pp. 29-50; P. Sillitoe, 'On sticks and stones, vines and bones: some notes on the scope, history and future of techology studies in anthropology', *Journal of museum ethnography* 5, 1996, pp. 1-22. According to these and other authors, the heyday of technology and material culture studies during Victorian evolutionist anthropology was followed by a long period of decline, related to the practical and professional changes brought about by Malinowski's 'participant observation' revolution, and

also to the theoretical and ethical discredit of diffusionist anthropology — a matter I will examine in the later part of this article.

5. Mauss, 'Divisions et proportions', pp. 194-5; 'Les techniques et la technologie', p. 250ff.

6. E. Durkheim and M. Mauss, *Primitive classification*, trans. R. Needham, Chicago, 1963; Durkheim, *The elementary forms of religious life*, trans. K.E. Fields, New York, 1995. The marginal position of technology and material culture studies in the Durkheimian epistemological and theoretical frameworks is a far more complex issue than I can discuss here (a study is in preparation). It may, however, be noted that the causes and implications of this ephemeral status are quite different from those that have prevailed in the British and North American anthropological traditions (see note 4).

7. J. Benda, *La Trahison des clercs*, Paris, 1927, p. 40, *passim*. My emphasis on the Great War is not intended to imply that this specifically dated event necessarily constituted a radical and self-defined rupture, which alone accounts for subsequent developments. On cultural and political continuities across and beyond the war, see J. Winter, *Sites of memory, sites of mourning: the Great War in European cultural history*, Cambridge, 1995, and C. Prochasson and A. Rasmussen, *Au nom de la patrie: les intellectuels et la première guerre mondiale (1910-1919)*, Paris, 1996. These continuities granted, there are good grounds to refer several of Mauss's research concerns in the 1920s and 1930s to the formative experiences of the war.

8. The various events and motivations surrounding Mauss's voluntary engagement for the front, his reactions to the unfolding of the war and the increasing bloodshed are recorded in M. Fournier, *Marcel Mauss*, Paris, 1994, p. 359ff. Besides expressing his grief at the loss of friends and colleagues, Mauss also discussed the sentiments of fear and panic he had to endure, and his recognition of the physical and moral force of instinct, which animates or on the contrary discourages and isolates the individual during extreme moments. See Mauss, 'Real and practical relations', pp. 14-18; 'Body techniques', p. 99ff. In many respects, Mauss's experiences and reactions bear comparison with those of W.H. Rivers and other British anthropologists, as highlighted by H. Kuklick, *The savage within: the social history of British anthropology, 1885 - 1945*, Cambridge, 1991, p. 119ff.

9. O. Spengler, *The decline of the west*, London, 1923; N. Berdiaev, *Le nouveau moyen-âge*, Lausanne, 1924. To be sure, the Great War alone cannot account for the visions of these authors, but rather for their popular reception. See Winter's *Sites of memory* for a recent culture-historical analysis of the broad spectrum of 'modern' and 'traditional' responses to the Great War. Responses among French combatants and intellectuals are discussed by J. Cruickshank, *Variations on catastrophe: some French responses to the Great War*, Oxford, 1982; C. Prochasson, *Les intellectuels, le socialisme et la guerre, 1900-1938*, Paris, 1993; Prochasson and Rasmussen, *Au nom de la patrie*. A survey of twentieth-century literature motivated by an 'apocalyptic state of mind' can be found in F.L. Baumer, 'Twentieth-century version of the apocalypse', *Cahiers d'histoire mondiale / Journal of world history* 1, 1953, pp. 623-40, and see Winter, *Sites of memory*, p. 178ff.

10. P. Valéry, *Regards sur le monde actuel*, Paris, 1931, p. 214. On the impact of the machine, see notably Cruickshank, *Variations on catastrophe*; D. and M. Johnson, *The age of illusion: art and politics in France 1918-1940*, London, 1987; M. Adas, *Machines as the measure of man: science, technology and ideologies of Western dominance*, Ithaca, 1989.

11. H. Bergson [1932], *The two sources of morality and religion*, trans. R. Ashley Audra and C. Brereton, with the assistance of W. Horsfall Carter [1935], New York, 1956.

12. By 1935, the French text of *Les deux sources de la morale et de la religion* was at its seventeenth impression (see R.C. Gorgin, *The Bergsonian controversy in France 1900-*

1914, Calgary, 1988, p. 204)! Various facets of Bergson's wide-ranging influence have been discussed (in English) by H.S. Hughes, *Consciousness and society: the reorientation of European social thought 1890 - 1930*, New York, 1958; Gorgin, *The Bergsonian controversy*, in F. Burwick and P. Douglass, eds, *The crisis in modernity: Bergson and the vitalist controversy*, Cambridge, 1992; M. Antlieff, *Inventing Bergson: cultural politics and the Parisian avant-garde*, Princeton, 1993. As these and other commentators have stressed, Bergson should not be confused with 'bergsonism', a moral, religious, and political stance that was often construed in conservative and extremist terms which were alien to Bergson's own ethics and intentions.

13. Bergson, *Two sources*, p. 307ff.

14. 'If we could rid ourselves of all pride, if, to define our species, we kept strictly to what history and prehistory show us to be the constant characteristic of humanity and of intelligence, we would perhaps not say *Homo sapiens*, but *Homo faber*' (H. Bergson, *Creative evolution* [1907], trans. A. Mitchell, London, 1911, p. 146: translation slightly amended). These terms were indeed appropriated in a diagnostic taxonomic sense by such eminent prehistorians as Breuil and Leroi-Gourhan, who sought to make of *faber* and *sapiens* two successive species in the archaeological record. See N. Schlanger, '"Suivre les gestes, éclat par éclat": la chaîne opératoire de Leroi-Gourhan', in F. Audouze and B. Stiegler, eds, *Geste technique, parole, mémoire. Actualité scientifique et philosophique de Leroi-Gourhan*, (in press).

15. Bergson, *Two sources*, p. 56.

16. Ibid., pp. 26ff, 45, 100,.209ff, 235, 281. This conception can be fruitfully compared with the 'reactionary modernism' of O. Spengler and contemporary German thinkers. See J. Herf, *Reactionary modernism: technology, culture and politics in Weimar and the Third Reich*, Cambridge, 1984, p. 49ff.

17. Already in the first preface to the *Rules of sociological method* [1895], Durkheim castigated the *mysticisme renaissant* that threatened the rationalist sociology he aimed for. On the unfolding of the Durkheim/Bergson controversy, see S. Lukes, *Emile Durkheim: his life and work*, London, [1973] 1988, p. 363ff. This conflict was suspended during the Great War, when both authors collaborated in the patriotic effort.

18. Mauss, 'La sociologie en France depuis 1914' [1933], *Oeuvres*, vol 3, pp. 436-50, at 436-7.

19. Benda, *La trahison des clercs*.

20. Mauss, 'Divisions et proportions ...', p. 194, emphasis added. The '*vertu dormitive de l'opium*' alludes to Molière's famous mockery of pseudo-scientific terminology in his play *Le malade imaginaire*.

21. Mauss, 'Les techniques et la technologie', p. 254.

22. Mauss, 'Divisions et proportions', pp. 194-5.

23. Mauss, 'Fragment d'un plan', p. 332.

24. Mauss, 'Body techniques'[1934], p. 101.

25. Mauss, 'Divisions et proportions', pp. 184-5.

26. For example, Mauss, *Manuel*, pp. 36, 51ff.

27. Ibid., p. 68.

28. Mauss, 'Divisions et proportions', p. 197.

29. Mauss expressed his concept of *homme total* in his 'Real and practical relations', and in 'Body techniques'. For a recent re-reading and discussion of this concept, see B. Karsenti, *L'Homme total: sociologie, anthropologie et philosophie chez Marcel Mauss*, Paris, 1997, p. 99ff.

30. Mauss, 'Divisions et proportions', p. 214.

31. Mauss, *Manuel*, p. 9.

32. G. Bataille, 'Le gros orteil', *Documents* 1, no. 6, 1929, pp. 297-302; 'Le bas matérialisme et la gnose', *Documents* 2, no. 1, 1930, pp. 1-9. On the points of

contact and dialogue between surrealism and ethnography in the late 1920s and 1930s, see D. Hollier, ed., *Le collège de sociologie*, Paris, 1979; J. Clifford, *The predicament of culture: twentieth-century ethnography, literature and art*, Cambridge, 1988; J. Jamin, 'Introduction' to M. Leiris, *Miroire de l'Afrique*, Paris, 1996, pp. 9-59.

33. Mauss, 'La notion de matière', p. 164.

34. This intention can be fully appreciated in the last pages of Mauss's essay *The gift: the form and reason for exchange in archaic societies* [1925], trans. W.D. Halls, London, 1990.

35. Mauss, 'La nation', p. 613.

36. The stakes and implications underlying this development are evidently far more complex. See notably E. Hobsbawm, *Nation and nationalism since 1780: programme, myth, reality*, Cambridge, 1990, and R. Tombs, ed., *Nationhood and nationalism in France - from Boulangism to the Great War, 1889-1918*, London, 1991.

37 Charles Maurras, quoted in C. Prochasson, 'Les années 1880: au temps du boulangisme', in M. Winock, ed., *Histoire de l'extrême droite en France*, Paris, 1993, pp. 51-82, 67.

38. L. Marin, *Questionnaire d'ethnographie (table d'analyse en ethnographie)* (extracted from the *Bulletin de la Société d'Ethnographie de Paris*), Alençon, 1925; *Disparition des institutions traditionnelles qui, en Lorraine, transmettaient et utilisaient les vieux contes populaires*, Enquête de la Société d'Ethnographie de Paris sur la crise des traditions, Paris, 1942. On the radical origins of the Société d'Anthropologie, see M. Hammond, 'Anthropology as a weapon of social combat in late nineteenth-century France', *Journal of the history of the behavioral sciences*, 16, 1980, pp. 118-32. For twentieth-century conservative and right-wing developments see D. Lindenberg, *Les années souterraines, 1937 - 1947*, Paris, 1990, and particularly H. Lebovics, *True France. the wars over cultural identities, 1900 - 1945*, Ithaca, 1992.

39. On Montandon's anti-Semitism and racism, see W. Schneider, *Quality and quantity: The quest for biological regeneration in twentieth-century France*, Cambridge, 1990, and P. Birnbaum, 'Georges Montandon: l'anthropologie vichyste au service du Nazisme' in *La France aux Français: histoire des haines nationales*, Paris, 1993, pp. 187-98. Both the uniqueness of Montandon's manual and the caution needed to use it were expressed in Mauss's lectures; see his *Manuel*, pp. 10, 47, *passim*, as well as A.G. Haudricourt, personal communication, February 1996.

40. G. Montandon, *L'Ologénèse culturelle: traité d'ethnographie cyclo-culturelle et d'ergologie systématique*, Paris, 1934, p. 215.

41. Techniques can thus link the Ainu of Japan, in cultural as well as racial terms, with the 'occidentaloid civilisation'; see, for example, Montandon, *Au pays des Ainou: exploration anthropologique*, Paris, 1927; *La civilisation Ainou*, Paris, 1937; and *La Race, les races: mise au point d'ethnologie somatique* Paris, 1933.

42. While generally far more cautious than Durkheim in his approach to 'so-called primitives', there is no doubt that Mauss too sought in many of their activities and institutions the 'archaic' or 'incipient' manifestations of later developments. See discussion by W.P. Vogt, 'The uses of studying primitives: a note on the Durkheimians, 1890 - 1940', *History and theory* 15, 1976, pp. 33-44.

43. Mauss's criticisms are most explicit in 'La civilisation', and 'Les techniques et la technologie'. For Mauss's reviews of diffusionist authors, see 'La théorie des couches et des aires de civilisation selon Graebner' [1913], in *Oeuvres*, vol. 2, pp. 489-93; 'Le manuel d'éthnologie de Graebner' [1925], ibid. pp. 493-8; 'Morphologie des civilisations africaines selon Frobenius' [1925], ibid. pp. 499-502; 'La théorie de la diffusion unicentrique de la civilisation' [1925], ibid. pp. 513-23.

44. On Mauss's use of diffusionist methods and approaches, see for example his *Manuel*, chaps. 1-2, as well as 'An intellectual self-portrait', in the present volume. On Mauss's diffusionist teaching, see L. Dumont, 'Une science en devenir', *L'Arc* 48,

1972, pp. 8-22, 11; A.G. Haudricourt, 'Souvenirs personels', _L'Arc_ 48, 1972, pp. 89-90, and personal communication, February 1996.

45. Mauss's committed stance — which makes manifest the inevitable fusion of science and politics — has similarities with that of some contemporary Anglophone scholars such as the anthropologist W.H.R. Rivers and the archaeologist V.G. Childe. Childe in particular veered in the interwar period from an essentialist conception of culture (inspired by G. Kossina) to a more dynamic and interactive one, and he also recognised the practical importance of archaeology in the political sphere. See V.G. Childe, 'Is prehistory practical?', _Antiquity_ 7, 1933, pp. 410-18.

46. Mauss, 'La nation', p. 601.

47. Ibid., pp. 599, 621, 609, 611, 613.

48. Mauss, 'Divisions et proportions', pp. 196-7.

49. Mauss, 'La civilisation', pp. 462-3, 474, 477. As can be seen, the conception which Mauss tries to flesh out in this and other essays resembles the 'culture contact' research undertaken at about the same time by B. Malinowski in Africa.

50. A. G. Haudricourt, 'De l'origine de l'attelage moderne', _Annales E. S. C._ 8, 1936, pp. 515-22.

51. P. Rivet, _Les origines de l'homme américain_, Montréal, 1943, notably pp. 129-32. On Rivet's scientific and political activities, see J. Jamin, 'Le savant et le politique: Paul Rivet (1876 - 1958)', _Bulletins et mémoires de la Société d'Anthropologie de Paris_ n.s. 1, 1989, pp. 277-94.

Chapter 13

FORM, MOVEMENT, AND POSTURE IN MAUSS:

THEMES FOR TODAY'S ANTHROPOLOGY

Claudine Haroche

'The form of a civilisation,' wrote Mauss, 'is all that gives a special and distinctive character to the societies that make up that civilisation.' He then listed a great variety of phenomena which contributed to defining that form. His list extended from words to tales; from the manner of working the land to the interior or exterior structure of the house; from tools to gestures, or manners of walking. He concluded that 'everything has a pattern, a style, and even in many cases, beyond its essential and ideal form, a special way of being put to use'.[1]

Mauss's observations on the material forms of societies — on the gestures, postures, and movements in which the anthropologist perceives elements of these forms — are of major importance: they invite deep reflection, they encourage rigorous observation; finally, they raise once again questions which have remained fundamental. For all that they may be sparse, partial, incomplete and often generalised, many of Mauss's comments are still striking: he notes (regarding civilisations) that 'historical uncertainty in particular cases must not discourage research. The general phenomenon remains.'[2]

Mauss stresses the crucial role of the tangible, the material, stating that 'The abstractions of the sociologist are applied to phenomena that are concrete and full of movement.'[3] One should take these terms literally, and then assess the interest and significance of a study like that on 'Prayer'. Here Mauss shows that, with regard to prayer and its associated gestures, bearing, attitudes, and movements, 'its forms are exclusively social in origin'.[4]

On the question of the material forms of societies, of gestures and movements, and of their social origins, Mauss was influenced by the works of Hertz and of Durkheim. In his study of religious polarity originally published in 1909, Hertz drew attention to the preeminence of the right hand which he contrasted with the 'despised' left hand — considered to be inferior — and thereby suggested further investigation into the relationship between postures, positions, status, and space. To the right hand, wrote Hertz, 'go honours, flattering designations, prerogatives'; it is 'the symbol and the model of all aristocracy'.[5] It remains unexplained, he noted, 'why a humanly-instituted privilege should be added to this natural superiority'. Hertz emphasised 'that the two sides of our body possess therefore in an extreme degree the characteristics of a social institution', and a study which tries to account for this phenomenon belongs to sociology.[6] Observing the existence of relationships between the right and the left sides of the body and space, he said 'the right represents the high, the upper world above, the sky...' He went on to conclude: 'All these usages, which today seem to be pure conventions, are explained and acquire meaning if they are related to the beliefs which gave birth to them.'[7]

Durkheim, in *The elementary forms*, equally recognised that 'spatial organization was modelled on the social organization, and replicates it.' Far from being built into human nature, even the distinction between right and left is, in all probability, the product of religious, hence collective, representations.' Pointing out that space must be 'divided' and 'differentiated', Durkheim wonders about the origin of these divisions which are essential to it. Space in itself has no right, no left, no high or low, no north or south, etc.' And he emphasises: 'All these distinctions evidently arise from the fact that different affective colourings have been assigned to regions.'[8]

Later Halbwachs also applied himself to the study of material forms in societies and to their inscription in space, speaking of general, social, and political morphology. He states that every society 'indicates its place in the spatial milieu'. Observing that 'a political organisation is moulded by spatial conditions', and turning his attention to the relationship between the symbolic, material, and concrete in groups, Halbwachs stresses that it is thus necessary, along with the symbolic meaning, to take literally the expression 'the body of the Church'.[9] 'The collectivity of the faithful', he is effectively saying, 'is manifest as a material mass'.[10]

Mauss returned to the social nature of bodily behaviour in his later text on the techniques of the body. By these techniques, he wrote, one must understand 'the ways in which human beings, society by society, know how to use their bodies'. He claimed that 'These "habits" do not simply vary from one individual to another ... they vary especially between societies, educations, proprieties and fashions.' He also said, 'We have a set of permissible or impermissible, natural or unnatural attitudes. Thus we should attribute different values to the act of staring fixedly: a symbol of politeness in the army, and of rudeness in everyday life.' To know why a person makes one gesture rather than another, it is not enough to investigate physiology and psychology; 'it is also necessary to know the traditions which impose it'.[11] Movements, gestures, attitudes, even the use of the eyes are then in part governed by rules or principles whose origin is social. Although he was able to describe all these kinds of conduct, Mauss mentions his dissatisfaction at being unable to refer to them clearly. 'I did not know what name, what title, to give it all.'[12] Forms? Fashions? Attitudes? Habits? Modes of living? Mauss concludes that in all these modes of being, in 'all these modes of acting' — the expression he uses — one must see techniques: 'the techniques of the body'.[13] From all this it is essential to remember that forms, postures, gestures, movements are, fundamentally, acts that are social in origin.

As emerges very clearly from these modes of acting or kinds of bodily conduct, 'we are everywhere faced with physio-psycho-sociological assemblages of series of actions'.[14] Noting their more or less habitual and established character in an individual and in a society, Mauss then goes further: he sees in them means, instruments, and also ends. 'One of the reasons why these series may more easily be assembled where the individual is concerned is precisely because they are assembled by and for social authority'.[15] He recalls how, as a corporal, he taught 'the reason for exercise in close order, marching four abreast and in step'. He recounts how he ordered the soldiers one day 'not to march in step drawn up in ranks and in two files four abreast', but nevertheless to pass between two of the trees in the courtyard.[16] What happened next? 'They marched on top of one another'. He adds, 'They realized that what they were being made to do was not so stupid'. From this anecdote Mauss concludes: 'In group life as a whole, there is a kind of education of movements in close order.'[17] There is an apprenticeship in gestural action, bearing, self-control. In a few words, by means of a short and specific account, humorous to begin with, Mauss enables us to grasp the role of marching and of comportment. But beyond that, he demonstrates the necessity for some kind of order, in a word, for an etiquette or protocol to govern the conduct of people within society.[18]

In his *Introduction to the work of Marcel Mauss* Lévi-Strauss emphasised the impact of Mauss's ideas on modern anthropology.[19] Dumont also drew attention to this in his famous article on Mauss, noting that he 'never separated the study of exotic societies either from the study of our own, or from the study of culture'.[20] Thus Mauss still offers today many relevant themes for those who are undertaking critical anthropological study of aspects of our contemporary world. This is equally true for those working in historical, cultural, social and political anthropology who share a curiosity about the way in which people deliberately make instrumental and symbolic use of their bodies, and for those who participate in the deepening interest in the role of gesture, bearing, and posture. Coming from different starting points, regions, documents, and periods, these works allow us to discover and measure the profound role, the constant and often unnoticed role of specific gestural activity in clarifying the presence of order in society. In this area of studies of the body, Lévi-Strauss emphasises, 'nothing is futile, gratuitous, or superfluous'.[21]

We are not here seeking to establish academic 'filiations', to learn whether some of the works we have briefly referred to have been influenced by Mauss, and to what extent. We are attempting to detect proximities and similarities, to make connections between topics, questions, and problems like the ones made by Mauss.

The case of 'precedence'

In his studies of historical anthropology, Le Goff explores gestures as they appear in a fundamental institution of medieval society, namely vassalage. In paying homage, Le Goff stresses that the important thing is the more or less marked expression of subordination on the part of the vassal in relation to the lord: 'The inequality of rank and situation is made visible in the bodily actions of gesture.' 'In the gesture of the lord, beyond a promise of protection, there is ... the demonstration of superior power'. Conversely, 'in the gesture of the vassal, whilst there may not be humiliation, there is at least the sign of deference and inferiority'.[22]

Le Goff draws attention to the fact that within the symbolic space where the entry into vassalage takes place, 'a spatial re-arrangement of the contracting parties allows the performance of the vassalage'. The re-placing reflects the nature of the bond between the lord and the vassal: the vassal, the inferior, manifests deference to the lord by moving towards him'.[23] He further observes that one should bear in mind the relative position of the contracting parties during the course of the ceremony: 'Is the lord seated?' he asks, 'and on what kind of seat? Is he in a raised position? Is the vassal standing up or kneeling down?'[24] Le Goff then recalls Meyer Fortes's paper, 'On installation ceremonies', where Fortes specifically refers to a passage from *The gift* in order to define these ceremonies as 'total institutions'.[25]

Raymond Firth, too, in his work as a social anthropologist, analyses respectful gestures and postures in relation to status. He examines in detail this instrumental and symbolic use of the body, which is particularly manifest in certain situations. The rank or status of individuals in a society is most clearly apparent at moments of meeting and separation. A certain kind of greeting at the time of meeting gives an idea of the social position of one person relative to another. 'Forms of greeting or parting in which one person lowers himself, sets himself at a distance, or removes articles of clothing indicate inferior status to other persons who do not behave in this way, or do so only to a modified degree ... in accordance with the implicit principle that lower status is equated with disarrangement of the person'.[26] The act of bowing, of remaining at a distance, or indeed of removing one's hat, are all types of behaviour which 'metaphorically if not physically leave the individual relatively unprotected [and] emphasize by contrast the other person who is protected by height, distance and covering. So social inferiority is expressed symbolically by a simulacrum of physical defencelessness'.[27] The anthropologist therefore concludes that, generally speaking, status implies the material and symbolic use of postures and gestures. Height, degree of elevation, distance, the position of the body in space, all indicate the status of an individual: 'bodily elevation is correlated with social elevation'.[28]

In the same way Firth observes a general tendency in British and other Western societies: there has been a decline in respectful postures and in gestures requiring a deep bow. He finds a particularly interesting example in the curtsey. This respectful posture requiring bended knees and a bow appeared in the sixteenth century as a very general form of polite behaviour, but it then took on a much more specific significance. Firth notes that respectful attitudes and gestures have been transposed from general social situations to very formal ones, which take place in a ritualised context. He believes that we can attribute this evolution to an egalitarian current in modern social relations, a current tending to reduce the amount of movement in bodily postures and providing evidence for a levelling of distinctions.[29]

Gestures, bodily attitudes, positions in space and in society differ according to societies, historical epochs, and political systems. Nevertheless, we must note that the positions relevant to the question of status, convey and express themes, preoccupations, and basic aspirations, such as the desire to be close to positions of power, the desire for supremacy, indeed for precedence, all of which inhabit, to a greater or lesser extent, the economy of meaningful gesture and posture.[30]

It is by starting from this formal and material patterning through which a society delineates itself in a space, and from the question of gestures, movements, and postures indicative of social status that we can appreciate the importance of further investigation into the forms constituted by etiquette, protocol, and modes of precedence. Mauss in fact leads us to see that protocol, arising out of the general question of forms, can basically be understood as the shaping of political order.[31] So we are attempting to show that the power of the form — which Mauss claims is never so apparent as in the case of prayer — is decisive in etiquette and protocol.

To a certain extent we have been encouraged by the text that Lévi-Strauss devoted to the works of Mauss. We would like to demonstrate that aspects of precedence are among those apparently insignificant gestures which Lévi-Strauss suggested were 'transmitted from one generation to the next and protected by their very insignificance'. They constitute, he added, 'examples of an archaeology of body habits which, in modern Europe (and all the more elsewhere), provide the cultural historian with information as valuable as that of prehistory and philology'.[32]

Thus in protocol, precedence has traditionally been seen as a matter of trivial details, insignificant gestures which were the object of laughable preoccupations and ridiculous arguments. For all their insignificance, however, we are trying to show that these gestures convey memory, traditions, feelings, beliefs, in short a content that might be thought to have disappeared long ago from formal conduct subjected to pernickety customs.

We would like to analyse these neglected, forgotten links, and thus to reestablish a continuity between, on the one hand, the feminine noun *la geste* referring to the epic poem, the story, the historical narrative — these all narrate individual or collective actions and belong to a macrohistorical and macrosociological approach — and *les gestes* (the masculine singular being *le geste*) on the other, gestures or parcels of individual bodily conduct, which belong rather to the microhistorical and microsociological domain. The etymologies reflect this continuity.[33] What we must do is take the gestural activities that structure, symbolise, materialise, and illustrate *la geste*, the epic narrative, and consider them as the founding elements of legal and political institutions. We are thus seeking to clarify the role of posture, bearing, and movement in the models of collective behaviour and institutional systems, both legal and political, whether past or present.

A number of etymological studies help to illuminate the historical development of institutions by tracing shifts in the meaning of key words. Such etymologies are essential to the understanding of protocol: they enable one to perceive the link evoked above between posture and gesture, space and aptitude or capacity. So *précéder* which appeared in 1353, is borrowed from the Latin verb *praecedere*, whose literal meaning is 'to walk in front', 'to be anterior'. At the end of the fourteenth century it took on the abstract meaning of 'to prevail over', 'to have priority over', carrying the idea of hierarchy. But it is the etymology of the verb *seoir* (to sit) that I feel to be particularly revealing of the passage from the valorisation of space in the literal sense, to the value attributed to a person according to his or her place. This term appears with the meaning 'to be seated' at the end of the tenth century, and later comes to have the sense, among others, of 'to be situated, to be suitable' (end of the twelfth century). Similarly its derivative, *séant*, means 'seated' (late twelfth century), then 'decent, suitable', as in *séant à* 'suitable for (someone)', from the late fourteenth century.[34] It is interesting to note that a certain number of terms such as gesture, posture, to precede, to sit, imply by their very etymology the copresence of attitudes, movements of the body and actions, as well as places, positions, and states of mind. We now see that these terms which give rise to, and order, the question of precedence in protocol include a literal and often spatial component, to which one should add a psychological and political, figurative and symbolic significance.

We shall now look at the way in which etiquette in the parliaments of the seventeenth century expressed itself materially, physically, concretely. The rules of etiquette and protocol reveal themselves by external signs, in the body, in gestures, bearing, posture. Precedence essentially finds its expression in the use of *seoir* and *marcher* (to walk), assigns places, governs movements, constrains posture, becomes obligatory when one takes up a position and when one changes it, thereby imposing submission to a certain order. Basically, precedence is regulated by a demand: to defer or to precede, in order to respect the laws of etiquette. Under the *ancien régime*, protocol distributed individuals within the space of institutions — parliament in particular — according to precedence. It operated according to title, condition, rank, and office, imposing order both on bodies and between bodies.[35]

From among the many texts, legal treatises, writings of theorists of the monarchy with their particular conceptions of social order, which were elaborated, protected, defended, occasionally challenged, we shall focus here on the writings of Guillaume d'Oncieu, then on the celebrated work of Charles Loyseau and finally on the *Memoirs* of Saint-Simon. The latter reports the testimony of jurists in the various parliamentary quarrels which set them against the peers in matters of hierarchical order, etiquette, and precedence. A deep concern runs through these texts: how to mark, by external signs and by precedence, the bodies of individuals and the estates of society.

In 1593, Guillaume d'Oncieu, President of the Senate of Savoy, brought out a work worth examining for a moment even though it is forgotten by posterity: *La precedence de la noblesse*. The subtitle is enlightening: 'A work concerning the honours, forms of respect, arrangements for seating and precedence of the age, and the causes and reasons for them'. In it d'Oncieu stresses how seating, posture, and the sequence in which one stands and processes occur in an order regulated by precedence and deference, and translating a certain relationship with space. To precede implies deference in gesture, bearing, and movement on the part of those who follow behind. Noting the importance of precedence, d'Oncieu emphasises that the place one occupies in space, governed by precedence, has a value: it is a question of privilege. Of precedence, d'Oncieu says that it is 'nothing more than an act of respect due to and directed towards someone, because of which one can see that person ... pass ahead of others'.[36]

Precedence which requires distance in space, in elevation, a distance as symbolic as it is literal, thus sets the noble above other persons. It shows itself in external marks of respect, as in bending the knee before a person, baring one's head in their presence, letting them pass in front of oneself. This constitutes a set of rules, a visible device of hierarchy allowing one to distinguish those who are more and those who are less worthy of esteem and consideration.

Composed a short time later, Charles Loyseau's work on public power went through many editions. The magistrate began his work with a general observation on order: 'In all things there must be order, for the sake of decorum and for their control'. In this way he connects the necessity for order with what is fitting and with decorum; he also stresses that order is indispensable to the organisation of people within society and reminds us that if human beings 'cannot subsist without order', nevertheless order is 'changeable and subject to vicissitude'.[37] Order, the principle of organisation and of the general and concrete distribution of statuses and of duties, operates by visible adornments, and also by posture, position, and movement. Loyseau affirms that order is the source of two specific prerogatives: title and rank, within which he then distinguishes patterns of precedence. Rank, he states, 'is precedence in sitting or in walking'. He observes that 'the social orders [i.e., the estates] are the principal source of such precedence, 'for the very name 'order' denotes and signifies as much'.[38] Thus he returns to what d'Oncieu called precedence, and to the forms of priority that would be Saint-Simon's constant preoccupation.

It is the writer of the *Memoirs* who allows us to grasp the decisive role of the material dimension of precedence: the search for anteriority, elevation, and distance are for ever present in questions of precedence. The *Memoirs* thus illustrate, in relation to concrete facts, the theories and developments of d'Oncieu and Loyseau. Saint-Simon here gives lengthy details about postures and the order of bodily movements and displacements — the order in which one enters or leaves the session — in Parliament. Seated or standing, posture conveys rank, position, elevation, greatness understood in the literal as well as the symbolic sense: inequality in elevation is an essential element of protocol. So when it addresses the king, the parliament, as the Third Estate, must be bare-headed and kneeling, 'a deeply mortifying matter' wrote Saint-Simon, 'while [the jurists] could see the peers ... give their opinion whilst seated and with the head covered'.[39]

The numerous conflicts concerning precedence which put the presidents of the parliaments in opposition to the peers, most often arose from the question of posture, bearing, seats, their height, and their arrangement in space. The account of the 'affair of the bonnet', the undertakings relating to the removal of stuffing from the seats of the peers and its transfer into those of the presidents, constitute famous examples of how the presidents of the parliament endeavoured to equal the peers.[40] Bodily conduct and gestures, even the most trivial, such as wearing one's bonnet when addressing someone, are not innocent: it is a sign of power, a mark of superiority on the part of the person who dons the cap or, even more, of the person who never takes it off. Even the most apparently insignificant gesture may, in this way, become decisive at the level of political institutions. Saint-Simon reports how in 1681, Novion introduced a modification into the rules of etiquette, in a particularly insidious fashion.

> [He] began by pretending carelessly to drop his bonnet on the table, sometimes at the beginning, sometimes in the middle, occasionally towards the end of the roll call of the councillors, and he always avoided removing it when he called on the senior peer to speak. From there, he went further in his pretence of an oversight: he continued wearing his bonnet while calling on the first few peers, then took it off as if he had forgotten to do so, and finished calling on the others.

Saint-Simon concludes his story by recollecting that on the occasion of the reception of the Cardinal de Noailles, the Archbishop of Paris, at the Parliament in 1681, Novion 'gave himself away by keeping his cap on all the time that he was calling on the peers, and only removed it when he came to the princes of the blood'.[41]

Let us recall what was understood by the term 'peer of France' at the court of Louis XIV and had been from the beginning of the monarchy: 'one known ... by the name and title of peer of France was to be found sitting next to the throne'. Here, the Duc de Saint-Simon mentions that proximity to the king is an essential element of etiquette in the parliament. To be close to the monarch is therefore crucial. To touch the throne with the elbow is a privilege. The demand for equality in the matter of proximity and elevation thus provokes quarrels and conflicts regarding precedence which can often only be resolved by introducing or inverting inequality in elevation.[42]

Our reading of d'Oncieu, Loyseau, and the *Memoirs* of Saint-
Simon, with the attention they pay to precedence, has led us from the
observation of individual bodies, their movements, their gestures and
their posture, to grasp the general principle behind the historical fact;
more generally, we see the collective, the social in the individual, and
discover the habits, traditions, and customs that qualify, define, and
determine political bodies in a particular society. Modes of precedence
are social and political forms that link and separate people within
institutional space. They introduce distance between people and bring
them closer together, and by assigning distinct, specific places to them,
they distribute them according to their rank, position, and function;
they assemble and reassemble people into orders and groups. In this
way precedence, which expresses itself in concrete and material forms,
even physical ones, enables us to make more precise what Mauss had
once noticed in the forms of prayer and the techniques of the body,
namely the sequence of actions enjoined, ordered by and for social
authority. Thereby one also grasps the role of the gestures and
postures expressing power, domination and submission. So there are
moments and circumstances when according to one's rank it is
appropriate to sit down and thereby indicate a position of authority or
domination; conversely there are moments when one has to rise to
one's feet and remain standing so as to demonstrate subjection before
the holder of a superior rank.

The study of these sequences of action, of these techniques of the
body, of these gestures and movements in the institutional forms that
constitute precedence, makes it possible to clarify certain processes
underlying the development and functioning of political and legal
institutions. By means of precedence, protocol imposes, structures,
and orders relationships of deference which rest on the existence of an
order within every society. We are not far from those processes
'stamping a territory with ritual signs of dominance', of which Clifford
Geertz has written.[43]

The perspective is the same as the earlier one of Marc Bloch, who
had urged that we sketch out a history of people's bodies in society,
stressing the importance of the meaning of gestures; as with Bloch the
aim is to find fundamental constants in politics.[44] It is what Geertz, a
few years ago, strongly emphasised when he recognised that 'though
both the structure and expressions of social life change, the internal
necessities that animate it do not. Thrones may be out of fashion, and
pageantry too; but political authority still requires a cultural frame in
which to define itself'.[45]

The relevance of returning to and re-reading the texts of Mauss
and Hertz for today's anthropology is obvious: political anthropology,
legal anthropology, the history of the law, the relationship between

religion and the law, all raise questions that have remained fundamental. The formulations we find in Hertz or in Mauss, though often generalised, are nonetheless essential and still constitute crucial avenues for research, crowded with unanswered questions which can perhaps never be answered exactly. Firth very justly points out that 'the basic problem for an anthropologist does not consist in making pronouncements on ultimate reality. It consists in studying the forms of symbolic expression in an attempt to understand the system of ideas they express, the order of this system, and the effects produced by the use of these symbolic concepts.'[46]

It is therefore appropriate to ask oneself, as Firth himself has done, whether the abstract schemes of the modern social anthropologist have moved too far from empirical reality. He invites us to return to the concrete: 'We are concerned' he writes 'with models rather than with behaviour, with symbols rather than with custom and practice'.[47] Finally, let us think once again about the remark made by Mauss: 'The abstractions of the sociologist are applied to material which is concrete and full of movement'.

NOTES

1. M. Mauss, 'Les civilisations: éléments et formes' [1929], *Oeuvres*, vol. 2, pp. 464, 470.
2. Ibid., p. 469.
3. Mauss, 'La prière' [1909], in *Oeuvres*, vol. 1, p. 358.
4. Ibid., p. 378.
5. R. Hertz, 'The pre-eminence of the right hand: a study in religious polarity' [1909], in *Death and the right hand*, trans. R. and C. Needham, London, 1960, p. 89. (Revised version in R. Needham, ed., *Right and left*, Chicago 1973, pp. 3-31.)
6. Ibid., pp. 92-3.
7. Ibid., pp. 101, 107.
8. E. Durkheim, *The elementary forms of religious life* [1912], trans. K.E. Fields, New York, 1995, pp. 10-12.
9. M. Halbwachs, *Morphologie sociale* [1938], Paris, 1970, pp. 17, 27, 26.
10. Ibid., p. 26.
11. Mauss, 'The notion of body techniques' [1935], in *Sociology and psychology: essays by Marcel Mauss*, trans. B. Brewster, London, 1979, pp. 95-123, at 97, 101, 105, 109. Translations slightly amended.
12. Ibid., p. 103.
13. Ibid., pp. 103-4.
14. Ibid., p. 120.
15. Ibid.
16. Ibid.
17. Ibid.
18. See Y. Déloye, C. Haroche, and O. Ihl, 'Protocole et politique: formes, rituels et préséances' and Haroche, 'L'ordre dans les corps: gestes, mouvements, postures' in *Le protocole ou la mise en forme de l'ordre politique*, Paris, 1997.

19. C. Lévi-Strauss, *Introduction to the work of Marcel Mauss* [1950], trans. F. Baker, London, 1987.
20. L. Dumont, *Essays on individualism* [1972], Chicago, 1986, p. 196ff.
21. Lévi-Strauss, *Introduction*, p. 4.
22. J. Le Goff, 'Le rituel symbolique de la vassalité', in his *Pour un autre moyen âge*, Paris, 1991, pp. 367-8.
23. Ibid., pp. 396-7.
24. Ibid., p. 399.
25. M. Fortes, 'On installation ceremonies', *Proceedings of the Royal Anthropological Institute*, London, 1967.
26. R. Firth, *Symbols, private and public*, London, 1973, pp. 325, 322.
27. Ibid., p. 325
28. Ibid., p. 324.
29. R. Firth, 'Postures and gestures of respect', in *Echanges et communications, mélanges offerts à Claude Lévi-Strauss*, Paris, 1970, pp. 202-3, 206-7. Firth describes this article as a 'companion piece' to his chapter on 'Greeting and parting' in *Symbols*, p. 309.
30. Haroche, 'L'ordre dans les corps'.
31. Déloye, Haroche, and Ihl, 'Protocole et politique'. See also Pierre Bourdieu, 'Habitus, code et codification', in *Actes de la recherche en sciences sociales*.64, September 1986,as well as 'Les rites d'institutions' in vol. 43 of the same journal, June 1982.
32. Lévi-Strauss, *Introduction*, p. 9.
33. *La geste* (as in *chanson de geste*) is a loan (first attested in 1080) from the classical Latin *gesta*, 'actions' and particularly 'exploits'; *gesta* was then used in medieval Latin in the sense of 'narrative, story', as in the title of historical works (*Gesta Francorum*). *Le geste* (from *gest* ca.1213) is a loan from the Latin *gestus*, 'attitude, movement of the body' (*Dictionnaire historique de la langue française*, ed. A. Rey, Paris, 1992). On the history of gestures, see J.C. Schmitt, *La raison des gestes dans l'occident médiéval*, Paris, 1989. See also J. Bremmer and H. Roodenburg, eds, *A cultural history of gesture*, Cambridge, 1991, in particular Keith Thomas's 'Introduction', and the papers by Bremmer on 'Walking, standing and sitting in ancient Greek culture' and by Roodenburg on 'The hand of friendship: shaking hands and other gestures in the Dutch Republic'.
34. Rey, *Dictionnaire historique*. On the important role that etymology can play, see G. Duby, *Les trois ordres ou l'imaginaire du féodalisme*, in particular 'La chevalerie', including 'Ordonnances' and 'Prééminences', Paris, 1978, p. 352-70.
35. Haroche, 'L'ordre dans les corps'.
36. Guillaume d'Oncieu, *La precedence de la noblesse*, Lyon, 1593, p. 9.
37. Charles Loyseau, *A treatise of orders and plain dignities* [1610], trans. H.A. Lloyd, Cambridge 1994, p. 5.
38. Ibid., p. 14.
39. Louis de Rouvray, Duc de Saint-Simon, *Mémoires*, 8 vols, ed. Y. Coirault, Paris, 1983-88. Reference here is made to vol. 5, 1985, p. 47. A shortened edition is available in English, *Historical memoirs of the Duc de Saint-Simon*, 3 vols, ed. and trans. L. Norton, London, 1968. Vol. 2 of this edition is the most relevant to the present discussion. If some of the facts and interpretations presented by Saint-Simon have been sometimes judged excessive, even 'fanciful', it is nonetheless certain that his observations on the postures and movements involved in precedence reflect the anthropological realities of the situation. For the criticisms of Saint-Simon see N. Fustel de Coulanges, 'L'organisation de la justice dans l'Antiquité et les temps modernes', *Revue des deux mondes*, 1871; G. Ducoudray, *Les origines du Parlement de Paris et la justice aux XIII et XIV siècles*, 1902.

40. Saint-Simon, *Mémoires*, vol. 5, pp. 54-6.

41. Ibid., pp. 54-5.

42. Ibid., p. 7. Cf. Haroche, 'L'ordre dans les corps'.

43. C. Geertz, *Local knowledge: further essays in interpretive anthropology*, New York, 1983, chap. 6, esp. p. 125.

44. M. Bloch, *The royal touch: sacred monarchy and scrofula in England and France* [1924], trans. J.E. Anderson, London, 1973.

45. Geertz, *Local knowledge*, p. 143.

46. Firth, *Symbols*, p. 428.

47. Ibid., p. 165.

Chapter 14

MAUSS IN AFRICA:

ON TIME, HISTORY, AND POLITICS

Wendy James

Shaping time

Most discussions of time in the social sciences tend to separate out this topic from history, particularly from the unfolding of events and the sifting of their residues by the collective memory into stories. 'Time' lends itself rather to the construction of mathematical, diagrammatic abstractions, the commonest forms of which represent 'modern' time as linear one-way movement, and 'traditional' time as embedded in social life, cyclic in its intellectual representation and rhythmic in its practice. Edmund Leach's well-known essays on time inaugurated a lively field of such discussion, which has become increasingly sophisticated — especially in the recent work of Alfred Gell.[1] It is still rare, however, to find analyses which reach out from 'intellectual' or cultural representation of time shapes to the morphology of historical time, and the formation of social phenomena through it. An exception here is John Davis's work; he has helped to show how in this domain, abstract images of time are intermingled with tangible experience of the world, of the social past, present, and future. From this perspective the notion of culturally exclusive time worlds disappears, because over historical time, we are all connected. The distinction between 'traditional' and 'modern' time, which itself has shaped much writing in the social sciences, collapses into the history which has produced it: in particular, the history of the concepts of modernity and progress themselves, and in the special case of anthropology, the colonial encounter.[2]

Here, Africa offers perhaps the clearest example of the way that a traditional/modern dichotomy permeated scholarship: there was typically, during the middle colonial period, a complete opposition between the idea of the traditional social system (even perhaps with its very slow 'evolution' or its internal ideas of time shapes), and the idea of 'change' — surely about to affect it one day, as a result of the economic and political impact of the outside world. History was left to the historians, who typically investigated this type of impact, tracing past events in their linear succession and relying on 'the authorities' for their evidence, even when they first started to pursue field research. Anthropologists of the early to mid twentieth century typically thus shared with historians a 'modern' view of time.

It is my present argument that this dichotomous view of time also characterises the greater part of the work of the *Année sociologique*. For many parts of the world, such as the Americas or Australia, the opposition was unproblematic. There was no difficulty in perceiving the native peoples of those continents as traditional or 'ahistorical', in themselves; there was no discomfort in applying notions of the archaic or primitive, and accepting a total disjunction with the world of contemporary history. The ethnography of Africa, on the other hand, did not fit so comfortably into this 'modernist' division of time. Nor does it today. The Durkheim group were at first uncertain how to deal with the mixed scene that Africa offered, but Mauss led the way in formulating an approach which to some extent bypassed the archaic/modern divide, and managed to encompass both the internal and external historical relations which played a part in shaping social forms in Africa. In other words, he demonstrated a sense of historical morphology in his own writings on Africa, both in his reviews and in the short piece he published on his own brief field trip to Morocco (see below). In the face of those dilemmas which face Africanist anthropology in the postcolonial period, and indeed anthropology generally, it is very interesting to look back at Mauss's little-known writings on the continent, from which I think we can draw guidance.

Let me first sketch some of the foundational work which lay behind Mauss's response to Africa. The essay on time which was originally written by Hubert and published later under his name jointly with that of Mauss is a beautiful exposition of the 'morphological' mode of time.[3] Time is presented not as an intellectual or abstract schema, as Leach attempted in his later essays, nor as mechanically embedded in the rhythms of social life. While the morphology of festivals and regular gatherings indeed served as the pragmatic form of the social representation of time, they were capable of absorbing and adjusting to event and experience. It is suggested in the essay that even we in modern society struggle to bring experience in line with the rhythms of our time systems, which themselves retain aspects of the magical and religious. This experience includes historical events, which may receive marked places in the rhythmical scheme. This is a part of the way in which time, and duration, have a qualitative and concrete rather than a quantitative and abstract nature. The past is marked and celebrated in the time patterns of the present (examples are given of Moorish and English invasions in France; and of the founding saints of local churches) to the point where the recurrence of certain dates brings on a recurrence of the events themselves — as in haunted castles, when ghosts are expected at specific anniversaries.[4]

Myths, for Hubert and Mauss, are about things outside time, but we try to bring them into line with our regular time systems; thus myths are about the margins of time, the beginning or the end. But myths renew themselves in periodic ways through rites within the life of society, and in terms of human consciousness, time is thus a succession of eternities. There is always an adjustment of two series of representations, the calendar and the chronology — the mind tries to bring elements of the two series into the same tension; the collective consciousness brings a maximum of convention and minimum of experience to bear on the way this is done. Time is always a part of individual experience; and departing perhaps from what the text actually says, we could add that in the recognitions outlined in the essay lies a part of what could be called 'historical consciousness'. The essay does convey a sense of intellectual struggle going on all the time, 'adjustment' or the reconciliation of individual experience and the memory of event with the conventional cycle of 'critical dates', a cycle in which periods are emboxed one within another and form overlapping patterns. The preface refers to the 'travail collectif' of generations and societies and of the values which lie behind the 'movement of human groups'.[5] Within this essay, there is ample allowance for themes of renewal, of rewriting the past, and of the grafting of current events into the analysis of 'morphological' time. And yet the modern period seems to disrupt the slower flow of social life with which the essay is primarily concerned, and into which so much ethnographic writing seeks to situate itself.

A sense of disruption was a common marker of the modern, especially in relation to the imperial view of subject territories and their peoples. The colonial period in Africa, by comparison with the longer and more complex imperial encounter of Europe with the other continents, was relatively short and sharply defined. Nevertheless it was the African colonial period which gave shape to much British anthropological theory and practice. Anthropological writings on African society in the mid twentieth century tended, under the momentum of the urgency to be up to date, relevant, and politically acceptable, to operate with a very 'modernist' kind of dichotomy between past and present. The colonial period itself tended to prescribe its own rhythms, and to assume, if not actually create a sharp disjunction with the older past. The 'internal' time of African societies was not often a very intimate part of anthropological analysis, and most historians themselves tended to work with a distinctly external framework of time-reasoning, drawn from the dominant political events of the imposition, administration, and giving up of empire. The more embedded, 'archaeological' mode of enquiry into the experience and practice of time within African society, into the relevance of myths and rites, and the nature of historical consciousness, was rarely a part of any research strategy.[6]

It has been standard for most key practitioners of the discipline in Britain to look back to the formative influence of Durkheim and the *Année sociologique* as a whole (and increasingly to point to their supposed lack of historical insight). The Durkheimian group actually wrote very little about Africa, and little of what they did write has ever been read on the English-speaking side of the Channel, let alone translated. The 'formative influence' came mainly from texts dealing with other regions, such as the essay on the gift, that on seasonal variations of the Eskimo, or that on 'primitive classification'.[7] These were almost exclusively written within the frame of the embedded time of social practice, transposed into the discourse of African colonial times as 'tradition' mostly in need of updating. When I became aware of this puzzle and looked back to read more carefully what had been offered on Africa, I found that it actually had more of a 'historical' character than I had expected, and sometimes more so than much of the professional ethnography and analysis of the mid-century. In particular, I found some of Marcel Mauss's lesser-known writings on African ethnography particularly sympathetic to questions which anthropologists are pursuing today in their endeavour to analyse the historical or 'time' aspect of society and human events. This is now a major concern, though in our anxiety to escape the charges of naive functionalism and antiquarianism we have sometimes pursued the linear narratives of event-history so single-mindedly that we have lost sight of the continuities of social form as such. In accepting the criticism made of us in the colonial period, we naturally turned to economics, politics, and development studies for ways of including 'time' and 'change'.

However, as the colonial period has now receded in memory both for African peoples and for those who write about the continent, that period no longer seems the main source of change, or the backbone of all African history. The colonial period now seems a more 'contained' phase of the past, while older patterns are becoming more visible. At least this is the case in North East Africa, the part of the continent with which I am most familiar.[8] With this recognition of longer continuities, I believe, has come a more complex and interesting sense of what it is for a society to constitute itself within and through time. And this is where one comes to look again at the writings of Mauss on Africa, and to feel a need to explain the sense of recognition and relevance. Mauss was writing before the urgencies of colonial time helped to flatten the internal history of African societies. In his way of integrating a time dimension into his analyses, Mauss was I think building his own historical anthropology which in many respects seems to branch out from what have been later represented, at least in anthropology, as the Durkheimian orthodoxies.

A separate paper has been published on the treatment of African ethnography in the first series of the *Année Sociologique*.[9] It arrives at fairly negative conclusions, discussing why there was not more interest in the ethnography coming out of the African continent compared to other parts of the world, and why it was not used to a greater extent in the substantial general essays of the Durkheimian school. The problem cannot be explained solely by the relative lack of literature, though it is true that there were fewer historical and literary sources for comparison and the African material did not often lend itself to sensitive linguistic analysis. The failure to draw in Africa as a key region of reference in early Durkheimian scholarship can be attributed in part to the awkward intermediate place which it occupied in the explicit evolutionary schemata of the *Année sociologique*. But also, and in greater part I believe, it can be attributed to the difficulty caused for Durkheimian analysis by the perception of Africa as having been overwhelmed by a recent and often violent history. The traces of archaic human society had been covered over. By contrast, and ironically, Durkheim did not seem to have the same problem with Australia or North America, where history had if anything been more violent, more cataclysmic for the indigenous peoples. In those cases, I suggest that the older vision of primeval society remained intact because of the very profundity of the perceived gulf between the native peoples and those who brought the devastation of modern events to them; indigenous existence could be imagined quite outside the modern era. In Africa, the primal vision could not be kept separate from the turbulence of modern times; the internal and external admixture and interconnection between those of the continent and those outside it could not be imagined away. These various factors seem to have inhibited the inclusion of African data in the major comparative essays of the early *Année sociologique*, despite their undoubted influence on the later thinking and practice of both French and British field researchers in Africa.[10]

A tension between the two senses of time, the slower socially embedded kind of time treated quite positively and the modern quite negatively, can be traced in many of the reviews in the early volumes of the *Année sociologique*. For example, consider the following early commentary by Mauss himself reviewing Henri Junod's 1901 article on the Ba-Ronga of the coastal region of what is now Mozambique:

> The author was a missionary among the Ba-ronga, to whom he has already devoted several publications. These are the first substantial documents that we have on these tribes. Unfortunately, however, these communities are among the least interesting of the Bantu peoples. Living in the neighbourhood of Lourenço Marques, they have experienced European influence for three centuries, and particularly in recent times have undergone profound transformations. Thus we are not dealing with beliefs and practices free of all contamination. We should add nevertheless that there really does appear to be a kind of Bantu civilisation, and that all these tribes have interacted with each other; it is for this reason that certain tales seem common to them all. It is therefore necessary to submit the evidence about them to a rigorous ethnographic critique.[11]

On the one hand, because the various tribes had all been interacting with each other over a long period of time, they had created what we could truly call a Bantu civilisation; but the three most recent centuries of European influence had transformed them, contaminating their practices and beliefs and thus making them the least interesting of the Bantu peoples.

Now, in a native American or Australian context, these two contrasting sorts of time could perhaps plausibly be kept apart in the way one wrote, even in the early 1900s. But it is not so easy or so plausible for Africa. What constitutes the native or the immigrant population is not so clear. The East African coast provides a striking example, a region where Arab and other Muslim influence goes back centuries; in fact the date of this influence has been put back further by recent scholars than was known to the *Année sociologique* writers. Compare however the way that Durkheim and Mauss respectively write about the Swahili, the coastal people whose very origin lies in this contact. Relative to Durkheim, Mauss had long had a more sympathetic 'historical' eye in the modern sense for African communities. I think the difference is clear. Durkheim writes: 'The Swahili, a population of eastern Africa who are at present part of the region of the German protectorate, have been formed of two elements: on the one hand the natives, and on the other the immigrants. The former belong to the large Bantu family, the latter mainly Arabs.... The Swahili are the product of the crossing of these two races.'[12] Of the same people, on the basis of the same sources, Mauss observes in a very different vein:

The phenomena relating to Swahili religion and customary law, and their present traditions, are in a condition that is interesting for us to note. For many centuries already, this population of Bantu origin has been exposed as part of the Sultanate of Zanzibar to all kinds of influences, especially Arabic and Islamic, but also in recent times European and Hindu. The civilisation and social organisation of this society is by now simply the resultant of multiple interferences which, here and there, have certainly produced novel phenomena. For example, the rites of divination and magic present a curious compromise between Islamic and Bantu forms (... amulets, horoscopes ...). Similarly, Islamic law has not entirely replaced the former penal practices, and part of the civil law seems to have developed in a truly autonomous fashion.[13]

Mauss also communicates a sense of internal historical change in reviewing Alice Werner's work on Central Africa:

The tribes under consideration have all been subject to profound changes; centuries of wars and migrations in all directions have had an impact, not only on the institutions, but on the very size and shape of these societies, of which some have more or less disappeared, while others have become a kind of nobility in the midst of servile peoples, maintaining themselves only through a harsh exercise of authority. Such are the Ngoni.[14]

The reviews of African ethnography were not many in the first few volumes of the *Année sociologique*. Just before the Great War, however, in vol. 12 (for 1909-12, published 1913), there was a sea change, and a whole series of fresh and interesting reviews appeared, particularly by Mauss but also by Bianconi and Hertz. These writings were marked by a new historical sensibility, evidently stimulated by the African material. There were two particular clusters of related commentaries, treating on the one hand the central East African region and on the other the 'Guinean' or coastal belt and forested interior of West Africa. Mauss made the key contributions to both sets of reviews, emphasising in both cases the regional and temporal interconnection of social phenomena. For reasons mainly of space I focus my discussion here on his work on the ethnography of the East African interior as it was being published in English and in German. Several accounts of this region were appearing in the early twentieth century, describing settled peoples and kingdoms, and also pastoral nomadic peoples. Mauss came to see these various communities as interlinked in politically complex ways. This fresh interest might in turn have influenced the general development of ideas in the Durkheimian tradition, but it came too late to take root before the work of the *Année sociologique* was so suddenly cut off. Mauss, however, took up the discussion of African ethnography again in the interwar years and it is possible to see how his realisation of its historical character helped shape some of his general writings.

Mauss's Africa reviews and the encompassing of history

The earliest text on eastern Africa which Mauss had considered carefully was a 1902 article by the Rev. J. Roscoe on the Baganda, reviewed in vol. 7 of the journal, in 1904.[15] He immediately considered this work important; it documented the 'high degree of civilisation' of the Baganda.[16] Each clan had its religious and administrative functions at the royal court, which were related to it through modes of classification like those he and Durkheim had studied the previous year (i.e., in the essay on primitive classification[17]). Among the cults he notes especially that devoted to the spirit (*génie*) of the king, which he compares to those of ancient Egypt and of Rome, and he also notes points of comparison with Rome in the field of law.[18] He considered that one of the most profitable lessons the sociologist could draw from this study of a very characteristic system of royalty was that one could grasp, from a political point of view, the shape (*la forme*) of Bantu societies.

Two years later, in 1906, Mauss published what we would call a review article considering from several angles the differences between two books which had just appeared on the Masai, one by Merker, the other by Hollis (compare the discussion by W.S.F. Pickering in chapter 3, this volume). One might have thought, Mauss suggests, we were back in the days when ethnography was not a science. The contrast provoked an important critical question for ethnography: the books differed in so many respects that, were it not for the proper names, the photographs, and certain irreducible features specific to the Masai, they scarcely seemed to be about the same nation. 'One might even doubt whether it is a matter of a single tribe, or even tribes of the same family. The comparison of the two sources shows the dangers which sociology, like any experimental science, risks at the time of observation.'[19] The authors were well prepared, yet it was impossible to tell from them whether or not the non-pastoral Wandorobo hunters, scattered through the territory, were a part of the Masai ('Thus, even the very structure of the Masai nation is uncertain'). No wonder Mauss finds confusion and contradiction in collating the more subtle references to myth, religion, and magic. He does, however, make the interesting judgement that one of Merker's legends about the succession of ritual leaders is modelled on mission teachings about the Bible, and that one of Hollis's incorporates partisan accounts of a recent civil war between rival claimants.[20] While passing over Merker's judgement on the Semitic origin and migration of the Masai, he notes this ethnographer's opinion that Masai beliefs and mythology are analogous to the Judaeo-Babylonian tradition. They are presented as having a monotheistic cosmology and a single creator God who gives commandments; and each individual has a guardian angel. Hollis on the basis of closely recorded texts offers a quite different picture, of a black and a red divinity and other manifestations. How, he asks, should we account for the irreconcilable differences between these two ethnographies?

It is true, says Mauss, that the Masai nation is very extensive. It covers areas of both German and British East Africa. It was formerly even larger, but the loss of herds from recent disease had caused devastation and a famine, and these events had changed the morphology of the whole tribe. Furthermore there had been links with Protestant missionaries for more than twenty years, and much older links with the Swahili Muslims. Galla [the people termed Oromo in today's language] and Arabs were scattered through the country. Merker had not made sufficient effort to eliminate the recent — Mauss means 'Biblical' — elements in Masai mythology; Hollis reached fewer conclusions, even including two different versions of the myth about the origin of cattle, one from German and one from British territory. The conditions of observation, Mauss notes, were not the same.[21] However, the descriptions we have of rites, of celebrations, of age classes, are more or less the same (though Hollis tells us that the operator in circumcision rites is a Wandorobo).

Here Mauss elaborates for the first time his interest in the Judaic parallel. Dismissing Merker's idea of the Jewish provenance of the Masai, he points out that Merker has missed an aspect of Masai ethnography which would have supported his thesis. They have a system of food prohibitions which is almost the same as that of the Jews, including a taboo on mixing certain foods. They leave the flesh of wild animals, including that of fish and birds, to the Wandorobo and to their Bantu neighbours; and most of their legends referring to foreign peoples portray them as violating Jewish food prohibitions. Like the ancient Hebrews among the peoples of Canaan, the Masai raise domestic animals, upon which their survival as a distinct people depends. These animals are the object of a system of positive and negative observances, and there is no reason, Mauss suggests, why we should suppose that the same causes have not produced the same effects in the Nilotic world and in the Semitic, as in the Hindu (Toda and Arya) worlds (this comparative theme is taken up in later reviews on East Africa, as well as his later piece on the ancient Hebrews,[22] which I discuss below).

Mauss does not hesitate to use the term 'domination',[23] nor to point to the military organisation of East African societies, based mainly on age-sets with rigorous initiation procedures. Military organisations have external as well as internal consequences; they stimulate reponse in those who face them, sometimes provoking the formation of comparable institutions in self-defence. In reviewing four books published in 1909-10 on various East African peoples, Mauss draws attention mainly to the links between them; in particular, the influence of the Masai upon a whole series of settled neighbours (Chagga, Akamba, Kikuyu, and Nandi).[24] All share a similar strong military organisation, which encompasses (*recouvre*) other forms such as the tribe, clan, and family. 'The organisation of armed men is all-powerful.'[25] Such is the influence of 'Nilotic civilisation' that even the Masai name for God has passed to their Bantu neighbours, who have erased all theological principles of their own which might contradict this monotheism.

In relation to the character of that strongly symbolised central authority we are accustomed to call 'royalty', Mauss tends to perceive power and strength in the way that a conventional historian might, rather than remaining content with a 'morphological' analysis; he notes for West Africa that the Dahomeyan kings did not remain invisible, they went to war.[26] He made several comparisons of kingship in the eastern regions which noted their political effectiveness, including one such reference to the Shilluk.[27] The contrast with the later famous 'functional' analysis of Evans-Pritchard which rested on the maxim that the Shilluk king 'reigned' but did not 'rule' is clear.[28] The occasional ferocity of precolonial kings (often forgotten during the later, liberal colonial period) was visible to Mauss and is easier to recall from our later 'postcolonial' viewpoint; ideas and institutions of royalty and its paraphernalia of ritual power are perhaps not so far from the social imagination of some parts of Africa today, and they are little to do with simply 'reigning'.

Mauss clearly appreciated, perhaps more than the present-oriented British field anthropologists who followed, the political character of royal authority — the power even of divine kings. He recognised that Roscoe had given himself the task of reconstructing the past of Buganda in his book of 1911, as it was before the arrival of Arab merchants and the tumultuous events of recent decades, and that his work inevitably raised more questions than it had solved (here we find again the challenge of bringing time scales together): 'And in fact [Roscoe] arrived almost too late. The nation of the Baganda is already no more than a memory of itself. The country has known, over the last forty years, the worst horrors of civil and religious war and of sleeping sickness; it has lost two thirds of its population which has in addition become converted to Christianity and civilisation with surprising speed.'[29]

Nevertheless Mauss interprets the old kingdom of Buganda as having a historical existence of its own, shaped by the dynasty itself, and he might have been less surprised than some later progressive commentators have been that the son of a former exiled King of

Buganda was welcomed back to his country in the 1990s. Mauss presents elements of the religious system as testimony in themselves to the prior political history of the kingdom. The national, and especially royal, cults, show parallels with peoples both to the west and to the south, and these two currents of Bantu civilisation, characterised by monarchical institutions, appear to converge among the Baganda.[30] Buganda is, however, quite distinctive. Mauss distinguishes three levels of religious system which have contributed to the kingdom as represented by Roscoe. At the lowest is a flourishing layer of totemism (which was commonly perceived by the *Année sociologique* writers to 'survive' in most parts of Africa); above this is a layer of 'naturism' in which rites are devoted to elements of the environment; and finally there are the national cults of the royal gods. This dynastic religion is a 'secondary formation', grafted upon the more archaic forms; but it has encompassed and assimilated these. For example, the creator god, Katonda, and the gods of the moon, earthquakes, and death are linked genealogically with the royal dynasty. The great national god, Mukasa of Lake Victoria and its islands, is thus identified with Cwa, the second king. Mauss thus arrives at a very 'Durkheimian' conclusion, though he has taken a 'historical' route and the emphasis should perhaps be understood to be upon the centralising process: 'The god to whom, more and more, the national religion tends to address itself is the nation itself personified by the royal family'.[31]

I do not think an abstract notion of 'evolutionary time' is the key to understanding Mauss's formulation. I believe that he is using a tangible notion of historical time which links the Baganda more closely with 'us' than any variant of evolutionary theory. A crucial aspect of 'our' historical time, sometimes reserved exclusively for the modern world and denied for the traditional, is perhaps the evidence of human agency: the idea of power exercised by human beings as a mechanism by which the world is changed. This idea is present in his discussion of the king.

Mauss emphasises that (despite prevalent theories of 'divine kingship' in anthropology) the king of Buganda is not a god in himself while he is alive, though he is the object of many rites, including human sacrifice, which confer health and long life. One of his 'future relics', the umbilical cord identified with his spirit (*génie*), is the object of rites even during his lifetime. The political significance of his physical strength is clear. He is chosen after a traditional trial by combat; those princes not chosen are put to death. He is able to exercise some control even over the gods, pillaging their temples when he is not pleased with them. Only after death, indeed, does he fully acquire the spiritual character which makes a god of him. Mauss compares him to Alexander or Caesar in that he then becomes the object of a ceremony which introduces him into the pantheon. The surroundings of the palace are scattered with the graves of kings, 'like those of the former Mikados'. Mauss suggests that there may be graves of kings even more ancient than those whose history Roscoe traces, and suggests that it would be interesting to excavate them.[32]

Mauss laments the sparsity of oral tradition offered by Roscoe for the Baganda. By contrast, commenting in another review on a contemporary German ethnography of the Baziba, to the south, he praises the author (Rehse) for his editing of a long oral historical text, offered in the original Kiziba with both interlinear and free translation.[33] He even extends Rehse's commentary by noting the importance of an idiom which represents the king, at his enthronement, as 'eating the country', an idea paralleled in the Buganda context (and, in the context of my present argument, a very potent image of political agency). Rehse's work reinforces what has been learned from the traditions of other peoples of the region. Mauss exclaims 'Let us hope that we have now finally done with the old image (la légende) of "peoples without history", especially in Africa.'[34] He remarks further on the interconnections between the myths of the various neighbouring kingdoms: a god who is the son here, is the father there — as is only natural, Mauss suggests, between rival dynasties which express their national pride through myths. 'We have here a precious example of these mythological traditions which have come to mask historical events. These discoveries tend to confirm certain interpretations which have been proposed for Egyptian, Hindu, or Greek myths.'[35] The African data, thus, because of their evident historicity, can provide insight into the contexts which have helped shape classical mythology. Interestingly, Mauss picks out as one of Rehse's best chapters the one dealing with Kiziba traditions of chronology and the calculation of time.[36]

In 1925 Mauss took up East African comparative themes again, stimulated by the publication of three more studies by Roscoe on Ugandan peoples who could be regarded as nations, together with notes on a range of other tribes, including some 'Nilotic' peoples like the Bateso.[37] Some peoples, like the Basoga, were formerly under the domination of the Banyoro and the Baganda but resisted it and have remained fairly democratic. Other points noted by Mauss, clearly bearing on the historical linkages of this region of the East African Lakes, include the salt industry and trade of the Bakonja [Bakonzo] in the far west.[38] He also draws attention to the ties of affiliation between various peoples of the region and the king of Rwanda, who he reminds us was under German before Belgian rule. He remarks that these new studies point to the need for further research, especially on the tribes in the north of Uganda and the south of Abyssinia. From Roscoe's two

main new monographs on the Banyankole and Bakitara (Banyoro)
Mauss suggests that it is possible to extract a kind of comparative
sociology, from the religious as well as from the juridical point of view.
They are 'composite societies' of the Masai type [i.e., taking the Masai
region as a whole]. A society of pastoralists, known as Bahuma
[variously Bahima, Watutsi, etc.] in each case, has conquered a society
of agriculturalists and artisans, of serfs, Bahera [variously Bahutu,
etc.]. While Roscoe like most authors tends to regard this situation as
the result of invasion by 'Hamites', this cannot be the only hypothesis
(for example, the Nkole language is 'neither Bantu nor Hamitic'). 'The
turbulent history (*l'histoire mouvementée*) of these peoples is perhaps
greater than we have assumed, or described.'[39] In Ankole and Bunyoro
the population strata are more unified than the Masai with their
Wandorobo, but less so than the people of Buganda, and this is also
clear in the form of their religion.

Mauss notes that Roscoe's enquiries were mainly confined to the
centre of each country and do not reflect variations of locality and
caste (which by implication would have thrown further light on the
history of these kingdoms). He compares the forms of stratification in
the region to the 'double morphology' of the Eskimo or the American
North-west. He also uses the expression 'dominant caste' of the
pastoralists of the region, though he draws attention to the fact that
even with regard to language, the substrata have exerted their own
influence, the conquered sometimes assimilating the conquerors, the
cultivators and artisans the pastoralists. After touching on the
Israel/Canaan parallel again,[40] Mauss finally discusses the importance
of Roscoe's new work on this region as it bears on the question of royal
power. Roscoe himself, Mauss mentions, has followed Frazer in
emphasising the religious side of the king's functions. He is in effect a
kind of living god, and an officiating priest to the gods. But he is
surrounded by a 'sacred guild', consisting not only of pastoral chiefs
but also ministers, senior officials, and 'grands feudataires'. This body
governs during the interregnum and to some extent exercises control
over the king.[41]

These reflections reach their mature expression in Mauss's use of
East African ethnography in his contribution to the special issue of the
Revue des études juives offered to Israël Lévi in 1926. Sketching the
interrelation of mythical motifs and peoples in the ancient Middle East,
he points out that we are far from the savages of McLennan or the
rustics of Renan. The geographical area was immense, but it was full
of settlements, many fortified, from the third and fourth millennium,
and encompassed rich pastures, where great families of active agnates
founded tribes and clans and in places furnished the chiefs and
ancestors of defined societies. The ancestors of Israel conducted trade

across the deserts and formed alliances with settled kingdoms as do the Bedouins and Tuaregs of today. From their 'entry into history', as far back as any evidence goes, the Semitic peoples with their elegance of language and in a land so rich in goods, in human beings, and in timeless (*éternelles*) ruins from the past, have always been civilised.[42]

The second part of Mauss's essay draws in detail upon the East African ethnography, which by analogy illuminates the analysis from Biblical times. From Tigre and Abyssinia to Uganda there extends a variety of societies speaking languages of many different families, some of them mixed. Among these are excellent examples of the kind of social organisation which we can call 'composite', races or groups being grafted (*accolés*) one upon another. This kind of society was very widespread in antiquity, in India as well as in the Biblical lands. Today we can see in Africa, particularly among the composite societies of southern Ethiopia and Uganda, the way in which the ancient Israëlites lived, nomads, herders, warriors, usually disdaining the earth, the noble sons of a noble race, taking pride in their flocks, their horses and the camels, their diet and their cult of meats and milk.[43] These East African societies lived, as the Israelites did, in the midst of other peoples who did not share the same relationship with their God. Mauss goes into considerable detail to demonstrate the analogy, emphasising for example the way that endogamy played a part in building up the dominance of the pastoralists. This was how Israel secured its position, first between Mesopotamia and Egypt, and then moving between Egypt and Canaan, in the manner of the kings of Rwanda and Nyoro, even to installing priests, judges, and kings in the various settled places. 'The analogy between this social morphology and that of the Hebrews is profound.'[44] Similar conditions of life, Mauss concludes, have produced similar effects; and moreover, the African case suggests that many of the details of the Biblical texts, formerly taken as purely legendary, may have some basis in the history of the patriarchs. The pastoral peoples have played a very important role since the end of the neolithic age and have very often established superiority in relation to sedentary communities, dominating them strategically in their towns and countryside, not only by force but also through wealth, commerce, and industry.[45]

I do not have space here to add an extended commentary on the way Mauss developed his analysis of the regional interconnections of West Africa. This part of the continent, however, stimulated his interest over a long period, from his early reviews of Mary Kingsley[46] to the enthusiastic welcome he gave the work of German ethnographers and others in Togo and other areas of West Africa. He even compared the revelations of the new German ethnography to the great Australian expeditions.[47] He noted the connectedness of apparently discrete phenomena in the region: for example, mixed combinations of patrilineal and matrilineal filiation across West Africa, and the circulation of religious ideas and cults.[48] He drew on this ethnographic region in several of his later general review commentaries, particularly when developing themes of the 'international' transmission and circulation of currencies, especially cowries, and the connection between religion and money.[49] One does wonder why some of this material was not used in his essay *The gift*.[50]

Political complexity and civilisation:
Mauss's use of African data

Nick Allen has already drawn attention to Mauss's paper of 1931 on social cohesion in 'polysegmentary' societies.[51] Here, he seems driven to demonstrate the internal complexity of what might otherwise be classed as simple or amorphous social forms, by a need to complicate Durkheim's vision of mechanical, as distinct from organic solidarity. In developing his argument he draws on several earlier pieces, and upon African data along with ethnography from other regions. He notes in passing that he views African societies as very advanced in many ways, even more so than the early Germans and the Celts.[52] He also seeks to explain that the dilemmas of authority, and of its transmission, are present everywhere, at least in the forms of opposition between the sexes, ages, and generations, as well as between local groups.[53] This point might be thought, Mauss suggests, to contradict the gregarious and purely collective view that Durkheim had of the clan: but adds that this understanding was implicit in the work they had done together. These oppositions might work against one another; 'the lines of opposition cross-cut those of cohesion' as in the joking relationships of North America and the Bantu peoples; 'the groups are interwoven one within another (*s'imbriquent les uns dans les autres*)'.[54]

Mauss gives a particular instance of a system of quadripartite division as reported by Labouret among the Lobi peoples of Upper Volta, represented as groups A1 and A2, B1 and B2. Mauss considers this form similar to the marriage classes of Australia, where a tribe may be divided into two phratries, each again divided into two, usually by generation. Regretting that Labouret has not been able to record the pattern of exogamy or marriage of the Lobi clans, Mauss considers that the four divisions would once have seen their relationship to each other as either brothers-in-law, or fathers- and sons-in-law (he makes comparative reference here to Ashanti). However, a 'political' account is given by Labouret; when A2 is fighting with B2, it is the people of B1 who stop the A2s from fighting, and the B2s stop the A1s when necessary.[55] To Mauss, this pattern suggests the exercise of generational authority across the lines of affinal division, where brothers are set against brothers-in-law. One generation-class has the right to police the built-in oppositions of the other. Mauss's rendering thus transforms the principle of categorical opposition and engagement from the idiom of those who marry each other, to those who fight each other. He extends further this 'political' reading of the Lobi ethnography with a commentary on the way that authority is built up and exercised by elders in families. The patterns of chiefship are not, however, the only principle of organisation. He goes on to discuss education, tradition, as passing on things and practices, even collective representations, in different contexts; and the overriding importance of notions of peace within subgroups and the complex relationships of a society, even those assumed amorphous.[56] It is scarcely necessary to point out the foreshadowing in this piece of Evans-Pritchard's classic work, and that of his students, on African political traditions and especially those of the Nilotic peoples.[57]

A focus on internal political complexity is complemented by Mauss's vision of the wider interconnectedness and material interdependence of communities within 'civilisation'. In collaboration with Durkheim, he offered a note on the notion of civilisation in Vol. 12 of the *Année sociologique*. Here he made it quite clear that while studying social phenomena in themselves and for themselves, an important principle to be followed was not to leave them in the air, but always to link them with a definite substrate, that is a human group occupying a particular geographical space.[58] Of all such groupings, the largest, which frames and envelops all the forms of social activity, seems to be political society, the tribe, the population (*peuplade*), the nation, city state, modern State, and so on. 'It seems at first sight that collective life can develop only within political organisms having distinct contours and clearly marked borders, and that sociology cannot recognise social phenomena of a higher or more general order.'[59] However, patterns of social connection are not everywhere very clearly delimited; they can 'cut across political frontiers and extend into less easily determinable spaces'.

Mauss developed his vision of 'civilisation' as an essentially intersocietal field of connection in an essay prepared in 1929.[60] Setting his argument against the general theories of evolution and 'culture history' of the time, he here insists that sociologists, like historians and geographers, should link the phenomena of civilisation not to a hypothetical idea of human evolution but to the chronological and geographical interconnectedness (*l'enchaînement*) of societies.[61] He recalls that 'civilisation' is derived from *civis*, citizen. Not all social phenomena are those of civilisation; many signal the specificity of societies and mark them off from others: China behind its wall, the

Brahman within his caste. The Hebrews and their descendants, the Jews, distinguish themselves from other Semites by concentrating within themselves. These examples prove that it would be better not to speak of 'civilisation' when one is referring to phenomena restricted to a single society as such. But even in the most isolated societies there are common features which have a connected history. Techniques and arts pass from one group to another; music, dance, stories, and special cults circulate over wide areas (one example he gives are the griots of West Africa). The cowrie money or copper wire of central Africa are examples of 'truly international' phenomena, and long-distance circulation of valuables was known in the middle Paleolithic. 'Military institutions are necessarily 'borrowed' along with techniques of armament, right up to our own era and our own mode of life. A particular phenomenon can impose itself beyond the society and the time when it was created. The "phenomena of civilisation" are thus essentially international, extranational.'[62] Mauss comments further that the phenomena of civilisation are common to several societies linked (*rapprochées*) in some degree; they may be linked by prolonged contact, by permanent intermediaries, or by derivation from a common source in the past. As Nathan Schlanger has emphasised in chapter 12 with respect to techniques and material culture, for Mauss the phenomena of civilisation have a foundation in the past, in history, but this historic past is more than the past of a single nation. By studying them one can perceive connections and establish a genealogy of facts, or more or less certain sequences, without which it would be impossible to conceive either history or human evolution.[63]

In these texts Mauss outlines a view of human society as existing and being formed through time in a recognisably modern sense, a view which, however, does not abstract time from the social forms of human life. This is an anthropological view which can be accommodated to some archaeological approaches to the past, and to some relatively recent views of social and cultural history (as distinct from the political event-led kind of history that used to fill the textbooks). It presents an interesting foil to some modern writing in anthropology which seeks to intensify particularity in local human interaction and experience, but which has been hijacked by a popular discourse of contrast and relativism in society, culture, and identity, a discourse of difference which is often 'naturalised' and thus akin to the racism of earlier times.[64]

Mauss on sources, methods, and the emerging colonial context

In his sensitivity to ethnographic method, and to the colonial context and its formative implications for the personality and background of ethnographers and informants, Mauss is speaking directly to our current concerns in seeking to handle ethnography as a kind of 'history'. It is relevant to note here also his self-awareness, especially in his engagement with issues of psychology (see the various pieces translated by Brewster, and compare the discussions by Bruno Karsenti and Nathan Schlanger in this volume — chapters 5 and 12).[65] Moreover, his ear for language alerted him to the fact that the colonial situation in which so much ethnography was carried out had itself lent much of the seemingly appropriate terminology. 'When the history of the science of religions and of ethnography comes to be written, it will be astonishing to see the undue and haphazard role that a notion like that of "fetish" has played in theoretical and descriptive works. It corresponds only to a vast misunderstanding between two civilisations, the African and the European; it has no basis other than a blind copying of colonial usage, as embedded in one lingua franca or another spoken by Europeans on the West coast.'[66] In general Mauss is very critical of missionaries — especially Fr. Schmidt and his desire to see the religion of the Pygmies as the result of primitive revelation, rather than a process of historical development,[67] and of over-literary evocations of the primitive.[68] He is also against the heavy scientism of some established schools of the day, mounting a sustained critique of the German school of 'culture history', focused on Frobenius in particular. This began with a review in 1906,[69] and culminated in a harsh and sustained attack in 1925.[70]

In an early comment on a 1902 article in the *Journal of the Royal Anthropological Institute* on the Wagogo of (German) East Africa, Mauss took the author (the Rev. H. Cole, a resident missionary) to task for having adopted Frazer's standard questionnaire as the literal framework for his notes, a method which could not be accepted as 'ethnology' in the proper sense of the word. Even for a study in 'la sociologie religieuse' Mauss would regard such topics as commerce, kinship terminology, and the position of children, as being of equal importance to those questions posed concerning arithmetic, writing, the measurement of time, games and dances. He also regretted the lack of any questions bearing on temples and sacred places.[71] These comments are pertinent, incidentally, to our present argument that, *contra* Mauss, it is the late modern style of ethnographic research which separates out the intellectual construction of 'time' as a thing in itself from its social matrix.

In reviewing a Belgian compilation of data on the peoples of the eastern Congo, Mauss notes that most of the information was collected from former colonial administrators, and edited back in Belgium without being verified *in situ*. An Ababua informant, Tisambi, whose responses to a questionnaire were included, turned out to have been a servant in Antwerp and to have left home at the age of fifteen. With respect to another compilation on the Mandja of the French Congo, Mauss notes that the author was not afraid to allude to a horrible execution for which he and a colleague were responsible; this gives us an idea, he suggests ironically, of the quality of intimacy which could be expected between him and his subjects, and the degree of reliance which could be placed upon his enquiries.[72]

Mauss did not have a negative attitude to colonial rule as such or to the practice of anthropology under it. On the contrary he was rather in favour. Even in the early years of the century, in reviewing Casely Hayford's 1903 account of 'Gold Coast Native Institutions', Mauss approves of the focus on the conflict between forms of law, on the grounds that out of it there may emerge new phenomena:

> This book, the work of an indigenous lawyer, deals with the jural institutions of the Fanti and the Ashanti.... It is primarily concerned with the daily conflict between the social institutions of these people, already at an advanced stage of civilisation, and those imposed on them by Britain in the interests of colonial rule. The problem has a sociological significance; for these intricate contacts between different forms of law give rise to new phenomena which are well worth recording.[73]

In 1913 Mauss published an overview of ethnography in France and abroad, which called for a greater investment of resources and activity in the investigation of the life of the peoples of the French colonies. He noted first the older roots of interest among eighteenth-century French historians and philosophers in the life of 'primitives', but then its eclipse in the nineteenth century. By contrast, ethnography in England was developing fast with the discovery and conquest of colonies, throughout the nineteenth century. After the English contribution to ethnography came that of the North Americans, where it was institutionally organised. Ethnography was also being written in Germany and Holland. France was scarcely competing. Why? Although most of the New World colonies were lost after Napoleon I, Mauss claimed this was not a complete explanation. The scientific establishment was simply not interested. Mauss goes on to survey what was then known of different parts of the world, including Africa, and castigates the French in particular for not doing more. He did not regard the ethnographic project as merely a matter of recording a disappearing past, but included in its brief the observation of changing conditions in the colonies.

In the British Empire, field research in anthropology flourished in mid-century, but mainly within the boundaries established by the colonial administrations. Moreover, the close focus of local fieldwork, together with its intensely personal character and short time span, seemed to leave little room for regional relations and the depth of time which had become preoccupations for Mauss in his reflections on Africa. The first wave of criticism directed at colonial anthropology suggested that history should be brought back into focus by taking colonial conquest, domination, and administration into account; but this line of criticism itself stemmed from the modern, linear, political sense of time. It is only with the lapse of a substantial period since the end of empire that anthropologists can see more clearly the relevance of longer genealogies, the reemergence or at least continuing momentum of precolonial social formations, and the need not only to collect narratives and time-scales but to build a more morphological sense of time into social analysis. We no longer regard the presence or absence of analytical narratives about the past or intellectual models of time as a diagnostic factor in exploring historical consciousness. We look for it in a variety of embodied practices, in rites and symbolic representations, in 'performances', in spirit possession cults, and in prophetic evocations which transcend the regular time-bound events of the day to look to a moral landscape of past and future. These need not all be compatible with one another; we have learned that historical consciousness rests partly upon the recognition and enactment of different time scales and rhythms.[74] Here, I believe, we can go back to Mauss with great profit.

Partly because of his greater sensitivity to movement, renewal, and agency in society than Durkheim ever showed (and I realise this may be an unjustifiably crude way of making the point), Mauss responded in a lively way to the new material coming out of Africa. This new body of ethnographic data was so transparently evidence of history both past and present, both in the morphological sense and the modern sense, sometimes distinctly but sometimes conjoined. Events were themselves transcending this opposition. Mauss's eventual field trip was to Morocco, another region of the African continent with a notably heterogenous history.[75] In his short report on this visit it is clear that he was excited by the evidence before his eyes of a living testimony to a very ancient history, in the spirit possession cult he witnessed among black Hausa speakers in Morocco, descendants of a population movement northwards across the Sahara which had been renewed again and again since antiquity.

NOTES

1.   E.R. Leach, 'Two essays on time', in *Rethinking anthropology*, London, 1961. A. Gell, *The anthropology of time: cultural constructions of temporal maps and images*, Oxford, 1992.

2. J. Davis, 'The social relations of the production of history', in E. Tonkin, M. McDonald, and M. Chapman, eds, *History and ethnicity*, ASA Monograph 27, London, 1989, pp. 104-20. Cf. Davis's inaugural lecture, 'Times and identities', Oxford, 1991, and J. Fabian, *Time and the other*, New York, 1983.

3. H. Hubert, 'Etude sommaire de la représentation du temps dans la religion et dans la magie', Ecole pratique des Hautes Etudes, Section des sciences religieuses, Paris, 1905, pp. 1-39; reprinted under the names of H. Hubert and M. Mauss, in their *Mélanges d'histoire des religions*, Paris, 1909, pp. 189-229. An English translation is in preparation, to be published under the auspices of the British Centre for Durkheimian Studies.

4. Hubert, 'La représentation du temps', *Mélanges*, p. 196.

5. Hubert and Mauss, Préface, *Mélanges*, pp. xxxi, xxxiii.

6. It would not be easy to document fairly this sweeping generalisation; but if one representative collection of papers had to be selected, it would probably be M. Fortes and E.E. Evans-Pritchard, eds., *African political systems*, London, 1940.

7. M. Mauss, *The gift: the form and reason for exchange in archaic societies* [1925], trans. W.D. Halls, London, 1990. M. Mauss in collaboration with H. Beuchat, *Seasonal variations of the Eskimo: a study in social morphology* [1906], trans. J.J. Fox, London, 1979. E. Durkheim and M. Mauss, *Primitive classification* [1903], trans. R. Needham, Chicago, 1963.

8. See, for example, W. James, *'Kwanim pa: the making of the Uduk people. An ethnographic study of survival in the Sudan-Ethiopian borderlands*, Oxford, 1979; *The listening ebony: moral knowledge, religion and power among the Uduk of Sudan*, Oxford, 1988; *The southern marches of imperial Ethiopia: essays in social anthropology and history*, ed. with D.L. Donham, Cambridge, 1986.

9. W. James, 'The treatment of African ethnography in *L'Année sociologique* (I-XII), *L'Année sociologique* 48, 1998, pp. 193-207.

10. There was, in my view, a parallel problem for the continuing tradition of structuralism in French anthropology, signalled by the scant attention given to Africa at all in the work of Lévi-Strauss. Again I think the problem is that of the difficulty in accommodating 'modern' time into structuralism. For a detailed case analysis of 'exchange-marriage' in Africa which does attempt to incorporate 'modern' time, see my paper 'Lifelines: sister-exchange marriage among the Gumuz', in *The southern marches of imperial Ethiopia*, pp. 119-47.

11. M. Mauss, *Année sociologique* (henceforth, *AS*) 3, 1900, p. 220, repr. *Oeuvres*, vol. 3, p. 126.

12. E. Durkheim, *AS* 7, 1904, pp. 421-2.

13. Mauss, *AS* 8, 1905, p. 305.

14. Mauss, *AS* 11, 1910, pp. 108-9.

15. Mauss, *AS* 7, 1904, pp. 396-8.

16. Ibid., p. 397.

17. Durkheim and Mauss, *Primitive classification*.

18. Mauss, *AS* 7, 1904, p. 398.

19. Mauss, *AS* 9, 1906, p. 184.

20. Ibid, p. 185.

21. Ibid, p. 188.

22. Mauss, 'Critique interne de la légende d'Abraham' [1926], *Oeuvres*, vol. 2, pp. 527-36.

23. See also 'L'organisation religieuse des pasteurs Bantou' [1925], *Oeuvres*, vol. 2 , p. 550.

24. *AS* 12, 1913, p. 142ff.

25. Ibid., p. 143.

26. Ibid, p. 398.

27. Ibid., p. 146.
28. E.E. Evans-Pritchard, 'The divine kingship of the Shilluk of the Nilotic Sudan' [1948], repr. in *Essays in social anthropology*, London, 1962, pp. 66-86.
29. *AS* 12, 1913, p. 128.
30. Ibid., p. 129.
31. Ibid., p. 131.
32. Ibid., p. 130.
33. Ibid., pp. 132-4, repr. *Oeuvres*, vol. 1, pp. 587-9.
34. Ibid., p. 132.
35. Ibid., p. 133.
36. Ibid., p. 134.
37. Roscoe, J., I: *The Bakitara of Bunyoro*; II: *The Banyankole*; III: *The Bagesu and other tribes of the Uganda Protectorate* (Report of the Mackie Ethnological Expedition to Central Africa, 3 vols, Cambridge, 1923, 1924).
38. *AS* n.s. 1, p. 433, repr. *Oeuvres*, vol. 2, pp. 550-1.
39. Ibid., p. 434.
40. *AS* n.s. 1, p. 599, repr. *Oeuvres*, vol. 2, pp. 553-4.
41. Cf. *AS* 12, 1913, p. 391.
42. Mauss, 'La légende d'Abraham'.
43. Ibid., p. 533.
44. Ibid., p. 535.
45. Ibid., p. 536.
46. See *AS* 1, 1898, pp. 179-83; *AS* 3, 1900, pp. 224-6; *AS* 6, 1903, pp. 182-3.
47. *AS* 11, 1910, pp. 136-7.
48. *AS* 12, 1913, p. 398.
49. 'Les origines de la notion de monnaie',*Oeuvres* [1914], vol. 2, p. 106ff.
50. Mauss, *The gift*.
51. Mauss, *Oeuvres*, vol. 3, p. 11ff. See N. J. Allen, 'The division of labour and the notion of primitive society: a Maussian approach', *Social anthropology* 3, 1995, pp. 49-59.
52. Mauss, *Oeuvres*, vol. 3, p. 12.
53. Ibid., p. 13.
54. Ibid., pp. 19-20.
55. Ibid., p. 21.
56. Ibid., p. 24.
57. E.E. Evans-Pritchard, *The Nuer: mode of livelihood and political system of a Nilotic people*, Oxford, 1940; J. Middleton and D. Tait, eds, *Tribes without rulers*, London, 1958.
58. *AS* 12, 1913, p. 46, repr. in *Oeuvres*, vol. 2, p. 451.
59. Ibid.
60. Mauss, *Oeuvres*, vol. 2, p. 456ff.
61. Ibid., p. 475.
62. Ibid., p. 460.
63. Ibid., p. 461.
64. See W. James, ed., *The pursuit of certainty: religious and cultural formulations*, London, 1995.
65. M. Mauss, *Sociology and psychology: essays by Marcel Mauss*, trans. B. Brewster, London, 1979.
66. Mauss, *AS* 10, 1907, pp. 308-9, repr. *Oeuvres*, vol. 2, pp. 244-5. Bruno Karsenti kindly drew my attention to this passage.
67. Mauss, *AS* 12, 1913, pp. 65-8, repr. *Oeuvres*, vol. 1, pp. 504-7.
68. Mauss, *AS* 12, 1913, pp. 139-40.
69. Mauss, *AS* 9, 1906, p. 290, repr. *Oeuvres*, vol. 2, pp. 488-9.
70. Mauss, *AS* n.s. 1, 1925, pp. 302-6 (repr. *Oeuvres*, vol. 2, pp. 499-502), 441-6.

71. Mauss, *AS* 7, 1904, pp. 238-9.
72. Mauss, *AS* 12, 1913, pp. 139-42.
73. Mauss, *AS* 8, 1905, p. 391.
74. Davis, 'Times and identities'.
75. M. Mauss, *L'Anthropologie* 40, 1930, pp. 453-6, repr. *Oeuvres*, vol. 2, pp. 562-7.

SELECT BIBLIOGRAPHY

A. Reading Mauss in French

Mauss's original publications are very widely dispersed, but the greater part of his early work appeared in the twelve volumes of the Année sociologique published between 1898 and 1913. For instance, these volumes contain more than 450 of his longer or shorter reviews of books or articles. He attempted to relaunch the journal in 1925-7, but this second series soon lapsed and a successful revival had to await the later 1940s. Mauss himself never published a book, and a number of his manuscripts remained unpublished at his death. Most of his surviving work, published or not, has subsequently been collected in six volumes. When citing these volumes, it is usually helpful to include in references an indication of when the text was originally published (or written).

Sociologie et anthropologie, Paris, 1950, with a two-page *avertissement* by G. Gurvitch and a well-known 'Introduction à l'oeuvre de Marcel Mauss' by C. Lévi-Strauss, pp. IX-LII. All parts have been translated (see section B).
Part 1. 'Esquisse d'une théorie de la magie', written with H. Hubert [1904], pp.1-141.
Part 2. 'Essai sur le don. Forme et raison de l'échange dans les sociétés archaïques [1925], pp.145-279.
Part 3. 'Rapports réels et pratiques de la psychologie et de la sociologie' [1924], pp. 283-310.
Part 4. 'Effet physique chez l'individu de l'idée de mort suggérée par la collectivité (Australie, Nouvelle-Zélande)' [1926], pp. 313-30.
Part 5. 'Une catégorie de l'esprit humain: la notion de personne, celle de "moi"' [1938], pp. 333-62.
Part 6. 'Les techniques du corps' [1935], pp. 365-86.
From the third edition (1966) onwards: Part 7. 'Essai sur les variations saisonnières des sociétés eskimos: étude de morphologie sociale', with H. Beuchat [1906], pp. 389-477.

Oeuvres, 3 vols, (1968-9), presented by V. Karady, Paris.
Vol. 1 *Les fonctions sociales du sacré.*
Vol. 2 *Représentations collectives et diversité des civilisations.*
Vol. 3 *Cohésion sociale et divisions de la sociologie.*
The following list is a selection of the most substantial and/or best-known texts, and includes the majority of those referred to by contributors. However, there is also much of value among the texts not listed. The titles have been translated.

Vol. 1.
'Introduction to the analysis of some religious phenomena', written with H. Hubert [1908], pp. 3-39.
'Essay on the nature and function of sacrifice', written with H. Hubert [1899], pp. 193-307. (See section B.)
'Prayer' [1909], pp. 357-477 (the opening of Mauss's unfinished thesis).

Vol. 2.
'On some primitive forms of classification: a contribution to the study of collective representations', written with Durkheim [1903], pp. 13-89. (See section B.)
'The origins of the notion of money' [1914], pp.106-112.

'(Primitive mentality and participation)' [1923], 125-31.
'Conceptions which preceded the notion of matter' [written 1939, published 1945], pp. 161-66.
'Art and myth according to Mr Wundt' [1908], pp. 195-227.
'The origins of magic powers in Australian societies: analytical and critical study of some ethnographic documents' [1904], pp. 319-69.
'Civilisations: elements and forms' [1930], pp. 456-79.
'Internal criticism of the 'Legend of Abraham" [1926], pp. 527-36.
'Semites and Africans in Morocco' (Mauss's report on his study trip to that country) [1930], pp. 562-7.
'Anna-Virāj' [1911], pp. 593-600.
'Religion and the origins of penal law according to a recent book' (by S.R. Steinmetz), [1896], pp. 651-98.

Vol. 3.
'Social cohesion in polysegmentary societies' [1932], pp.11-26.
'An ancient form of contract among the Thracians' [1921], pp. 35-43.
'Gift-gift' [1924], pp. 46-51. (See section B.)
'On a text of Posidonius: suicide, the supreme counter-prestation' [1925], pp. 52-7.
'Joking relationships' [1926], pp. 109-124.
'Sociology' (encyclopaedia entry), written with P. Fauconnet [1901], pp. 139-77.
'Divisions and proportions of the divisions of sociology' [1927], pp. 178-245.
'The obligatory expression of sentiments (funerary oral rituals of the Australians)' [1921], pp. 267-78.
'Methodological note on the extension of sociology: a statement of some principles in the light of a recent book' [1927], pp. 283-97.
'Fragment of a plan for a descriptive "general sociology"' [1934], pp. 303-54.
'Ethnography in France and abroad' [1913], pp. 395-434.
'Sociology in France since 1914' [1933], pp. 436-50.
'In memoriam: the unpublished work of Durkheim and his collaborators' [1925], pp. 473-99.
'Sylvain Lévi' [obituary written in 1935], pp. 535-45.
'The nation' [written 1920?, first published 1954], pp. 573-625.'
'The problem of nationality' [1920], pp. 626-34.

Manuel d'ethnographie, Avertissement et préface de Denise Paulme, Paris, 1947. These are essentially notes for a course of lectures addressed to students, and would not have been published in this form by Mauss himself. The pagination in the first edition differs from that in subsequent editions (2nd 1967, 3rd 1989).

Marcel Mauss: ecrits politiques, intro. and ed. Marcel Fournier, Paris, 1997. (Many of these texts were originally published in journals that were not primarily academic.)

Uncollected work. Most of the texts that have not been collected can be traced via the bibliography in *Oeuvres*, vol. 3, or the slightly fuller one in Fournier's biography (see section C).

B. Work by Mauss available in English

The gift: forms and functions of exchange in archaic societies, trans. Ian Cunnison, intro. E.E. Evans-Pritchard, London, 1954; and more recently *The gift: the form and reason for exchange in archaic societies*, trans. W.D. Halls, foreword by Mary Douglas, London, 1990. (*Sociologie et anthropologie*, part 2.)
Primitive classification (written with E. Durkheim), trans. and intro. Rodney Needham, London, 1963. (*Oeuvres*, vol. 2.)
Sacrifice: its nature and function (written with H. Hubert), trans. W.D. Halls, Foreword by E.E. Evans-Pritchard, London, 1964. (*Oeuvres*, vol. 1.)
'On language and primitive forms of classification', trans. D.H. Hymes, pp. 125-7 in D.H. Hymes, ed., *Language in culture and society: a reader in linguistics and anthropology*, New York, 1964 [1923].

'Note on the notion of civilisation', trans. and intro. B. Nelson, pp. 808-13 in *Social Research*, 38, 1971.

A general theory of magic (written with H. Hubert), trans. R. Brain, foreword by D.F. Pocock, London, 1972. (*Sociologie et anthropologie*, part 1.)

Sociology and psychology, trans. Ben Brewster, London, 1979. (*Sociologie et anthropologie*, parts 3-6. Part 6 originally appeared in *Economy and Society*, 2, 1972. Part 5 was retranslated by W.D. Halls in Carrithers et al. eds; see section C below.)

Seasonal variations of the Eskimo: a study in social morphology (written with H. Beuchat), trans. and intro. James J. Fox, London, 1979. (*Sociologie et anthropologie*, part 7.)

'A sociological assessment of Bolshevism (1924-5)', trans. and annotated Ben Brewster, pp. 164-225 in Mike Gane, ed., *The radical sociology of Durkheim and Mauss*, London, 1992, reprinted from *Economy and society* 13, 1984, pp. 331-85. (Mauss's *Ecrits politiques*, pp. 537-66, 699-721.)

'Gift, gift', trans. Koen Decoster, pp. 28-32 in Alan D. Schrift, ed., *The logic of the gift: towards an ethic of generosity*, New York, 1997. (*Oeuvres*, vol. 3.)

'An intellectual self-portrait', see chap. 2, this volume.

C. Selected secondary sources

A certain amount on Mauss can be found in the copious English-language literature relating to Durkheim (see currently the journal *Durkheimian studies/Etudes durkheimiennes*), and a little in the introductions to English translations of works by Mauss. There has been considerable English-language discussion of *The gift*. However, most of the other secondary literature is in French.

In English

Besnard, P., ed., *The sociological domain: the Durkheimians and the founding of French sociology*, Cambridge, 1983. (On the scholarly world within which Mauss worked.)

Carrithers, M., Collins, S., and Lukes, S., eds, *The category of the person: anthropology, philosophy, history*, Cambridge, 1985. (A collection of essays focusing on Mauss's 1938 essay – see *Sociologie et anthropologie*.)

Davis, J., *Exchange*, Buckingham, 1992.

Dumont, L., Chap. 5 in *Essays on individualism*, Chicago, 1986.

Lévi-Strauss, C., *Introduction to the work of Marcel Mauss*, trans. Felicity Baker, London, 1987 (originally in *Sociologie et anthropologie*). (Sometimes thought to tell us more about Lévi-Strauss than Mauss.)

Lukes, S. 'Marcel Mauss' in D. Sills, ed., *International Encyclopaedia of the Social Sciences*, vol. 10, 1968, pp. 78-82.

In French

L'Arc, no. 48, 1972. (Special number devoted to Mauss; contains thirteen articles.)

Cazeneuve, J.. *Sociologie de Marcel Mauss*, Paris, 1968.

———, *Mauss*, Paris, 1968. (Both of Cazeneuve's books are quite short.)

Fournier, M., *Marcel Mauss*, Paris, 1994. (The standard 767-page biography, includes in addition a 45-page bibliography of Mauss's work.)

Revue européenne des sciences sociales, vol. 34, no. 105, 1996. (Proceedings of a conference on 'Mauss: hier et aujourd'hui', held in Lausanne. Eds G. Berthoud and G. Busino. Contains fifteen articles and a valuable bibliography of secondary literature on Mauss in several languages.)

The journal *Revue du MAUSS*, edited by Alain Caillé, is dedicated to pursuing the insights of Mauss, though the title also alludes to the *Mouvement anti-utilitariste en sciences sociales*. The *Année sociologique* (3rd series, started in 1949) will be marking the centenary of its original foundation.

Three recent studies on specific aspects of Mauss's work:

Godelier, M., *L'énigme du don*, Paris, 1996.

Karsenti, B., *Marcel Mauss: le fait social total*, Paris (1994).

———, *L'homme total: sociologie, anthropologie et philosophie chez Marcel Mauss*, Paris, 1997.

CONTRIBUTORS

NICHOLAS ALLEN, Reader in the Social Anthropology of South Asia at the University of Oxford, has published on the ethnography of the Himalayas (dealing especially with language, ritual, and myth), on the evolution of systems of kinship and marriage, on aspects of the Durkheimian tradition, and on Indo-European cultural comparativism. He is currently working on a study of the common origins of ancient Indian and ancient Greek epic.

PAUL DRESCH, Lecturer in Social Anthropology at the University of Oxford, has specialised in the study of Yemen and the Arab world. His publications include *Tribes, government and history in Yemen*, Oxford, 1989, and papers on politics, poetry, and tribalism. He is currently working on the Arab Gulf.

ALEXANDER GOFMAN is Professor at the Higher School of Economics in Moscow, and Head Researcher at the Institute of Sociology in the Russian Academy of Sciences. Among his many publications on the history of sociology and the sociology of industrial design and fashion are *Fashion and people: a new theory of fashion and fashion behaviour*, Moscow, 1994, and *Seven lectures on the history of sociology*, Moscow, 1995/1997 (both in Russian). He has presented and translated into Russian works by Durkheim, Mauss, and Bergson.

CLAUDINE HAROCHE, Directeur de Recherche at the Centre National de la Recherche Scientifique (CNRS), has for some years been studying the relation between bodily postures, psychological dispositions, moral attitudes, and political behaviour. Her publications include (with J.J. Courtine) *Histoire du visage*, Paris, 1988/1994; (as editor) *Le for intérieur*, Paris, 1995; (with Y. Déloye and O. Ihl) *Le protocole ou la mise en forme de l'ordre politique*, Paris, 1997; and *Civilidade e polidez: ensayos de antropologia politica*, Sao Paulo (in press).

WENDY JAMES, Professor of Social Anthropology at the University of Oxford, has carried out ethnographic research in various countries of North East Africa, and has also pursued a number of general themes in historical anthropology. Her publications on Africa include *The listening ebony: moral knowledge, religion and power among the Uduk of Sudan*, Oxford, 1988; and she has worked on several edited volumes, including *The pursuit of certainty: religious and cultural formulations*, London, 1995. She is currently working on a series of papers linking anthropology with the fields of philosophy and the study of emotion.

TIM JENKINS is Dean and Fellow of Jesus College, Cambridge. He was trained in social anthropology at Oxford, and has carried out fieldwork in south-western France and south-western England.

BRUNO KARSENTI, formerly a scholar of the Thiers Foundation, is Maître de conférences in Philosophy at the University of Lyon III. He has published *Marcel Mauss: le fait social total*, Paris, 1994, and *L'homme total: sociologie, anthropologie et philosophie chez Marcel Mauss*, Paris, 1997, and has presented several classics from the sociological tradition — Tarde's *Les lois d'imitation*, Paris, 1993, and Durkheim's *Sociologie et anthropologie*, Paris, 1996.

JONATHAN PARRY, Professor of Social Anthropology at the London School of Economics, has specialised in the ethnographic and analytical study of Hindus in India. His publications include *Caste and kinship in Kangra*, London, 1979 and *Death in Banaras*, Cambridge, 1994, and he has coedited (with M. Bloch) *Death and the regeneration of life*, Cambridge, 1982, and *Money and the morality of exchange*, Cambridge, 1989.

W.S.F. PICKERING was formerly Lecturer in Sociology at the University of Newcastle upon Tyne. Since retirement he has founded and worked for the British Centre for Durkheimian Studies at the Institute of Social and Cultural Anthropology at Oxford. His publications include *Durkheim on religion*, London, 1975; *Durkheim's sociology of religion*, London, 1984, and (as coeditor) *Debating Durkheim*, London, 1994.

NATHAN SCHLANGER completed his Ph.D at Cambridge, focusing on prehistoric technology and cognitive archaeology (1994). Alongside archaeological fieldwork in the Netherlands and Turkmenistan, he has studied historical, conceptual, and ideological dimensions of material culture studies in archaeology and anthropology, in both French and Anglo-Saxon traditions. His publications include papers on gas masks during the Gulf War, on Levallois flint-knapping technology, on Piaget's genetic epistemology as related to Leroi-Gourhan's technology, and on pre-Boasian studies of native American techniques.

ILANA FRIEDRICH SILBER has taught as lecturer in the Department of Sociology and Anthropology at the Hebrew University of Jerusalem. She is interested in comparative historical sociology, sociology of culture, and sociological theory, and is currently working on religious gift giving in the 'great' traditions and its implications for gift theory. Among her recent publications is *Religious virtuosity, charisma, and social order: a comparative sociological study of monasticism in Theravada Buddhism and medieval Catholicism*, Cambridge, 1995.

ALAIN TESTART, Directeur de Recherche at the CNRS, has published numerous works on Australia, on hunter-gatherers, and on more general topics in social anthropology. Among them are *Les chasseurs-cuilleurs ou l'origine des inégalités*, Paris, 1982; *Pour les sciences sociales: essai d'épistémologie*, Paris, 1991; *Des dons et des dieux: anthropologie religieuse et sociologie comparative*, Paris, 1993.

INDEX

Abraham, 51, 59 n.44, 246 n.22
action, 5, 13, 19-20, 22, 53, 68, 74, 89, 111, 117-
  21, 182, 198, 200, 215-16, 218, 222
Afghanistan, 126-7
Africa, 22, 34, 103-4, 108, 132 n.64, 121, 227-
  45; Northern: Berbers, 38,125; Morocco, 131
  n.35, 227, 245; Tuareg, 125, 239; Egypt, 237,
  239; Eastern: Ethiopia/Abyssinia, 237, 239;
  Galla/Oromo, 234; Nuer, 13-14, 19, 52, 167,
  Shilluk, 235; Swahili, 231-2, 234, Baganda,
  233, 235-8; other Interlacustrine Bantu, 237-
  8; Masai, 51-2, 233-5, 238, Chagga, Akamba,
  Nandi, 235; Wandorobo, 233-4, 238, Wagogo,
  243; Central and Southern: 242; Azande, 13;
  Bantu, 51, 236, 238, 240; Ngoni, 232,
  Mozambique, 231, Baronga 231; Western: 38,
  232, 235, 239, 242; Dahomey, 235; Lobi,
  Ashanti, 240-41, 244; Fanti, 244; Hausa.
  245; Congo, 152, 243-4, lower Congo, 103;
  Ababua, 243, Mandja, 244
agency, 5, 15, 68, 89, 236-7, 245
agriculture, 7, 125, 128, 207, 238; sedentary
  communities, 51, 235, 238-9
Allen, N., x, 12, 15, 21, 29, 131 n.31, ch. 11
  (175-91), 188 n.3, 189 n.17,190 n.28, 191
  nn.61 and 63, 240
Alliance Israëlite Universelle, 45, 49
alliance, 115, 123, 125, 239
alms, 112-18; see also charity, philanthropy
altruism, 138, 148 n.18
America, 7, 50, 81 n. 15, 135, 139-46, 158,
  195; American writers, 48; Chicago, 156;
  New York, 143; see also anthropology
  (American), Amerindians, philanthropy
  (American)
Amerindian peoples (Native Americans), 11,
  207, 227; Omaha, 189; Zuñi, 13; North-
  western: 34, 37-8, 90, 135, 238, Kwakiutl,
  99-101, 105-8; Haida, Tsimshian, 105, 108;
  N. California, 101; Northern, 230, 240
ancient world, 4, 96, 98, 105-6, 119, 135-6,
  158, 179-80, 188, 126, 238-9; see also
  Greece, Rome
Anderson, J., 125, 128, 130 n.8
Andler, C., 29
Année sociologique, 3, 7-9, 33-4, 36, 152, 180,
  227, 230-37, 241
antagonism, 17, 37, 38, 240-41
anthropology, British, ch. 1 passim (3-26), 193;
  French, 3, 4-6, 8, 9, 244; French school, 4,
  9-10, 12, 18, 34, 45, 153, 192, 197, a new
  foundation for, ch. 5 passim (71-82);
  American, 14, 21, 80, 208 n.4, 209 n.6;
  German,8, 203-4, 207, 233-4, 237, 239,
  243-4; see also biology, ethnography,
  sociology, history, psychology, humanities
anti-Semitism, 46-7, 154, 203, 211 n.39
Appadurai, A., 156
Arabs, Arabic, 111-18, 122, 125-7

archaeology, 4, 31, 212 n.45, 207, 210 n.14,
  237-9, 242; 'archaeology' of bodily habits,
  218; of notions of time, 229
archaism, archaic societies, 67, 112, 119, 135,
  153, 178, 230; civilisations, 38, 120, 137;
  forms, 40, 138, 144, 226, 236
Ardener, E., 19
aristocracies, 38, 216-19; see also elite,
  stratification, kings
Arnove, R., 148 n.15
art, artists, 23, 41, 142, 144, 149 n.32, 195-6,
  200, 205, aesthetics, 38, 144, 200;
  surrealism, 200 n. 32; see also primitive arts
  and techniques.
Assayag, J., 154-5
Australia, 7, 13, 22, 38, 52, 177, 227, 230, 239-
  40; Aranda/Arunta, 39,53; Wonkanguru, 81
autonomy, 18, 112, 122, 125, 127-9, 158, 165-
  6, 168, 188
Avestan, 36, 180
Balfour, H., 7
Bali, 183
Baluchistan, 116, 123, 125-6
Banaras, 165, 183
Barnes, R.H., xi
barter, 39, 87, 121, 125, 127
Barth, F., 17
Bataille, G., 86, 200
Baumer, E., 209 n.9
Bazin, J., 94
Beattie, J., 17
Beck, B., 171 n.65
begging, 116, 98, see also soliciting
Bellah, R., 172 n.97
Benda, J., 195, 197
Benveniste, E., 88
Bergson, H., 66, 196-9, 207
Berthoud, G., xi
Besnard, P., ix, xi-xii, 29
Best, E., 34
Beuchat, H., 14, 31, 37
Bianconi, A., 232
biology, 66, 73, 76, 80, 86-7, 92, 96, 203,
  biological anthropology, 202-3, 211 nn.39
  and 41
Birnbaum, P., 46, 211 n.39
blacksmiths, tinkers, 133 n. 64
Bloch, Marc, 222
blood, 52, 132 n.41, 133 n.50, 206, blood-
  donations, 135, 138, 148 n,18
Boas, F., 37, 105-8
body, 15, 20, 75-7, 165, 198, 214, 216-22, body
  techniques 14, 41, 55, 65, 193, 222;
  body/soul, 15; body of society, 185; see also
  Mauss (Body techniques), techniques
Bolshevism, 45
Bonte P., 132 n. 38
Bordeaux, 30, 35, 46, 48, 56
Bouglé, C., 155